STILLWATER TROUT

Contributors

DONALD BALTZ
GEOFFREY BUCKNALL
FRED EISERMAN
BOB ELLIOT
DAVE ENGERBRETSON
JIM GILFORD
HAL JANSSEN
LEFTY KREH
JOHN MERWIN
PETER MOYLE
STEVE RAYMOND
DAVID RICHEY
EARL WEST

STILLWATER TROUT

EDITED BY

JOHN MERWIN

Illustrated by Victor Ichioka

NICK LYONS BOOKS
DOUBLEDAY & COMPANY, INC.
GARDEN CITY, NEW YORK
1980

All photos of flies by John Merwin

ALL RIGHTS RESERVED
First Edition
2 4 6 8 9 7 5 3 1
PRINTED IN THE UNITED STATES OF AMERICA
ISBN: 0-385-17140-4
Library of Congress Catalog Card Number: 80-492
Designed by Ruth Kolbert Smerechniak
Composition by Publishers Phototype, Inc., Carlstadt, N.J.

NICK LYONS BOOKS
is a division of
BENN BROTHERS, INC. New York

FOR
John Henry Treadwell,
the grandfather who got me started

CONTENTS

Introduction by John Merwin

INTRODUCTION

PONDS AND LAKES ARE THE POOR SISTERS OF AMERICAN TROUT FISHING. Our tradition of fishing writing reaches back more than one hundred and fifty years, and all through that time brooks have laughed and rivers have offered songs to the anglers who fished them. And our quiet waters have remained quiet. The astounding number of fly-fishing books published since the 1930s have become the foundation of an angling technocracy that centers around streams. Books are now almost as important in our tackle as a rod or a reel; we all look to them for answers, for ideas, and for fun. But there has been no broad-based book in which I could find such things about ponds and lakes—and that is the reason for this one.

Stillwater trout fishing in this country has no experts in a conventional sense; the most widely traveled, frequently published writers have fished and written mostly about streams. That's why much of this book is an anthology, a collection of ideas from writers well-known for solid advice on tactics, but whose stillwater experiences have often been concentrated in one part of the country or another.

The many books in print about fly-fishing for trout offer information in three basic areas: historical and contemporary perspectives on the sport, aquatic ecology, and advice on tackle and tactics. So that's how this book is constructed: the first part to show you what's going on in this country and elsewhere, the second to give you a better understanding of the biology of lakes and ponds (which will help you fish them better), and a third covering the tackle and tactics needed for most of the stillwater situations you might encounter. I should add right away that this is not a where-to-go book. Stillwaters containing trout are numerous and easily found, especially when you consider that almost every famous trout stream has one or more equally good stillwaters within the same watershed, ranging from clear sloughs and beaver ponds up to the giant western reservoirs.

I make no pretense about this being a comprehensive book; in putting it together, I often found more questions than answers. One especially wide-open area is the entomology of trout ponds and lakes. Tens of dozens of fishing writers have worked hard over a span of centuries at correlating the insect life of trout streams with hatching times and fly patterns. Such work in stillwaters has been almost nonexistent in this country. It will be decades more before such information becomes widely available as increasing numbers of fly fishermen start including stillwaters in their fishing plans and start making note of what they find.

There are a couple of things you might expect to find in these pages that you won't. One is trolling with flies, most commonly done in the Northeast. That's usually boring, and so our fishing in this book is done by casting. Lake trout are discussed briefly; but except for the Far North and a few high-altitude lakes, they are generally out of range of the fly caster.

I suppose the question of whether I would rather fish a stream or a lake is inevitable. I see that question as like being asked to choose between my two children, and I refuse to make the choice. Happily, I can have both.

JOHN MERWIN
Dorset, Vermont
July, 1979

Part One

A PERSPECTIVE

1

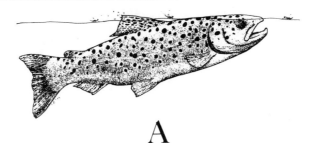

A
STILLWATER
SAMPLER

John Merwin

A POND NEVER HURRIES. THE BROOKS THAT LEAVE IT RUSH TO BECOME streams, streams impatient to become rivers and rivers that run to the sea. Flowing waters demand that life within adapt to their strategy; stillwaters are more accommodating. The pond is a philosopher.

Birches, maples, and the mountain are all perfectly duplicated on this windless afternoon, the pond's quiet reflection unbroken. Where the afternoon sun lights the bottom, various pondweeds can be seen, their tops within a foot of the surface. Bright-green grasses grow along a brief section of shoreline, and winking reflections of sunlight at one edge betray a hidden inlet stream. The underwater channel of the little stream is a dark, deep scar visible across the shallower weeds, and it extends for almost fifty yards in an outward meander from shore. A half-dozen tree swallows dive and bank against the birches on the far side, flashing light-tan when they turn toward us. Reeds are scattered in the shallows along that shore. Just in front of them a heavy wake appears briefly and disappears.

There are brown trout here. We've heard and we have faith. We also think we've seen a fish. John slides the canoe into the water carefully. I sit in the bow and look on the surface for the pale shucks left by hatching mayflies or midges.

They are numerous and varied. Nothing seems to predominate, and that's little help. I tie on a little dark-colored nymph and sit watching the reeds as we glide closer.

Another wake—this time for a distance of about five feet and ending in a swirl. Another wake, shorter this time, and another swirl. A muskrat, the disappointing alternative, doesn't act like that. John stops the canoe a long cast from the edge of the reeds, and we watch. Small, pale mayflies are popping off the surface here and there among the reeds, and the trout is apparently chasing their nymphs. The wake is now almost on the bank, then heading farther away. The fish turns and parallels the shore in front of us, and finally we see it, a brown trout of a couple of pounds.

I cast and drop the fly about ten feet from where I expect the fish to be. The wake turns and heads in the opposite direction. I bring the fly back and cast again, trying for an interception in the fish's erratic cruising pattern. Once again the fish goes the other way. Finally the fish works about fifty feet down the shoreline, but will probably be cruising back. I cast far back in the reeds without retrieving, and we wait.

As a general case, stillwater trout are harder to catch than trout in streams. It's not that trout in one instance are smarter than in the other, of course, but because of differences in physical circumstances governing trout behavior. In streams, the waters moves and the fish don't. In lakes, the fish move and the water doesn't. That's a commonly made observation, but its implications are relatively unexplored. It means, for example, that stream trout can often be located easily, their holding places defined by visible and obvious currents and cover. The flat surface of a trout pond offers no such clues, especially if no fish are rising. Faced with the obvious difficulties of finding fish in a silent pond, most fly fishermen give up quickly and head for the nearest trout stream. They have been doing so for more than three hundred years, which is why the history of fly-fishing is a history of stream fishing.

It's curious that a fisherman who spends an entire day working a trout pond with no more than a hit or two will often become turned off to stillwater trout in general. The same thing often happens on trout rivers, even the very famous ones, and yet here people seem more persistent, which yields occasional successes. In the stream is a target—riffle, rock, or eddy—to which the fisherman can dedicate his effort. It's a tangible goal, and part of our angling mythology holds there to be no such goals in stillwater, a myth that this and subsequent chapters should help to dispel.

The fish is cruising back toward us once again, its wake turning this way and that slowly through the reeds. My fly still rests on the bottom. When the fish is about six feet from the fly, I start moving it in a series of slow twitches.

"Here he comes!" John whispers, and from six feet away the trout pushes a deliberate wake toward the fly. The wake starts moving faster. I twitch the fly.

"A pond never hurries." *John Merwin*

Then the wake moves really fast and when I think it is close to the fly I panic and strike and the fly line flies back and piles around my shoulders. And the fish swirls hard where the fly has been.

"You had him coming and you struck too soon!"

"I know." And I sit still for a moment and wait for my knees to calm down. The fish is still working, farther down the shore now, and we can see its wake weaving among the reeds. A kingfisher flies by about six feet over the water and the trout spooks instantly, speeding past the canoe out into the pond. The bird laughs. So does John.

"That was just like bonefishing. I think I was as excited as you were. Ever been bonefishing?"

"No," I answer, and start winding up the coils of line.

"Well, it's just like that was. Really spooky fish in shallow water. The excitement is incredible."

(15)

I mutter something about understanding what he means and John pulls his paddle out of the muck and starts us down along the shore.

Brian Clarke, the English writer whose book *The Pursuit of Stillwater Trout* is a remarkably original work, once observed that nobody is making rivers anymore. In England, shrinking stream mileage and increasing numbers of fishermen have produced a stillwater revolution, fed by increasing numbers of manmade reservoirs that are stocked and intensively managed as trout fisheries. Clarke also wrote that such a revolution was inevitable in this country as shrinking rivers would force American anglers into stillwater. I think the observation was made without a real perception of the amount of stream fishing available in this country, a perception that most American fly fishermen seem to lack as well. Our best-known trout streams get vast amounts of publicity, and the various threats to their well-being—dams, chemical pollutants, agricultural diversion—are also well known. Many people automatically assume that all of our hundreds of thousands of miles of flowing trout waters are subject to similar threats and gradual deterioration. That is simply not true. They are all valuable resources requiring guardianship and management, and given such care, we will have them tomorrow. Within the forseeable future, stillwater fly-fishing for trout in this country will remain a matter of choice and not necessity.

A British visitor, well versed in the English reservoir scene, got his first look at the immense Pepacton Reservoir, part of the New York City water-supply system in the Catskills. Such a reservoir, he observed, if intensively managed for trout, could comfortably provide fly-fishing for all the angling hordes from the cities nearby. He may have been partly right. But the big Delaware, Beaverkill, Willowemoc, Mongaup, Neversink, and numerous smaller trout streams are just as close to those cities, offer good fishing, and many miles of some of them don't see a fisherman for days on end.

I'm not trying to talk you out of fly-fishing in stillwater, but rather to point out that it's not a last resort. Our best stillwaters for trout, like our best streams, are biologically productive, have consistent and predictable fly hatches, and trout—sometimes very big ones—can be taken on both dry flies and nymphs. Pepacton is really a bad example; like many reservoirs, it is subject to wide fluctuations in water level and its shoreline drops steeply below the surface. On a season-long basis, the shallows and weeds of a lake are where the hatches occur. The steep banks and changing levels of Pepacton keep those at a minimum, and its substantial population of large brown trout get that way by eating free-ranging alewives, a small forage fish often stocked in reservoirs as trout food. It is quite possible to take such trout on flies, but not easy. And knowing that, I doubt that I'll ever bother to try. I will find instead a small, cool pond with a stable water level and sufficient shallows to produce insect life in quantity. Such ponds are numerous from Maine to California. In a way, they're like starting your fly-fishing on a small stream where the problems at hand are much better defined.

There is a vague rippling of the water a few feet from shore, visible only as the reflected sky catches the tops of the wavelets and produces a changing light pattern. We paddle over for a look, once again stopping about fifty feet from where we think a trout might be. Once again, a slight humping of the water, and then nothing. Another cruising fish apparently, but the water is a little deeper and the disturbance much less. I don't cast, afraid of spooking the fish because I don't know where it is. A few feet to the left is a swirl and a splash in the reflection of a birch. I cast, twitch, and nothing happens. I start fanning the water toward shore with a series of casts. Still nothing, and we are puzzled. Once in a while the water tilts slightly—not a ripple or a wave, just a barely perceptible tilt—against a log about twenty feet away, but it looks like water disturbed by what small movement we make in the canoe. I finally make a cast—a bad one—over there and hook the fly on the log. I grab the line and pull the canoe over to free the fly. As the canoe moves toward shore, a brown trout, larger than the last one, goes steaming out of there, clouds of silt marking his passage through the underwater weeds. The fish had been in that small area for several minutes, apparently taking nymphs, and although the subtle rocking of the water should have told me, I simply hadn't realized what I was seeing.

The sun is on the shoulder of the ridge now, and the tops of the birches hold its light while the pond is in shadow. Several trout are rising over where we had earlier seen the channel of the inlet stream. The pattern of the riseforms seems to follow the underwater channel exactly, and it is almost certain that the different depth and vegetation there are producing a hatch not yet taking place on the rest of the pond. We paddle over and anchor this time, parallel to the channel and about fifty feet away, so we can both cover it with a series of casts.

There have been few glorious tales written about eight-inch trout. Yet even on the best of American trout streams, the *average* size of the fish in a day's catch of thirty or more is most likely no more than a foot. It's a startling thought, and first pointed out to me by Phil Wright one late June as we fished Montana's Big Hole River in the midst of its famous stonefly hatch. We caught some good-size fish, up to three or four pounds, and we caught some little fish, about eight or nine inches. The average was indeed about a foot.

I mention that to point out that the average size of the trout you catch in a pond, while not huge, is apt to be larger than those you'll take in a nearby stream. It may be a twelve-inch brookie from a Maine pond instead of a six incher from a feeder stream. Or it may be a twenty-pound brown trout from Flaming Gorge Reservoir in Utah, instead of a five-pounder from its tailwaters. Those are extreme examples, but it remains a valid generalization that stillwater trout get bigger faster. A four-year-old brown trout from Lake Michigan may weigh as much as twenty pounds, while a healthy brown of age four from Michigan's famed Au Sable River may be sixteen inches or less.

Ponds offer a more accommodating environment than streams. Moving water is kind neither to a trout nor its food. Summer heat, bottom ice in winter, floods in spring and droughts in late summer, plus the sheer fact of a current, all require the expenditure of energy for survival. In stillwater, all a trout has to do is swim around and eat. Depending on the relative productivity of a particular body of water, aquatic insects, freshwater shrimp, and other forms of trout food may be available in astounding numbers, their life cycles uninterrupted by the sudden environmental changes so characteristic of many trout streams. Forage fish—alewives, smelt, shiners, shad, or others—may also be available in substantial quantities. Each baitfish represents a big nutritional package, and trout that feed on them heavily grow at phenomenal rates. The brown trout that manages to catch a small dace in a stream benefits, to be sure, but that's nothing like a brown or rainbow that gorges on fat alewives in a lake day in and day out.

We can see the riseforms along the channel, but reflected sky still hides the fish. Looking straight down, we can see an occasional dace or shiner darting here and there over the weedtops. The rises are sporadic, not the strung-together rise-forms that can mean easily intercepted fish. Small, light-colored caddisflies appear as if by magic here and there on the surface, then take off with their typically erratic flight.

We both spread casts over the channel; John uses a little caddis dry fly, while I stay with the small nymph that had drawn interest earlier. He finally hooks a small fish that turns out to be a little brown, encouraging because we know the pond hasn't been stocked for many years, and the little fish means that spawning has taken place in the small tributaries we'd found.

As it gets darker, fish rise with increasing frequency all over the pond. Caddis still hop off the water, but my little nymph draws nothing. I do my best fishing in a pond called hindsight, and there I would have used a little tan caddis pupa, brought back in rapid twitches just below the surface. But it is almost dark, so I cut the leader back to a larger diameter and tie on a big white-winged dry fly,

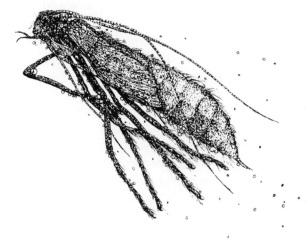

Caddis emerger

casting and retrieving it in twitches. Nothing. I still don't know why not. John does the same thing with a big White Wulff, and the first cast brings a slashing strike that breaks his leader instantly. A couple of half-decent fly fishermen turned idiot by rising fish. I finally decide to try a big marabou leech, crawled just under the surface in the growing darkness.

There are two keys to finding trout in a lake or pond. The first is asking somebody where they are. The second is persistence.

Although I was quite small, I can remember clearly my father asking a stranger on the shore of a Maine pond about where in the pond we should fish for brookies. I think I remember it so well because the hood of the guy's old black Chevy had muddy black-bear footprints going up one side and down the other. He was very proud of them, and never having seen a bear track, let alone a bear, I was all eyes and ears. He pointed to the far side of the pond.

"See that sapling sticking out of the water? That marks a springhole. Fish there." He finished tying his canoe on top of his car, being very careful of the tracks on the hood, and drove away. We all piled into the canoe, anchored by the sapling, and used little bucktails to catch what were then zillions of brookies. Probably a dozen or so.

In subsequent years, I've often found trout in a strange pond simply by drifting with the wind and trailing a small wet fly on a sinking line. It's a simple and effective locating method. Check local laws, though; in some of Maine's fly-fishing-only ponds, for example, this is considered to be trolling, which is illegal. And often I've been able to find fish simply by going to a pond known to hold trout and looking in the early morning or late evening, when they're most apt to be rising. At other times, a simple tackle-counter question lets me find out that "the boys do pretty good with bait off that point," where a deeply fished nymph may do just as well. Sometimes the answers are more obvious than they appear.

And other times they're not. I tossed hair-bugs for shoreline bass in a small pond near home for more than a year before I realized that the rises in the middle of the pond were being made by trout. So I started trout fishing there instead. It took a trip or two each week for three months before I got on to the various morning and evening feeding patterns of those fish, and only after that could I go there with any confidence of catching fish. Any fisherman is at a definite advantage on his home water; the more he fishes it, the more likely he is to take fish. This isn't so much because he's reduced the odds by sheer persistence, although that also helps, but rather because he's learning more with every outing.

The leech makes a plopping noise when it hits the water, and I bring it back in short, slow strips, fully expecting to have the rod yanked out of my hand at any moment. It doesn't happen. It is almost completely dark now, and the moon is starting to show through the spruces. The trout have stopped rising except for an occasional dimple. We sit and watch the quietness. A tremendous splash snaps our heads around in time to see the ending of a big swirl halfway between us and the shoreline. Little waves lap against the canoe and the pond is quiet again. The grandfather of all trout and the demise of a dace. We laugh and make jokes about big Rapalas and rigged shiners. But we don't fish for him then. We have promises to keep, and we go home. And I am haunted by that fish.

There is an old saw about 10 percent of the fishermen catching 90 percent of the fish. It often seems to be true, but even more true is that less than 10 percent of *that* 10 percent consistently catch big fish. Even fewer people seem proficient at catching the larger fish in lakes than in streams, perhaps because more fly fishermen fish streams. Del Canty does catch big fish in lakes, and in the last couple of years he's become something of a legend. Charlie Meyers of the Denver *Post* did a story on Canty for *Outdoor Life* magazine more than a year ago. A story of a relatively short, quiet man taking rainbow and brown trout well over twenty pounds in lakes on flies. With a regular fly rod and a shooting-head. From a float tube out in a huge western reservoir. Alone and sometimes in the middle of the night. It was—and is—a hell of a story. I subsequently got my friend George Gerkhe, a neighbor of Canty's in Colorado, to do an interview with him, and we ultimately made a magazine story out of it. The following are a series of quotes from Canty, extracted from that interview.

"Big fish aren't stupid; they're experienced about boats. With a float tube, you have the added advantages of surprise and of being quiet. Let's say I'm paddling along, and I see an interesting little shore section and notice a little bit of disturbance. You *know* a fish is there. You can move around and get the position you want. No paddles in the hands; your feet just go. You can watch that spot all the time as you turn yourself just right. I can't stress how much more accurately, I think, you can cast from a float-tube system. You can't afford to blow that one-time cast. It may be the first time, and the last time, you'll ever see a thirty-pound brown. In a boat, you may be right on him, but because the boat is turned around, you can't hit him. The fish is moving, always moving. It's a question of the right equipment."

For Canty, the right equipment consists of a multiple-chambered float tube in which he sits, propelling himself with a pair of swim fins. He's wearing foam-cell wet-suit underwear, warm-up pants, and sometimes more clothing, covered by a pair of chest waders and waterproof upper garments. He carries a sleeping bag and cooking gear, and may be on or in a big reservoir for days at a time.

"If you go to the water with good equipment, a good set of clothing that you know protects against hypothermia, you go there with confidence. If you're inside your waders with just a pair of pants and you feel that cold water on you right away, you're not confident enough to venture very far from camp. You're limiting your chances. Also, you can't go out there saying, "Well, I'm after this big fish and this is all I want to do." You can't just say that. Doesn't work. You have to enjoy the surroundings. You have to be able to get out there in the middle of the night and not be afraid of the night. To be capable of saying this is really beautiful. To really enjoy seeing a bunch of grebes feeding. And to wonder

Del Canty of Colorado with a twenty-six-pound rainbow taken on a fly from Utah's Flaming Gorge Reservoir. *Photo courtesy of Del Canty*

what they're feeding on. Then you're starting to put two and two together because of your mental attitude."

Canty recently took a twenty-six-pound Kamloops rainbow on a fly, a state record, in Utah's Flaming Gorge Reservoir.

"We arrived at Flaming Gorge at Antelope Flats and got our gear together. We talked it over and decided to do basically a reconnaissance job that day. We took our rods, of course, but did a lot of looking around. We knew the rainbows were spawning and we figured they would be on points where there was gravel. I had found a redd where some rainbows had tried to spawn, when a storm started to come up. I had nothing better to do, so I went out again and started to look around for fish. The waves had started to crest a little when I saw a fish of about five pounds in them about thirty feet away.

"The storm was picking up and it was getting windy. More fish started showing up. They really like that oxygen in the whitecaps! I cast to a couple of fish, but the wind was blowing me around so I couldn't get to them accurately. Then there he was. Right in the waves. I could see the whole fish. I was lucky; the fly fell right in front of his face. He turned a few inches and had the fly before I had really recovered. I hit the fish three times to set the hook."

That sort of hook-setting is usually associated with big, tough-mouthed fish like tarpon or big bass and not dainty little trout. Canty's explanation was a little chilling.

"I gave him three short jerks for a certain reason. That's the way they operate in killing bait. They have teeth on the tongue and on the bone in the roof of the mouth that mesh. When they take a minnow, they mash the minnow to the roof of their mouth and they push their tongue forward—to kill it and to break it up—and they do it two or three times. You can see their head working, moving it around. When they do this, your fly is pinned in extremely powerful muscles. When you first strike, there's no way you're going to move it. So you keep striking to move that fly during a relaxing of pressures between the tongue and the roof of the mouth.

"Then I relaxed the pressure and fought him gently. The main thing is not to apply tremendous pressure or you're going to panic him. He ran a bit and got me scared, but he finally stopped and started swimming back and forth. I got close to him again and he got used to me. They will get used to you if you don't push them and don't go after them. That's about it. I used the waves to help keep him off balance and wear him out. I just kept him worried and using energy until finally I was able to scoot him out onto land."

Canty has taken a large number of browns and rainbows over fifteen pounds, many of them over twenty pounds. He releases most of them. He is using a six-pound-test tippet. Considering the size of the fish, his flies are relatively small. I have one of his flies in front of me, which he calls a Zonker. It took his big rainbow. It's tied on a number-six 4XL streamer hook: a simple, tinsel body, some sparse yellow hackle at the throat, and a strip of beaver fur (still on the hide) about an inch and a quarter long by one-eighth-inch wide, tied in at the tail and at the head. The head is lacquered black thread. A few of his flies are long—six or seven inches—tandem-style streamers tied with hook sizes six and eight. Some of them look like little trout.

"Most lakes are stocked with trout because trout can't spawn in them. Find out when the stocking trucks come. It's a bait truck anyhow, but they won't admit to it. Like clockwork, those big hogs will show up for dinner a day before the truck arrives. So start fishing in the morning before the trucks get there, and you'll see these big fish showing up for breakfast. It's just conditioning."

Those are just a few comments from a forty-page transcript on my desk, but I think you've gotten the idea. I should add that Del Canty has a reputation for not telling fibs. And besides, he has pictures.

Of all the first-time trips I've made to various trout ponds and lakes, the single afternoon's fishing that I scattered through this chapter was probably the most typical. A few fish caught and a few chances muffed. I learned a few things about the place, and the next time there will be better. It was at times very exciting, at others merely pleasant. I would say the same thing about all of my stream fishing. I don't really choose between them or place one above the other. The only real frustration is the general lack of information about trout in stillwaters, which we've already started to remedy.

2

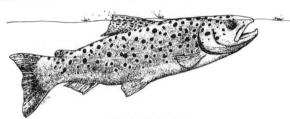

THE
AMERICAN
BEGINNINGS

Bob Elliot

BIBLIOGRAPHIES OF AMERICAN TROUT FISHING SHOW A DECIDED EMPHASIS on stream fishing for trout extending well back into the nineteenth century. The first American edition of Walton's *Compleat Angler* (1847) contained a description of American fly-fishing written by George Washington Bethune, its editor, which treated fly-fishing in stillwaters as a casual aside, and that type of reference has persisted in American fly-fishing books to the present day. Yet there was a tremendous growth in American field sports in the last half of the nineteenth century, and fly-fishing for trout in stillwaters was a part of it. During the final quarter of that century, stillwater fly-fishing became a significant activity, and during the first few years of this century, it put down roots and flourished to a remarkable degree.

Although tackle of the times was primitive by contemporary standards, the lack was often compensated for by the enthusiasm and numbers of the trout. The following anecdote is a good example of both. It is by a Mr. W. Thomson, appearing in *Fishing with the Fly* by Charles F. Orvis and A. Nelson Cheney (1883).

"I stood up and made my first cast along the edge of the reef. No result! but I thought I saw a faint suspicion of a shadowy form or two, and a slight movement of the water just behind my flies. Have been too quick, I thought; and so tried again, letting the flies this time rest until they sank an inch or so below the surface, when I *attempted* to draw them slowly in. I say attempted, because they had not moved six inches when first the dropper and then the tail fly were taken in a rush, by two large trout which didn't draw towards me worth a cent, for some fifteen minutes at least. On the contrary they darted away as if the Old Nick was after them with a red-hot frying-pan; pulling in unison like a pair of well-broken colts and severely trying my rather too light tackle. Any decided check was out of the question. I could only put on such pressure as the single gut leader would bear, and that was sufficient to make a half-circle of my rod. I had beautiful open water in which to play the fish, but as they rushed along and down the face of the submerged cliff, I did not know what hidden dangers might lurk in the unseen depths, nor at what moment a sharp, jagged rock might cut the line, or some profound recess furnish a retreat from whence it might be impossible to withdraw my prize. . . . When the wildest of this flurry was over, I drew them cautiously to the boat and dipped up both at once with my landing net. An immediate application of my pocket scale proved their weight to be twenty-nine and thirty-three ounces respectively . . . By ten o'clock I had secured fifteen beauties, some running close upon three pounds.''

Several things contributed to the growth of stillwater enthusiasm. Some, such as the marketing of six-strip cane fly rods by Leonard in the 1870s, were a part of the general evolution of fly-fishing in this country. Others, such as the tremendous size of the eastern brook trout then found in Maine's Rangeley Lake region, were often unique to stillwaters. Most important, this was a time when the frontier became a romance instead of a struggle, especially in the Northeast where luxury hotels, sporting camps, and rail and stage travel in the northern areas were heavily promoted in the travel sections of metropolitan newspapers and magazines.

In terms of numbers of fishermen, stillwater fly-fishing probably attracted more attention at this time than did streams, and one reason was the length of those early fly rods. Only the more dedicated angler would suffer the tribulations of snagging flies, gut leaders, and even a rod tip in the confines of comparatively narrow rivers, let alone those brooks bordered by brush and trees. As late as 1880, twelve-foot rods were commonplace. In 1885, for example, Fred D. Divine of Utica, N.Y., advertised his "Divine Bethebarra and Lancewood rods," which were awkward sticks except on open water and much used for trolling from boats and canoes in preference to the new-fangled wisps of cane. Even in 1901, the appearance of fly rods as short as eight feet and as light as three-and-one-half ounces startled most sportsmen, and guides were prone to tell them that such light bamboo was not adequate to bring any respectable trophy to net. Still, the golden days of American rod-making had begun, and American casters developed an affection for the shorter, lighter equipment that was to play a significant role in the subsequent growth of stream fishing.

The transition to casting flies in preference to the use of various baits for trout and landlocked salmon was actually remarkable. The Maine woods trips by Hen-

Clay Bartlett landing a rainbow. *John Merwin*

ry David Thoreau in 1846, 1853, and 1857 were routed by his guides in canoes over some of the more productive fishing waters (Moosehead Lake, Allagash headwaters, Katahdin ponds), yet he carried with him only lines, hooks, corks, and pieces of salt pork for the taking of trout. The publication of his books, however, was a factor in motivating other anglers to seek out the magical places he described. In one instance, for example, he told of encountering some men haying at Maine's Telos Lake, who had shut down a nearby dam in order to entice brook trout into the waters it held.

The lumberman's need to hold river water until it was time for a downriver log drive led to the building of dams throughout the northeastern woods, creating ponds and lakes that soon teemed with brook trout and, in some areas, landlocked salmon. The lumbering industry that created so many stillwaters in the Northeast also provided guides for the resort areas that were then growing in the Adirondacks, Maine, Vermont, and New Hampshire. And it was those woodsmen, many of whom were of recent Scottish or English origin, that brought to the region their Old World affection for the casting of flies in preference to the use of bait. Thus the oldest stillwater traditions of northern Europe—those of the lochs—became briefly part of our own in the Northeast.

In many instances, it was those trappers and loggers from northeastern Canada, who had come to the American Northeast to work the woods, who ultimately made the sporting camps themselves. Those canny Scots and others were quick to see the possibilities of catering to fly fishermen, and they built what is still the typical layout of a northeastern sporting camp: several cabins for sleeping quarters and a larger cabin for dining, nearly always on the shore of a lake. The fishing was right at hand and the breezes over the lake kept black flies and mosquitos hopefully at a minimum.

To advertise the accommodations, camp operators often cooperated with existing railway lines, and travel packages were widely promoted in various travel guides and newspapers. Stage lines often met the trains at outposts and conveyed families to within comparatively easy distance of the fishing lodges. In one 1885 travel book, for example, the Main Central, Boston and Maine, Sandy River R.R., and such stage lines as those carrying guests from Kingfield, Maine, to Eustis (site of a "resort" farm house; $1.50 per day, which also offered accommodations for ladies and children) were among those listed. Those visiting the more plush hotels in the Adirondacks arrived by similar routes, often using such now-defunct companies as the Utica & Black R.R. or the Ogdensburg & Northern. Two hotels at Plattsburgh, N.Y. (on Lake Champlain) were said to offer every luxury and could be reached by steamer from Burlington, Vermont, or by railroad from Montreal. At one of these more notable hotels, guides and sports could travel by boat over 160 miles of lakes and streams, most of which had excellent trout fishing.

The railroads, stage lines, and grand old hotels had their heyday during the nineteenth and early-twentieth centuries. Almost all of them are out of business now, the hotels demolished for the most part and old railway beds weeded and rusting in the woods. Gravel roads, at the least, now serve sportsmen who drive their own cars to fishing lodge doors.

One of the big attractions at the time were the size and numbers of fish to be found in northeastern lakes and ponds, perhaps none better known than in Maine's Rangeley Lake region. In 1878, for example, records of eastern brook trout taken by some anglers there were compiled by the Oquossoc Angling Association. One week's score was as follows.

DATE (October)	NUMBER OF TROUT	AVERAGE WEIGHT	LARGEST
2	11	4 lbs.	10 lbs.
3	4	5½ lbs.	7½ lbs.
4	12	5 lbs.	8 lbs.
5	17	4½ lbs.	9 lbs.
7	10	3 lbs.	7 lbs.
8	4	5 lbs.	9 lbs.
9	5	5 lbs.	8 lbs.

Along with the exhibition at the 1867 Philadelphia Centennial of a ten-pound Maine brook trout, statistics such as those just given drew sportsmen to the Rangeleys and other parts of Maine in appreciable numbers. Fly-fishing was favored by a majority of the visitors and encouraged by the guides. Stillwaters always produced the heaviest fish, often during fall spawning time and where a stream entered a lake. By 1885, and perhaps earlier, there was a closed season on trout and landlocked salmon in Maine to protect the big spawners from October 1 through May 1. However, fish were so abundant that the limit was fifty pounds of trout and/or salmon in possession.

In this same period—the late 1800s—there was a tremendous growth in outdoor publications, books, and of available tackle. *Forest and Stream,* for example, was one magazine that thrived during that period, publishing both fishing tales of the Northeast and elsewhere along with an astounding number of advertisements for both tackle of all sorts and for places to use it. Guide books were also a thriving industry, and were the work of such early authors as A. W. Robinson, who in 1885 published his *Sportsmen's and Tourists' Guide to the Dead River Region of Maine.*

I like to think, however, that it was the old-time fishing guide with his strength, endurance, patience, and quick wit who primarily influenced early fly fishermen that stillwater trouting was better done with feathers and silk than with bait. In 1949, I talked with William Grant, an elderly gentleman himself then, whose father had carried him into Kennebago Lake through the woods in a packbasket when Will Grant was an infant. He remembered fascinating things that happened while he grew up at the fishing lodge that his father maintained—one of which was a ten-pound brook trout that hit a fly in the quiet water at the mouth of Kennebago Stream.

"I think, perhaps," he told me, "that those big brookies got that size from feeding on blueback trout in these waters. When landlocked salmon were introduced into the Rangeleys, the bluebacks disappeared."

Brook trout still dimple the smooth evening surface of many Maine ponds, but the ten pounders of legend are gone now, along with the old resort hotels and railroads. Such legacy as remains from those early stillwater days in the Northeast is largely found in the streamer-fly patterns that originated in the Rangeley region—the Black Ghosts, Gray Ghosts, Supervisors, and others that ultimately found their way into American trout streams from coast to coast and that still play an important role in contemporary fly-fishing for stillwater trout.

Editor's note

To find a history of stillwater fly-fishing for trout concentrated on the Northeast doesn't mean, of course, that it was never practiced farther west at the same time or shortly thereafter. The native brook trout of Michigan, for example, were certainly the target of nineteenth-century sportsmen in stillwaters as well as streams, and it stands to reason that the native cutthroat of the Rockies were caught in the lakes as well as the streams of that area by sportsmen around the turn of the century. However, in terms of the relative intensity with which stillwater fly-fishing was practiced at the time, other areas offer little comparison to the flurry of activity that took place in the Northeast.

In a sense, that stillwater fishing was a social fad, as were the railroad tours and the grand wilderness hotels. That romantic era of American sport largely ended with the First World War, and with it ended such widespread enthusiasm as was ever felt for stillwater fly-fishing in this country. The technical development of fly-fishing for trout, both in England and in this country, took place on streams, largely because the problems of stream-fishing for trout are better defined. Thus we have no stillwater tradition, no shelves and shelves of books on stillwater technique where one author has built upon another as has been the case with stream fishing. And even though stillwater fly-fishing has roots stretching far back in northern England, the mainstream of English fly-fishing writing has been just that: a stream. Only major and recent changes in England—far more fishermen and far fewer streams—brought about their stillwater revolution as described by British writer Geoffrey Bucknall in the following chapter. And just as this country took and built upon British stream technique sixty years ago, so might we also emulate their interest in trout from quiet waters

In reading Bucknall's description of the British reservoir fisheries, American anglers should keep some basic differences between their waters and ours in mind. The stocking density, and hence numbers of trout available to fishermen, is quite high on many British waters. Most fishing is on a fee basis, usually the equivalent of a few dollars per day or a few hundred dollars for a season. Finally, the British reservoir system must by law be made available for recreational use, something that's not always the case in this country.

3

THE
BRITISH
EXPLOSION

Geoffrey Bucknall

THE GROWTH OF STILLWATER FLY-FISHING IN ENGLAND HAS BEEN BOTH explosive and recent, but its immediate roots go at least as far back as the beginning of this century and the emergence of several important fly-fishing trends. In northern England (Scotland and Wales), fly-fishing was based on rivers with stocks of wild trout. They were becoming hard to catch, and W. C. Stewart was developing the upstream wet-fly method out of which grew modern nymph techniques. In southern England, imitative dry-fly fishing was being raised to a high art form by F. M. Halford and his associates. This was based on the false assumption that one could make a totally perfect imitation of the trout's floating insect food. The feeding behavior of trout is now better understood, but Halford's dry-fly doctrine dominated trout fishing for the decades that followed. It caused fly-tying and fly-casting to be raised to high levels of skill, but it unfortunately caused a mystique to be implanted into anglers' minds that fly-fishing was to be confined to the intellectually gifted.

The works of both Halford and Stewart were instances of giant steps in stream-trout technique that never ruffled the surface of then-contemporary stillwaters. All this time anglers had been fly-fishing on the grand lochs of Scotland and the larger natural lakes of northern England and Wales. Both the flies and methods were simple. The flies were either sea trout patterns, or scaled-up versions of popular attractor-type river flies, and if any attempt were made to imitate a hatch of insects, it was only in the most rudimentary form. It may well have been true that loch fishermen neither knew nor cared why drab flies such as the Greenwell, Mallard and Claret, or the Blae and Black fared so well on occasion, though plainly they were related to forms of aquatic life.

The method was invariably fishing a drift in a boat before the wind, with a team of wet flies fished and worked on a shortish line. The team of wet flies would be three or four in number, fished as droppers with the highest fly normally well-hackled—a palmer fly that could be dibbled seductively in the ripple. The common phrase of the time was "to bring the fish up." It was primitive, but it was also, and still is, a most effective method. Few books of the time describe it, perhaps because surface fishing with such flies would have been contrary to the perfect-imitation school so treasured by the gentleman of leisure in Britain's last golden days before the First World War.

War did come, and the resulting industrialization of Britain increased the demand for water. The Second World War accelerated the process. Concurrently, there was a gentle social destratification, which had three important effects on stillwater fly-fishing. The first was the spread of personal transport, allowing all classes of people to visit even the remotest lakes. The second was a leveling of incomes to the extent that ordinary people expected to share in leisures hitherto the sole province of the fairly well-off. The third was the need for water authorities to placate those who were dismayed to witness large tracts of rural Britain disappearing under reservoirs.

They had a model in the Blagdon Reservoir. This lake had been constructed at the foot of Somerset's Mendip Hills at the turn of the century and was famed for its fast-growing rainbow and brown trout. The odd truth is that right at the beginning, anglers didn't know how to fish it, so big were the trout. The glass-cased specimens from that time often contain the Atlantic salmon fly that was used. Fish usually grow fastest when the land is freshly flooded, and as the years go by, the average weight settles down. Anglers then settle down themselves to work out finer techniques, and the first attempts at actual imitation of stillwater life were probably made at Blagdon. These were copies of Chironomid larvae and pupae, commonly known as buzzers, which probably form the largest proportion of stillwater-trout diet in British lakes.

Already some positive changes were apparent in angler attitudes toward stillwaters. The first developed from the introduction of American rainbow trout, which have been with us ever since. Halford would never have encountered the fast-growing rainbow on his native River Test dry-fly water where he fished for a mixture of previously stocked brown trout and the same species bred naturally in the river. The rainbow was ideal for the reservoirs because it grew quickly and rose freely. Brown trout in our richer lakes tend to be dour bottom feeders, unpopular with those addicted to the surface rise.

Anthony Groome of Newport lands a rainbow below the dam in Blagdon Reservoir. *Photo courtesy John Wilshaw*

Fish can grow to large size—like this twelve-pound five-ounce rainbow—in fertile reservoirs such as Grafham. *Photo courtesy of John Wilshaw*

In many countries the word "reservoir" conjures mental images of a concrete bowl. Blagdon set the new pattern: a water-supply reservoir that was guilty of decimating the countryside must be a thing of beauty in its own right. The planner of that reservoir set his eyes on the creation of a Scottish loch deep in the heart of our southern scenery, and before long the writers of the day so rhapsodised on the enchantment of the place that it became a pattern for others to follow. Postwar industrialization of our midland areas produced a second generation of vast tracts of impounded water, open for fly-fishing.

There were some curious spin-off effects. People from other countries, whose fishing habits were more practical, watched with amazement what they considered to be the growth of fly-fishing snobbery among the "lower classes," who now took to the sport in earnest. Sales of trout-fishing gear waxed at the expense of bait and spinning equipment. This was no more than was also happening in sports such as golf, but in Europe it was, and still is, completely misunderstood. The French, whom I admire dearly, would have filled such lakes with pike and zander to the pleasure of the bait angler, for instance. The explosion was not simply the availability of water and leisure time; it was also the result of our national characteristic of relating sporting rewards to the overcoming of self-imposed limitations. If you think about it, this is what the more doctrinaire Halford era was all about, too.

Now there is hardly an urban area of Britain whose inhabitants have not got stillwater fly-fishing within an hour's drive. Generally the quarry will be rainbow trout. In larger reservoirs the stocking policy, plus the dispersal time and available space, will allow the fish to make some natural growth and to survive long enough to overcome the conditioning effects of the stew ponds. The summer fishing can be excellent with stocked trout that have learned to feed naturally and to be wary of man. This allows for the stalking of fish and for imitative fly-fishing.

Unhappily, we're faced with an ethical problem. The explosion of reservoir fly-fishing brought about the creation of smaller, sometimes very commercial lake fisheries. Many Britons don't yet realize that this ethical problem exists, but already some criticism is being leveled at certain aspects of these commercial fisheries. Selective breeding and intensive feeding can raise rainbows (and other species) to artificially high weights. These fish are then released into confined areas of water where they fall victim to the fly before they have had time to develop natural wariness or feeding behavior. When some of them are caught, it's probable that the last man they saw was the one who fed them. The ethical problem crops up when such fish are claimed as national and international records, as is presently the case. Fortunately, no one has to fish these smaller waters. Although I am involved in the management of one such fishery (Sundridge), I prefer the challenge and solace of the large natural or impounded waters.

Trout-population densities and stocking practices vary considerably here with different fisheries. At one extreme we have lakes in our remote Pennine hills where no stocking is necessary. Although the wild fellside scenery is magnificent,

Some of the very big rainbow trout raised to high weights in "stews" before being planted out into smaller commercial fisheries. *Bill Goddard*

these lakes are so lightly fished that natural breeding in the moorland becks, which tumble into these lakes, is quite sufficient. Some small bands of devotees, among which I number myself, will make the long pilgrimage to fish the trout that only God's hand nourished from the day the egg was fertilized.

On the great lochs of the Isles of Orkney, off the north coast of Scotland, a thriving fishing association repopulates the streams with fry and fingerling trout. One could never say exactly what density of fish Loch Harray would hold, but it always is sufficient to satisfy the local anglers. It's sobering that the air fare from London to Orkney is not far from the fare from London to New York; hence, the rainbow fever has not yet bitten the quiet Orcadians.

(33)

In more southerly English reservoirs, stocking is so intensive that twenty to fifty fish per acre are possible. During most of the season, early spring being the exception, the acclimatization of stocked fish is good enough to maintain the reality of proper fly-fishing for reasonable worthy opponents. In high summer, for instance, I often fish with a graphite rod and a five-weight line to pick off visible fish with dry fly or nymph at the surface. Some of these reservoirs, Grafham for instance, have large bird sanctuaries where none may fish. These areas hold some of the fish population in reserve so that the opening-day massacre is less punitive. The bird sanctuary may well be the shallowest, most prolific food larder in the lake. It holds a good head of fish from which the main body of the lake will constantly draw a trout population already conditioned to natural feeding behavior.

When such an example is applied to the small commercial lake fisheries the problems become complex. I have touched on the ethical problem of the so-called super-strains of fish from these lakes upon which reputations are based, both for the fishery and the individual fisherman. Although the phrase "shooting fish in a barrel" is, for us, a transatlantic introduction, it does apply to these fisheries where the stocking rate may be in excess of a hundred fish per acre. Since the commercial success of these fisheries depends on high rod pressure, this level is maintained by continual replenishment. It has its comical side. I constantly hear subjective rationalizations—even plain self-deceptions—to justify the situation. I have read, for example, theories by writers who frequent these fisheries to the effect that fish become instantly wild on introduction, which is patently absurd.

However, even while enduring the excesses of the British equivalent of the dude fishery, some more enlightened managers try to improve the sporting standards. In my own twenty-acre lake, I know that a newly introduced fish will start to feed naturally, that is by recognition of its food, after about twenty-one days. The ideal situation is when a private syndicate decides on a natural-fishing policy such as fry stocking or fallow periods. At the famous Two Lakes fishery the owner cordons off areas of his lakes with chicken wire, and artificial food is withheld from the inhabitants for the last three weeks or so before release. Even so, we have a problem posed by extremes of artificial conditions, and while the angling public sometimes seems intoxicated by reports of huge fish from such hot-houses, others realize that while such places contribute to available facilities, they pose problems of sportsmanship that are, as yet, barely recognized, let alone resolved.

Fortunately most fly fishermen are intent on mastery of the larger waters. From such shorelines, the problem is that of reaching the fish, and distance casting is essential. We are probably mistaken in equating distance casting with long rods and heavy lines, rather than improved technique. I have been reading recently the debates between English and American writers in the columns of the *Fishing Gazette* before the First World War. The famous G. E. M. Skues was even then sold on the American light rod, but failed to convince his contemporaries. There is something in our national fishing mentality that rejects ultralight fly-fishing equipment, and our now-traditional reservoir fly rod would literally stop a runaway horse in its tracks.

A line-up typical of many British reservoir fisheries *Photo courtesy of John Wilshaw*

We have taken to the American streamer and bucktail, but this is often confined to the early part of the season before aquatic fauna emerges from dormant
stages. Smaller, imitative flies have grown in popularity, and some of our ama-
teur angling entomologists like C. F. Walker and John Goddard have preached
the religion of fairly exact imitation on stillwater.

For the future, the development of technique may well favor lighter rods with
shooting-head systems. As early as 1968, I was urging this on the British angler
in my *Fly Fishing Tactics on Still Water.* In contrast to America and Scandina-
via and excepting private lessons, facilities here for learning advanced distance
fly-casting are poor. Even so, by virtue of printed article, a small number of us,
committed to the improvement of casting technique, have managed to convince a
growing minority of the value of a scaled-down version of the tournament dou-

ble-haul method, especially for reaching out for distance from the bank. We still have a long way to go in combatting the popular fallacy that distance fly-casting results from a combination of heavy equipment and brute strength. The advent of graphite rods might have ushered in an era of ultralight tackle, but already the traditional trend is exerting itself in the demand for longer, more powerful rods with thicker walls, thus negating the single great advantage of the new material.

In broadly imitative terms we have made some strides with fly patterns. British fly-tying tends to be practical more than artistic, a state of which I heartily approve. There is little gain in painstakingly weaving the body of a nymph to fish for a primitive creature with an instinctive reaction to food. On stillwater we expect the fish to react to fairly simple copies of the aquatic fauna, providing that the flies are basically accurate in shape, color, and size. The feeding behavior of trout is widely understood now, because weekly papers such as the *Angling Times* devote much space to popular trout fishing, in addition to further information supplied by such magazines as our *Trout and Salmon* and others.

As an example of this, some years ago, before imitation was considered important, I found that the standard copy of the Chironomid pupa was too inaccurate to catch surface-feeding trout at Blagdon. The body of the natural fly is both segmented and hook-shaped; the artificial was of smooth silk and straight. I made a copy by winding alternate strands of black and white horsehair forward from the hook bend, dubbing in a pinch of mole's fur as the thorax and a turn or two of peacock herl for the head. This fly became known as the Footballer due to its striped jersey. I deliberately left out materials to copy emerging wings, legs or breathing tubes, because the fishing method was to cast the fly so that it cleanly pierced the surface immediately in front of a fish seen to be feeding with preoccupation on the natural pupae. It worked well, and I cite it here to exemplify the combination of imitation and practicality typical of our modern technique, a far cry from the pedantry of Halford so many years ago on the chalkstreams.

In a historical sense, it's curious that in the last century W. E. Stewart, the famous Scottish border angler, had his disciples fishing upstream with short lines and skimpy wet-fly patterns. From this first great change in method evolved nymph fishing, first through Skues and subsequently renewed in the postwar era by Frank Sawyer. Frank is a chalkstream keeper and mainly interested in river fishing, but on a trip to Sweden he applied his Gray Goose nymph to lake fishing with resounding success. Of course, followers of his teachings applied his other stream patterns, such as the Pheasant Tail, to reservoirs. Although not sharing the same dietary importance as the Chironomids and caddis, various lake and pond olives (mayflies) do exist on our stillwater fisheries. They are sufficiently close in appearance to the river flies so that the same imitations are taken freely by trout in lakes and reservoirs. This was how our stillwater nymph fishing developed.

On the debit side, we undoubtably have a fair proportion of anglers who automatically strip lures such as streamers throughout the season, and it is from them that the heavy-tackle philosophy comes. However, many of these are people who

Pete Wring with three rainbows taken from Blagdon Reservoir
Photo courtesy of John Wilshaw

trout fish for the small period of time when the closed season for our coarse fish and the opening of the trout season overlap. When some of these anglers become converted to trout fishing, they soon yearn to catch the fish in a method requiring more finesse. You may rightly gather from this that our rules are catholic; providing an orthodox fly rod, reel, and line are used, almost any type of fly or lure is allowed. This causes no problem on large expanses of water; it's simply sad that so many lose out on the true pleasure of fishing, as if one's golf were confined to a driving range with wooden clubs.

The real blessing of our stillwater fisheries is that most allow anyone to fish by almost any fly-fishing method. Even a dry-fly purist could quite happily work through a season, and on his day, when caddis and buzzers abound, might well outscore his companions. The mechanical lure-stripper, who has found a substitute for spinning, will be equally happy, though finding dour periods in high summer when natural food is prolific enough to bring about preoccupied feeding behavior on insect life. Those are the two extremes.

My personal philosophy—though I have reached middle age, when I want to fish more and preach less—consists of two themes. The first is that the essential conditions for distance casting should come out of a lighter tackle system and better casting technique. Second, one derives more pleasure from selecting fishing tactics according to the behavior of the trout, rather than by adopting a rigid preference in advance. This tactical theme is suited to a lake because it offers such a wider choice than a river. The behavior of river trout, especially on a chalkstream, is circumscribed by the physical and biological limits of the fishery. Almost any lake is wider in both senses, and the mysteries of trout fishing are that much increased. That is the fascination of lakes as well as the frustrations they may offer.

When I used to fish the River Test, I could note the positions of trout holding stations in the stream, and by keeping an eye on the finny inhabitants of a particular beat, when a rise started it would be comparatively easy to solve the fishing problems. A vast reservoir offers no such easy formula. On many a day there may be no surface rise at all, and the fish must be located by understanding the geography of the lake floor and the unseen feeding behavior of the fish in relation to the local fauna. At first it's much like Churchill's description of the politics of the Soviet Union: " . . . a secret wrapped in an enigma and shrouded in mystery."

I believe I have described accurately our stillwater scene, from the lochs in the far north, as old as the rocks that surround them, to the new scoopings out of our shrinking countryside. In trying to evaluate the British scene, I leave this warning. The techniques and artificial results from the smaller commercial fisheries exert an influence out of proportion to their place, just as the chalkstreams did decades ago. There is no harm in this except as it distorts the situation facing the average British angler fishing his local loch or reservoir. While the angling press naturally sensationalizes the twenty-pound rainbow trout from one or two privileged small fisheries, most of us are going to continue to be delighted with catching stillwater trout between one and three pounds. The odd specimen of four to six pounds from richer areas such as the vast Grafham water will be in the nature of a red-letter bonus. This is the true perspective, and as it still represents the best stillwater trouting in Europe, I have no complaint.

(38)

Part Two

AN ANGLER'S ECOLOGY

The more you know about a lake and its inhabitants, the better you will be able to fish it. The following three chapters are all by scientific professionals, written for the express purpose of giving anglers a better understanding of the lakes and ponds they fish. The chapters are designed to be read in order. Jim Gilford's contribution and the first in this series is really a basic discussion of lake and pond ecology; it defines terms that are used without further definition in the subsequent chapters. High-altitude lakes, discussed by Fred Eiserman and Earl West, are special, extreme situations by virtue of their altitude, and a fascinating contrast to those more typical, fertile western waters that are covered by Peter Moyle and Donald Baltz.

Some readers will find this section too technical and will probably want to skip it. Others will be as delighted with it as I am. The complex web of ecological events that ultimately leads to the simple catching of a trout is fascinating. Even a partial understanding inevitably leads to better fishing.

4

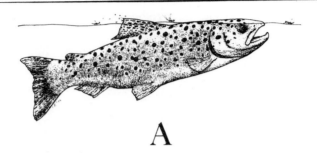

A
BASIC
UNDERSTANDING

Jim Gilford

THE CHALLENGE OF STILLWATER FISHING IS BARELY BEGINNING TO stir the interest of American trout fishermen is shown by the absence, in contemporary angling books, of basic information on the characteristics and ecology of stillwater habitats. While stream and river anglers can refer to a large volume of published information on the ecology of flowing water as it relates to fishing for trout and salmon, there is nothing of a comparable nature in popular print for stillwater habitat.

A great deal has been learned over the past fifty years about the physical, chemical, and biological characteristics of cold-water lakes and impoundments. The fundamental concepts of lake ecology that have evolved as a result of this knowledge are a logical basis for understanding the habits and behavior of stillwater trout and salmon. So versed, an angler is better prepared both to fish these waters and to understand what is involved in their management and conservation.

The undisciplined observer has a tendency to look on lakes as being much the same wherever they are found. That is not the case. Stillwater areas vary from one another as much as do streams or rivers. Features such as size, shape, depth, surface-to-volume ratio, chemical composition, and a variety of others differ sufficiently, alone or collectively, that the ecology of one lake may be distinguished from that of another. In spite of these differences, stillwater habitats share certain other characteristics equally important in shaping their ecology. So both differences and similarities need to be considered.

A typical freshwater lake located in a region of temperate climate, such as that found in the northern United States, contains three distinct zones, the littoral, limnetic, and profundal. The makeup of each zone, the habitat conditions that develop within them, and the plant and animal life they produce are related to the shape of the lake basin and the physical and chemical properties of the water within it.

The littoral zone consists of several marginal bands of rooted aquatic vegetation extending from the shoreline lakeward. The first of the these bands occupies the shallow water close to shore and its rooted vegetation usually is the emergent type such as rushes and cattails. The second band occupies slightly deeper water beyond this zone of emergent vegetation; in most temperate lakes, the surface area of this band is taken up by the floating leaves of water lilies and pond weeds. Beyond this is the third band of littoral-zone vegetation. It consists of submerged aquatic plants such as elodea, myriophyllum, and potamogeton, which are characterized by finely divided leaves.

Attached to the submerged parts of the vegetation in the littoral zone are microscopic diatoms and filamentous algae, which are important food organisms in the aquatic environment. Also living among the rooted vegetation in this zone are a variety of aquatic animals that feed on the algae and diatoms as well as on the submerged parts of the rooted plants and each other. Included in this community of bottom-dwelling animals is a diversity of aquatic insects—beetles, freshwater shrimp, mayflies, caddisflies, dragonflies, and damselflies. In fact, of all the lake zones, it is the littoral, because of the abundant shelter and food found there, where the greatest variety of species occurs.

The limnetic zone occupies the central area of the lake, encircled by the aquatic vegetation of the littoral zone. Vertically, the limnetic zone extends from the surface to the bottom of the lake, where it overlays the profundal zone. It consists of two layers, the depth of the upper one extending to the lowest level of light penetration. Typically, this layer is inhabited by mixed populations of microscopic plants, mostly single-celled algae, known as phytoplankton, and microscopic animals called zooplankton. The lower layer of the limnetic zone is below the level of light penetration, a condition that excludes plant life. The inhabitants of this layer frequently are adapted to living under conditions of little or no oxygen. In very shallow lakes, or in those with very clear water, light may penetrate to the bottom, in which case the limnetic zone is composed of a single layer.

The profundal zone is that portion of the lake bottom under the limnetic zone. Usually light rays do not reach this level and the immediate environment of this zone is low in oxygen but high in carbon dioxide. This is especially true in those lakes that are highly productive and where the soft, ooze-like bottom contains a large amount of organic material. Bacteria are abundant as are tubifex worms, fingernail clams, and certain insect larvae that are tolerant of low-oxygen conditions.

The phytoplankton community of the limnetic zone, along with that of the littoral zone and the rooted vegetation found there, is the starting point of the food chain or nutrient cycle that nourishes all of the animals that inhabit the lake, including the larger fish. The exact kinds of algae present will vary from lake to lake and from one time of the year to the next. In many lakes, seasonal pulses occur in the abundance of the plankton. These pulses, which are known as blooms, may appear one to several times during the year and it is not uncommon to observe two conspicuous blooms, one in early spring and the other in autumn. The appearance of algal blooms, it is believed, is related to temperature changes and increases in the amount of nutrients, especially phosphate, which the algae need for growth.

The next step in the food chain occurs when a variety of animals, including microscopic zooplankton, the young of some species of fish and certain plankton-eating baitfish, feed on the algae. These algal feeders in turn are fed on by larger members of the lake's animal community and they in turn are eaten by still larger inhabitants of the lake. Eventually, large predator fish such as trout and salmon join the food chain. Several different chains may furnish food for these larger predator fish, forming a food web linked through the feeding habits of the predator. Lake trout, for example, which feed on a number of different baitfish, top off such a food web.

Planktonic organisms, both plant and animal, which are not eaten, eventually die and settle to the bottom where their bodies are decomposed by bacteria. Baitfish that escape being eaten and the large predatory fish, as well, eventually die and decompose in a similar manner. Rooted vegetation, which grows in the littoral zone during the spring and summer months, dies back during the fall and winter. And that organic matter, too, settles to the bottom of the lake where it will be decomposed by bacteria. The breakdown of all this organic matter releases into the water minerals and nutrients that will again be taken up by the phytoplankton and reintroduced into the food chain. The amount of essential minerals and nutrients present in a lake is limited. And it is through the bacterial decomposition that this material is recycled.

The littoral, limnetic, and profundal zones are interrelated and their functions collectively have much to do with determining the ecological conditions that exist in the lake. To appreciate these relationships fully and to understand lake ecology, it is necessary to consider certain unique features of water that play a major role in shaping the character of the aquatic environment. Water exhibits certain thermal characteristics that are important ecologically. It changes density with changes in temperature. It is heaviest at 39.7°F. and it becomes lighter at temperatures above or below that point. This is the reason why a lake ices over rather than freezing from the bottom up.

Water has other thermal properties relevant to lake ecology. It is able to ab-

The littoral zone is a pond's food factory; trout cruise these shallows in search of the abundant insect life. *John Merwin*

sorb large quantities of heat without becoming appreciably warmer itself. For a lake to warm up a single degree, it must take up large amounts of heat from the sun and nearby land mass. In a similar vein, before ice can form or before it can melt, the lake water must give off or take on considerable quantities of heat. In practical terms, the cooling of a lake in the fall and the eventual formation of the ice cover, followed by ice out in the spring and warming of the surface water, involves large exchanges of heat between the lake and its surroundings.

Due to the nature of these heat exchanges, temperature differences in stillwater habitats typically are gradual and slow. This explains why, for example, large inland lakes in more northern regions do not become ice covered until December or January even though winter conditions set in much earlier. It also explains why ice-out sometimes does not occur until well after the onset of spring weather.

Water evaporates. In the process both vapor and heat are given off to the atmosphere. Evaporation takes place at all temperatures and it continues day and night. The amount of evaporation, however, and consequently the amount of heat lost, varies with the conditions that control the rate of evaporation such as temperature, wind, and relative humidity. Due to evaporation, there is a constant removal of heat from a lake and this helps offset daily heat gains from the sun and thereby maintains a relatively stable heat balance.

Water is a poor conductor of heat. The surface of a lake absorbs the heat of the sun's rays and becomes warmer. To a limited extent, this heat is transferred to the underlying water by conduction. But the most effective distribution of the heat absorbed from the sun is accomplished by the action of the wind as it agitates and circulates the upper layers of lake water.

The thermal properties of water have special significance when considering the natural cycle of seasonal changes that occurs in lakes in the temperate areas of the world. These cyclic changes, influenced as they are by the thermal properties of water, are especially important to the stillwater fisherman because they determine the distribution, movements, and feeding patterns of both baitfish and predatory gamefish.

In most lakes that freeze over in winter, a pronounced vertical temperature stratification becomes established during the summer months. Summer stratification may develop in early spring and last well into the fall in more southerly climates. In northern lakes, on the other hand, stratification may not appear until late May or early June and may end by late August or September. Stratification can be demonstrated by taking temperature measurements at different depths in the lake from the top to the bottom. When a lake is completely stratified, it's possible to distinguish three distinct thermal zones or strata layered one on top of another.

The upper layer is known as the epilimnion. It will vary in depth depending upon a number of factors but frequently it extends downward some twenty to thirty feet or more and it is relatively uniform in temperature throughout. Immediately below the epilimnion is the second or middle layer known as the metalim-

Lake Davis in Oregon. *Valentine Atkinson*

nion. Within this layer, the water temperature drops sharply. Somewhere near the middle of the metalimnion is a narrow band of water, called the thermocline, in which the temperature changes nearly 2°F. with every three feet of change in depth. On the bottom of the stack is the third zone, known as the hypolimnion. This layer extends to the bottom of the lake and holds the coldest water. There is little temperature variation throughout this zone and virtually no circulation.

Because of the temperature/density relationships, the epilimnion layer contains the lightest water of the three while that of the hypolimnion is the heaviest. The metalimnion forms a density barrier between these two, preventing the circulation of heat, oxygen, and nutrients between the top and bottom layers. Once formed, this thermal stratification lasts throughout the summer.

As fall approaches, air temperatures begin to drop and the surface water cools. As it becomes cooler and therefore heavier, the surface layer sinks and is replaced by the warmer, lighter water beneath. This, too, cools, becomes heavier and sinks. This process, aided by strong fall breezes, continues until the temperature and density differences between the epilimnion, metalimnion, and hypolimnion disappear. At this point, the action of the wind is able to set up circulation currents that reach to the bottom of the lake. The temperature of the lake becomes nearly uniform throughout, nutrients stirred up from the bottom are redistributed and the oxygen of the lake is recharged. This period is known as the fall overturn and often it is associated with the appearance of a plankton bloom triggered by the redistributed nutrients.

With the arrival of winter, the water temperature of the lake continues to drop. Eventually the surface layer cools below 39.7°F., its point of greatest density. Now the surface layer is cooler but lighter than the underlying water, and it remains on the surface and continues to cool, eventually freezing. The water in the lake then shows a reverse temperature stratification, the coldest and lightest on top and the warmer but heavier on the bottom, but the temperature difference between the surface and the bottom is relatively small.

In the spring, as the sun warms the surface of the lake, melting whatever ice is present, the water temperature begins to rise. Heated by the sun's rays, the 32°F. surface water becomes heavier and sinks through the colder, lighter layer beneath it. This warming and sinking of the surface layer continues until, eventually, the temperature of the lake is 39.7°F. throughout. Spring breezes sweeping over the surface of the lake help mix the water and, when the lake temperature becomes uniform, these air movements are able to circulate water from the surface to the bottom, bringing about a complete turnover. This again results in a redistribution of nutrient materials from the bottom of the lake and a replenishment of the oxygen content of the water. This overturning of the lake is similar to the one that occurs in the fall. The nutrients it brings to the surface layers stimulate a marked increase in the plankton community; this increase is known as the spring bloom.

At this time, conditions throughout the lake are relatively uniform and the fish population is broadly dispersed. As the season progresses and the sun's rays continue to heat the lake, the surface water warms above 39.7°F. Becoming progressively warmer and lighter, the surface layer stays in place and the density difference between it and the heavier, colder water beneath becomes so great that the wind is not able to drive the lighter surface water through the heavier layers underneath. This eliminates the currents that created the spring overturn. Lacking this circulation, the lake begins to stratify thermally and once again the epilimnion, metalimnion, and hypolimnion form. Because the water temperature within the epilimnion is nearly uniform, surface breezes continue to circulate the water within this layer, thereby assuring an adequate supply of oxygen for those organisms that inhabit it.

The lower edge of the epilimnion also corresponds roughly to the lowest level of light penetration. Because of this, the epilimnion is the only layer in which photosynthesis, a process which requires light, can occur. This is also the reason why the phytoplankton population is found in the epilimnion. And since these organisms are the starting point in the lake's food chain, conditions in this stratum greatly influence the ecology of the other zones of the lake.

In the hypolimnion, the water stagnates. Organic matter that rains down from above, including the dead bodies of planktonic plants and animals, aquatic insects and fish, undergoes bacterial decay. Decomposition by the bacteria uses up the oxygen of the water and, as summer progresses, may deplete it. The hypolimnion then contains the coldest water in the lake but also the water lowest in oxygen; in organically rich lakes, it may even be devoid of oxygen. So although the cold temperature salmon and trout require may be present, they cannot live in the hypolimnion because there is too little oxygen for them to survive. With the onset of fall and cold weather, the surface water once again starts to cool, fall overturn occurs, and the annual cycle begins anew.

At the same time the cycle of stratification and destratification is taking place, several other cyclic changes are occurring that have an important impact on lake ecology. Two critical ingredients in the biology of stillwaters, dissolved oxygen and plant nutrients, are depleted and replenished at various stages in the annual pattern of events.

Most aquatic organisms must have oxygen to live. They obtain it from the water, which holds it in dissolved form. The amount of dissolved oxygen in the water, therefore, is critical. Cold water is capable of holding more oxygen in solution than warm water. As the temperature of lake water drops from 75°F. to 32°F., for example, it can hold approximately 40 percent more oxygen in solution. Other factors, such as salinity and barometric pressure, may influence the amount of dissolved oxygen in the water but, within the lake environment, their influence is less dramatic than that of temperature.

Most of the dissolved oxygen in lake water comes from two sources, the atmosphere and photosynthesis carried on by aquatic vegetation. Oxygen in the atmosphere in contact with the lake surface diffuses into the water and is dissolved. Wind, which agitates the surface of the lake, aids in the process of mixing air and water. The planktonic plants, as well as rooted vegetation in the littoral zone, give off oxygen as a byproduct of photosynthesis. This oxygen, too, becomes dissolved in the surrounding water.

During summer, when lakes are thermally stratified, the water in the hypolimnion ceases to circulate and becomes stagnant. When this occurs, the dissolved oxygen in that layer may be used up by bacterial organisms living in the profundal zone. Since oxygen-laden water from the surface layer of the lake cannot penetrate the metalimnion and because there is no photosynthesis taking place in the hypolimnion, the oxygen used up is not replenished until the fall overturn. As a consequence, the hypolimnion in lakes rich in organic matter may be unable to support fish life during the summer months because of the lack of oxygen.

In the wintertime, ice cover effectively blocks the diffusion of oxygen from the atmosphere into the lake. A sufficient amount of sunlight, however, penetrates the ice layer to enable the phytoplankton to photosynthesize and replace the oxygen being used by aquatic animals. If the ice becomes covered with a blanket of snow and remains so for a prolonged period of time, sunlight cannot then reach the plantlife under the ice, photosynthesis is reduced or stops altogether, and the level of dissolved oxygen in the water gradually diminishes. If this condition prevails for a period of time, the oxygen may become so depleted that many of the aquatic organisms suffocate, creating a condition known as winter kill.

Dissolved oxygen in temperate lakes is uniform and near the saturation point during the spring and fall turnovers. The oxygen content in the epilimnion normally is high during the summer since this layer is in constant contact with the atmosphere and continues to circulate. The hypolimnion is the zone that is subject to oxygen depletion. The likelihood of this occurring is greatest in those lakes that are relatively shallow and have a rich organic bottom. Oxygen depletion in the hypolimnion of cold-water lakes, which have little organic matter accumulated on the bottom, seldom occurs.

A number of natural elements essential to living organisms undergo seasonal changes in concentration and distribution within a lake; this is chiefly associated with the annual overturns. Phosphate, for example, which is a critical element in the nutrition of both phytoplankton and rooted aquatic vegetation, is present in limited amounts. Phosphates are liberated from the organic deposits of the lake bottom through bacterial decomposition. Then at spring overturn, they're dispersed throughout the lake. Most of this phosphate is quickly taken up by the aquatic plants and phytoplankton, resulting in increased algal growth, which produces the familar spring bloom. In this way, phosphate enters the food chain and passes from plants and phytoplankton to the animals that feed on them. It moves in turn to other animals that feed on the plant eaters and so on up the food chain. The bodies of dead plants and animals carry phosphates with them as they settle to the lake bottom. There bacteria release the phosphates as they decompose the dead organisms. In the meantime, while phosphates are accumulating on the bottom of the lake, they've been greatly depleted in the surface layer and the phytoplankton community responds to the lack of phosphate by diminishing the number of organisms present. With the fall overturn, phosphates once again are redistributed to repeat the cycle.

While lakes show individually distinctive characteristics, it is possible to classify those which are of interest to stillwater anglers into one of two types based on the amount of nutrient material in the water. Those rich in nutrients are called eutrophic lakes while those relatively poor in nutrients are called oligotrophic.

Eutrophic lakes typically are contained in shallow basins that have gently sloping banks and well-developed littoral zones. Being shallow, these lakes have a high surface-to-volume ratio, tend to be very productive biologically, and have rich organic bottoms. The hypolimnion of eutrophic lakes becomes oxygen poor during periods of summer and winter stagnation.

Oligotrophic lakes, by comparison, characteristically are deep, with sharply sloping shores and minimal marginal vegetation. This type of lake has much less organic matter deposited on the bottom, a low surface-to-volume ratio, and a low level of biological productivity. The hypolimnion of oligotrophic lakes generally does not become devoid of oxygen during periods of stagnation. The oligotrophic type of lake has a special combination of physical and chemical characteristics that create ideal habitat for trout and salmon.

Oligotrophic lakes, as a result of a slow, natural process known as succession, eventually become eutrophic. Organic matter carried into the lake by inlet streams and blown in from the surrounding land mass begins to fill the basin. In time, as the filling process goes on, the shoreline becomes shallower and rooted aquatic vegetation establishes itself. The littoral zone enlarges and the spread of aquatic plants there adds to the yearly organic loading of the basin. Also contributing to the filling of the lake basin are the algal blooms stimulated by the nutrients that come into the lake with the influx of organic matter. Although this aging process takes hundreds of years under natural conditions, eventually the character of the lake, the shape of its basin, and the organisms that inhabit it change from those of an oligotrophic to those of a eutrophic habitat.

Many eutrophic lakes, especially the shallower ones, are unable to maintain some species of cold-water fish during the warmer months because of high summer temperatures in the surface water and lack of oxygen in the colder water of the lower strata. While bass and other species having a tolerance for warmer water thrive in such lakes, members of the trout family may not. In some eutrophic lakes, however, the temperature and oxygen within the metalimnion are sufficient to carry brown trout and rainbows through the warm weather although often the trout fisheries in these lakes must be maintained through stocking programs. Frequently two-story fisheries develop as a result of the stocking programs; warm-water species occupy the epilimnion during the summer months while trout inhibit the cooler layers of the metalimnion below the thermocline. The extent to which stillwaters in the Northeast can support two-story fisheries depends upon the amount of food and oxygen available in the limited area of the metalimnion during the summer months.

The different aspects of lake ecology that have been discussed up to this point have an influence on the distribution, movements, and feeding patterns of those members of the trout family inhabiting stillwater environments. Members of the trout clan present in eastern stillwaters include lake trout, *Salvelinus namaycush,* landlocked salmon, *Salmo salar,* brook trout, *Salvelinus fontinalis,* brown trout, *Salmo trutta,* and rainbows, *Salmo gairdnerii.* All of these species are cold-water forms and they are widely distributed in the arctic and north temperate portions of the United States and Canada. Water temperature is a critical factor in the lives of these salmonids and this relationship provides the stillwater angler with a valuable clue to the whereabouts of these fish in lakes and impoundments. Lake trout and landlocked salmon prefer water temperatures between 40° and 50°F. Brook trout favor 55° to 65°F. water while brown trout like 55° to 70°F. and rainbows prefer 60° to 70°F. temperatures.

LAKE TROUT

Largest of these eastern stillwater salmonids is the lake trout. It is found throughout Canada except in Newfoundland, some parts of the prairie provinces, and the coastal areas of British Columbia. In the United States, lake trout are indigenous to the Great Lakes drainage and parts of northern New England, New York, Wisconsin, and Minnesota. In the northern part of its range, it is found in relatively shallow but cold-water lakes and occasionally in rivers. At the southern end of its range, on the other hand, the lake trout is confined to deeper lakes in which the hypolimnion is cold enough and contains sufficient dissolved oxygen to sustain the lakers during the summer when the surface water becomes too warm for them. Its preference for 40° to 50°F. water influences the movement and the location within the lake where this species may be found from season to season. These fish seldom remain in water warmer than 60°F. And they may go off their feed at temperatures between 50° and 55°F.

The relationship between temperature stratification and vertical distribution of lake trout is very marked. During the summer, lake trout abandon the warmer water of the epilimnion, retreating to the cooler region below the thermocline. In cold northern Canadian lakes such as Kree and Wollastan in Saskatchewan, where surface temperatures remain cool throughout the year, the vertical distribution of lake trout in the summer may range from just under the surface to a depth of 130 feet. In the southern extremes of its range, by comparison, lake trout, during the summer, are found concentrated at depths ranging from 60 to 300 feet. Although exceptions are known, lakers generally keep to deeper water, moving into shallow areas only when the surface temperature drops to the low 50s, a condition occurring there during the fall, winter, and early spring.

Lake trout are slow to mature, taking six to seven years in Lake Michigan and up to thirteen years in Great Bear Lake in the Northwest Territory. In general, lake trout grow more slowly in the colder water of northern lakes but live for longer periods of time. In Great Bear Lake, for example, lakers reach a length of twenty-five inches at twenty to twenty-five years of age. Some of these fish will live to an age of forty years or more and fifteen to twenty-year-old lake trout are not uncommon in these waters. Farther south in Alberta, lake trout from lower Waterton Lake have been found to reach twenty-five inches at only eight years of age.

The spawning period for lakers ranges from August to December but varies with latitude, water temperature, size, and race. Eggs are deposited on lake bottoms over rock and rubble where wave action and water currents keep them swept free of silt. The water depth where eggs are deposited also is variable, ranging from six inches, an observation made at Cold Stream Pond in Maine, to over 300 feet in Lake Superior. The eggs settle between the rocks and develop unattended. Incubation, which proceeds best at temperatures below 50°F., may require as long as four months. Fry hatching on shallow-water spawning grounds remain there for a few months before moving into deeper parts of the lake in summer as the surface area warms. In the northern fringes of the range, young lake trout may remain in shallow water for several years.

Lake trout feed on many kinds of aquatic organisms. The makeup of the diet depends upon the size of the fish and upon opportunity. Smaller fish gorge on zooplankton, aquatic insect larvae, freshwater shrimp, and various crustaceans. Although the aquatic insects and crustaceans continue to be part of their diet, baitfish are the principal food of adult lakers, once they exceed fifteen inches in length. While availability determines the bait or forage fish lake trout prey on, they'll feed on alewives, ciscos, whitefish, suckers, sculpin, smelt, perch, minnows, sticklebacks, and small trout.

Lake trout populations tend to be sparse because of their slow maturation, the low productivity of their cold-water habitat, and the high vulnerability of these fish to angling pressure.

BROWN TROUT

Brown trout are resident species in many cold-water lakes and impoundments. In general, they appear to grow faster in a stillwater environment and reach a larger size than they do in a stream habitat. They may weigh upward of ten pounds by the time they are three years old. Temperature has a marked influence on stillwater browns, too. They favor water close to 60°F. and during warm weather they retreat to that depth in the lake where the water is the preferred temperature. They'll move out of this temperature level to feed if it's necessary, and then return.

While brown trout will eat a variety of aquatic insects as the opportunity presents itself, they also prey on a number of different forage fish that are common to eastern stillwaters, including ciscos, lake chubs, sculpins, emerald shiners, alewives, and smelt. With the exception of the shiners, these forage fish prefer water temperatures ranging from 45° to 55°F. The shiners favor water between

A Lake Michigan brown caught during the day. *David Richey*

68° and 72°F; they'll school in large groups during the day and brown trout will move up into the warmer water to forage on the schools of shiners if other food is in short supply.

Unlike stream browns, which tend to feed and be more active at night, lake and reservoir residents are also active during the day. Their period of greatest activity is at dawn.

Brown trout spawn in the fall from October to December, depending upon the geographical location. They move out of the lake into tributary streams to deposit their eggs in gravel redds. The young trout from these spawnings remain in the streams for two to three years before making their way into the lake.

In the spring, when some of the forage fish are in the shallows near shore preparing to spawn or schooling up near the tributary inlets before starting upstream to spawn, brown trout will move into the shallow water to feed on them. In the Great Lakes, as an example, as alewives and smelt congregate inshore in preparation for spawning, brown trout, many of them of trophy size, will move in to feed on the baitfish. Once warm weather sets in, however, the trout will move out of the shallow areas far enough to find the cooler water they prefer. From that location, they will move in to gorge on the baitfish and return. Dropoffs close to shore are areas that brown trout frequent at that time of year.

LANDLOCKED SALMON

Landlocked salmon inhabit stillwater sites in Quebec, the Maritime Provinces, Maine, and in some larger lakes in other New England States, New York, and the Great Lakes region. The cold, oligotrophic lakes of these areas are ideal environments for both the salmon and its favorite food fish, the smelt, *Osmerus mordax.*

Although adult landlocked salmon will feed on other forage fish and aquatic insects, there is considerable evidence that this species has been able to establish itself only in those lakes in which smelt also were present. Adult fish of both species favor water temperatures below 70° F. and that preference has a marked influence on their seasonal movements and behavior.

Smelt spawn in the late winter or early spring. By ice out in many salmon and trout lakes of the Northeast, smelt have moved into the shallows to deposit their eggs or are schooling near the inlet streams in preparation for an upstream spawning run. Landlocked salmon move into the shallows to feed on the smelt at that time. Both the salmon and the adult smelt remain in the inshore areas during the first few weeks following ice out, until the surface water becomes so warm that it causes them to migrate into deeper, cooler water. In some stillwaters of Maine, such as Sebago Lake, this movement of the landlocks and smelt usually occurs between mid-June and early July. Farther north, where surface temperatures are later in warming, they may remain in the upper layers of the lake through much of July.

On occasion, smelt following the migrations of freshwater shrimp and water fleas on which they feed, may move upward or inshore during the summer but these ventures into warmer water occur at night and are short lived. Salmon, likewise, may follow the smelt or they may pursue emerging mayflies into the warmer surface waters now and then.

For the better part of the summer, however, the salmon and smelt remain in the cooler waters of the metalimnion and hypolimnion. With the coming of fall and the cooling of the surface water, the landlocks move into the upper levels of the lake and inshore to spawn in the gravel riffles of outlet and inlet streams. The time of spawning varies with the location, from mid-October to late November. The young salmon remain in the stream where spawning occurred for one to two years before migrating into the lake. They feed heavily on aquatic insects and crustaceans. Male landlocks mature at about three years of age, females at five years.

BROOK TROUT

Another native to the stillwaters of the Northeast is the brook trout. Brookies, however, never really become abundant in those lakes and ponds in which the water temperature exceeds 68°F. Even though this species can survive short exposures to temperatures in the low 80s, its preferred temperature range is 55° to 60°F.

Remarkably tolerant to both acid and alkaline waters, brook trout are able to inhabit a variety of stillwater environments. They are fall spawners and can spawn successfully both along the shoreline and in the spring-fed areas in deeper water. So successful is this species at spawning in stillwater that, in the absence of predator species such as walleyes and northern pike to reduce its numbers, brook trout in ponds and lakes often suffer from overpopulation.

Brook trout feed heavily on aquatic insects, freshwater shrimp, and forage fish. Availability appears to be an important factor influencing their feeding activities. While some strains of longer-lived brook trout are known, the life-span seldom exceeds four years. Where food and habitat conditions are suitable, brookies may reach several pounds in weight.

During warm weather, the vertical distribution of brook trout overlaps that of landlocked salmon where the two species share the same stillwater habitat. Brookies, however, feed on the surface with greater regularity during warm weather. In those lakes in which lake trout and brookies coexist, the brook trout occupy the shallower areas, partly because of competition from the lakers and partly because of the sparseness of aquatic insects in the deeper water.

The major threat to brook trout populations in the Northeast today appears to be acid rain. In the Adirondacks, aluminum leached from the mountain soils by acid rainfall has entered brook trout lakes in sufficient concentration to be toxic to the trout. As a result, the brook trout in some Adirondack lakes have disappeared completely.

RAINBOW TROUT

Through modern hatchery operations, rainbow trout are present in cold-water lakes and reservoirs throughout much of the Northeast. And as in the case with

other members of the trout family, the movements and behavior of stillwater rainbows are influenced by water temperature. Rainbows can tolerate temperatures in the low 80s for short periods but they prefer water in the 60° to 70°F. range.

To a considerable degree, rainbows will occupy the limnetic zone and when surface temperatures are below 70°F. they'll cruise the upper levels of the lake. As the surface water warms, the rainbows move down, keeping within the 60° to 70°F. band.

Most rainbows spawn at three years of age. Spawning occurs in the spring and takes place in gravelly riffles of inlet streams. Rarely are rainbows able to maintain themselves in lakes where they do not have access to such stream areas for spawning. Rainbows may live for a maximum of seven to eleven years depending upon the strain of fish and the locality, although most do not survive beyond the sixth year. Growth is greatest before the fish reach maturity and the maximum size reached depends on the quantity and quality of the food available to the fish. Rainbows up to thirty pounds have been caught in lakes that have abundant populations of forage fish.

While rainbows will eat a variety of foods, their diet is based on what is available. In more sterile stillwaters, plankton, diptera larvae, midges, and terrestrial insects make up much of the food consumed. Daphnia, or water fleas, are an important item in the diet of rainbows in some lakes. These tiny members of the

(57)

zooplankton community occur in large numbers in the limnetic zone, moving upward toward the surface at night and migrating down to cooler water during the day. Rainbows will follow the movements of these organisms to feed on them.

Larger fish of this species will feed on forage fish if they are fairly abundant. And, unlike other members of the trout family, rainbows will eat quantities of aquatic vegetation, particularly the filamentous forms of certain algae.

THE FOOD CHAIN

The alewife, a small silvery member of the herring family, is an important link in the food chains of stillwater trout and salmon in the Northeast. An anadromous species native to the Atlantic Coast, the alewife has become established in freshwater habitats over a wide area of the Great Lakes region, the New England states, New York, and even some mid-Atlantic states. Because of large population die-offs in the late spring or early summer, the alewife has been considered a nuisance in the Great Lakes, especially in Lake Michigan, where at times dead fish litter bathing beaches and clog water intakes.

In freshwater, adult alewives reach a length of three to six inches. They are plankton feeders and, in spite of the periodic die-offs, this species provides prime forage for many of the larger predator species, especially resident trout and salmon.

The life-span of the alewife in freshwater habitats is about four years. Adult fish move into shallow inshore water in the spring and early summer to spawn. They remain in those inshore areas until midsummer when they return to deeper regions of the lake to spend the winter. The young alewives, which have a greater tolerance for warm temperatures than the adults, hatch in late July and early August. They grow rapidly, reaching three to four inches before winter. The young fish congregate in large schools along the shoreline before migrating to deeper water for the winter.

Another link in the predator food chain of stillwaters in the East is the emerald shiner, found in freshwater habitats from Quebec to the Potomac River. In lakes, this species will suspend in the upper levels in large schools where brown trout will feed on them if more favored forage fish are not available.

Emerald shiners spawn near the lake surface in open water from June to mid-August depending on the locality. Spawning occurs earlier in the southern portions of its range and later in the northern areas. Eggs of this species hatch quickly, as soon as twenty-four hours. Freshwater shrimp and insects, both aquatic and terrestrial, are the major items in the diet of the emerald shiner.

Insects, both aquatic and terrestrial, constitute an available source of food for trout and salmon in stillwater habitats. The great majority of the aquatic insects in lakes and reservoirs are associated with the littoral zone, although a few important food insects live in the profundal zone in those stillwater areas where there is enough oxygen to meet their needs.

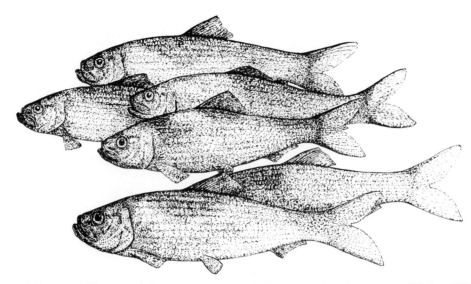

Alewives *(Alosa pseudoharengus)*

The nymphal stages of a variety of dragonflies and damselflies live and mature among the rooted vegetation in the shallow water along the shoreline. The larvae of a number of different species of case-building and retreat-making caddisflies belonging to genera such as *Phryganea, Ptilostomis, Polycentropus, Limnephilus,* and *Hydropsyche* and several different types of mayfly nymphs share the shallows with the dragonflies and damselflies. Included among the mayflies are small clinging forms such as *Siphlonurus, Callibaetis,* and *Cloeon,* sprawling forms such as *Caenis* and *Tricorythodes,* and large burrowing nymphs of *Ephemera, Hexagenia,* and *Ephoron,* which emerge in sufficient numbers to interest feeding trout. The burrowing mayflies and a few caddisflies will occupy portions of the profundal zone, provided there is enough oxygen.

Larvae and pupae of diptera, especially members of the midge and mosquito families, are found among the vegetation of the littoral zone and floating freely in the limnetic zone. Midge larvae may also be found in the profundal zone in abundance. Some of these larvae are bright red due to a hemoglobinlike pigment in their body fluids, which enables them to live in environments that have little oxygen.

The stillwater environment is a complex system supporting an equally complex array of life, the exact nature of which is determined by a number of physical and chemical parameters. Three of these—temperature, oxygen, and a suitable food chain—appear to be especially important in determining whether trout and salmon can occupy the environment. Stillwaters in temperate areas typically stratify during the summer months and trout and salmon as well as the fish they forage on respond to this phenomenon by moving to those depths in the lake or reser-

Mayfly nymph *(Callibaetis species)* *John Merwin*

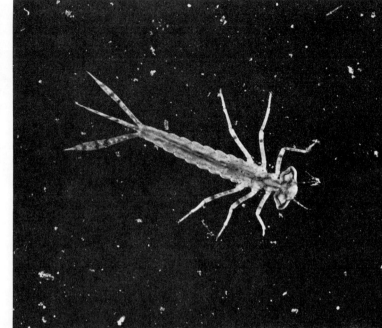

Damselfly nymph *John Merwin*

Dragonfly nymph *John Merwin*

(60)

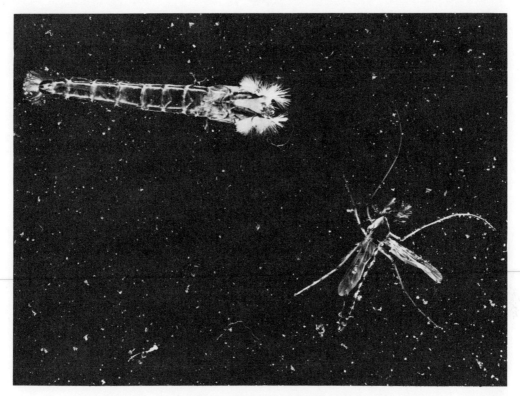

Adult male chironomid midge and its pupal shuck *John Merwin*

voir where the water temperature suits their preference. As long as oxygen and food are available, the fish remain there until the approach of fall and the breakdown of the temperature stratification. When the surface waters cool, whether it's fall or after ice-out in the spring, trout and salmon move into the shallow areas to spawn or to feed on forage fish that have schooled up there or on aquatic and terrestrial insects that are found in the inshore areas.

So while other physical and chemical conditions contribute to the ecology of stillwaters, the combination of temperature, oxygen, and food are the factors directly influencing the movements and behavior of the trout clan in stillwater. An understanding of this relationship is most useful to the stillwater angler.

5

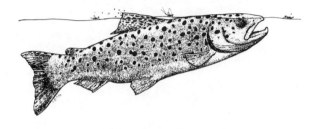

HIGH-ALTITUDE
LAKES

Fred Eiserman

REFLECT FOR A MOMENT ON A THOUGHT FROM *Walden:* "IS THE POVERTY OF our nomenclature such that we shape our perceptions of these stillwater places in mathematical terms." At least for this campfire conversation, I will not classify too far beyond the reader's correct image of these environments: unbelievably clean air, perpetually cool breezes, and nights that are enjoyed from the warmth of the sleeping bag under skies that go to eternity. These are the sky waters recently formed and reminders of the left-behind places of the snows and ice of the last age of perpetual cold. This chapter is about those isolated lakes found throughout the spines of mountain ranges in western North America, isolated in a biological sense by such geographic barriers as waterfalls, or rock-and-boulder subterranean water passages—situations that are impossible for fish to negotiate. And they are so recently isolated by elevation that the process of evolution and adaptation hasn't provided an opportunity for certain pioneer vertebrate species to occupy these ecological niches. This is in contrast to Canadian and Arctic regions, laced with river systems that connect with various life zones, where slow processes of adaptation have provided for numerous opportunities for colonization by invertebrates and vertebrates, including fish life to specialize in short-growing-season habitat.

Because any discussion of the bioecology of the aquatic environment (or a terrestrial environment) demands a synthetic organization, I must start by being somewhat esoteric. Our sky waters are scientifically classified by the rate at which energy is stored by photosynthesis and are called oligotrophic—lakes having few foods. They are characterized by having rocky shores and bottoms. Bottom sediments are present, but are usually poor in available nitrogen with little humus, and the amount of calcium varies depending upon the geology of the watershed. Many of these lakes have been formed behind terminal moraines, ridges formed by recent glacial action in which the water from melting ice or snow has been trapped. The color of these waters is usually a beautiful blue or emerald green with great transparency. Oxygen is usually close to saturation throughout the water column. The diversification of plankton is limited, and there are seldom so-called algae blooms. Nekton, the general group of larger free-living organisms (primarily fish), is limited and in most cases absent—that is, until the advent of the sport fisherman and the introduction of trout and, in some cases, forage species. In the majority of these lakes aquatic vegetation is insignificant. The differentiation between the shallows and the deep-water area is usually abrupt.

High-altitude lakes will probably be found in two life zones. The montane zone (not just the state) is typical of the lower elevation. This is the area of predominantly coniferous forests of spruce, fir, and lodgepole pine. In the Rocky Mountain region, the terrain is cut by deep canyons with extensions of peninsulas and rocky flats. The higher elevations of this zone are characterized by "benches," where lakes are generally surrounded by coniferous timber with occasional patches of willow.

The upper life zone is alpine. This country is characterized by bare rock, talus slopes, tundra meadows, and shallow soils. The lakes in this area are the least productive, and they are sometimes discolored by glacial flour and melting glacier-snowpack. In this zone of perpetual snowbanks the ice cover will often remain until the last of July or the first of August.

The temperature profile of both montane- and alpine-zone lakes is a function of time after ice-out for the first ten days. After this time daily weather conditions have a very important influence on thermal conditions that could govern the feeding cycle of the lake's fish population.

Now that we have satisfied the need for classification, let's direct the observations to more important issues: how and what the fish eat in these sky waters, the physical and chemical condition of their environment, and some of my own personal comments on how these fish might be caught.

Trout dominate the scene. Eastern brook trout are almost sure to occur in one or two or perhaps even more of the lakes of any drainage system. In some situations lake trout have been introduced in an effort to maintain a natural predator-prey relationship between these two species, and thereby achieve an equilibrium that might produce fairly good-size brook trout and mackinaw trout. All too often the fishing provided by the eastern brook trout is rather uninteresting to the fisherman because of stunting. I have often thought that the right variety of arctic

Beartooth high country, Montana/Wyoming
Engerbretson/Dvorak

char would produce a more interesting fishery by virtue of the fact that the habitat and the species' adaptation in general elsewhere would be matched at these elevations. Native trout species in the sky lakes are seldom encountered. Even the California golden trout, beautiful to look at and beautifully adapted to these high elevations, was originally a fish limited to the waters of the Kern River drainage in California. Cutthroat trout are the closest native in the Rocky Mountain complex of waters. In those situations where migration from prehistoric ice-age waters was possible, cutthroat trout of one subspecies or another are usually found. Unfortunately and in many cases, recent introductions (in the 1930s) of other salmonids, including other subspecies of cutthroat, have eliminated or diffused the gene pool of the original stock. Easy identification of the original native species is in most cases no longer possible.

Although just about every species of trout used in fish culture since the late twenties and thirties may be encountered, the eastern brook trout, cutthroat trout, California golden trout, and rainbow trout are the species most often taken by anglers. The only species that I haven't noted, excluding the salmon, are brown trout and lake trout—and they are certainly present. About the best that I can say about man's earliest efforts to add to the fishing in these waters was a philosophy of "stock-and-see-what-happens." As a result of this enthusiasm, today only the most remote lakes remain virgin waters.

Present-day fisheries managers are much more conservative in stocking programs, and introductions in almost all cases are based on the biological, physical, and chemical properties of the waters to be stocked. With the advent of the environmental movement, terms such as "natural," "pristine," and "primeval" also influenced fisheries management and subsequent stocking programs.

Although stocking has certainly been a factor in the development of a less-than-desirable fishery in many of the alpine lakes (and also some very exceptional fisheries), with the advent of fisheries-management programs since the early 1950s all state and federal resource agencies with responsibilities in aquatic habitat management have policies sensitive to the issue of so-called species pollution. The danger today of ecological disasters, especially in remote waters of wilderness areas, is from the do-it-yourself bucket brigade. The practice is, of course, illegal in all of the Rocky Mountain region. In spite of this, I feel that present-day users of the wilderness are usually quite informed about these especially fragile environments, and the threat of species pollution is less in the high-country lakes than in waters readily accessible by vehicle. I should also note that because most of the sky waters are in areas officially designated as wilderness and because trout are in most cases not native, the introduction of exotic fish to add to the wilderness fishing experience has been seriously questioned as not compatible with wilderness-area management. The question has been somewhat resolved by continuing with the use of trout as a management species in those waters stocked prior to the Wilderness Act. All waters not stocked prior to this date (1964) are evaluated for stocking on a case-by-case basis.

Elaborating on my previous comment about the occurrence of stunted populations, it has been noted that fisheries of this type are often correlated with the adequacy of spawning habitat. In the life-history requirements of the species, brook trout—a fall spawner—and in some situations cutthroat trout, are most susceptible to an ecological-climax level of overabundance. In a situation of this kind the fishery is often made up of adults maturing at from seven to eight inches and often smaller. On the other hand, where spawning habitat is limited and where brook trout are the management species, it's not uncommon for the fisherman to take fish exceeding one to two pounds.

Golden trout, spawning in late spring or early summer, are less apt to overpopulate. By the way, where brook trout are introduced into an established and healthy population of golden trout the results are almost always disastrous for the golden trout. Cook Lake in Wyoming's Wind River Range at one time produced world-record goldens, but it is now dominated by a population of small brook trout, the golden trout have virtually disappeared. A quick and simple fisheries management lesson: stay with the golden trout at higher elevations and refrain from stocking brook trout, a fall spawner, where spawning habitat is present. Cutthroat trout and/or rainbow trout, paying strict attention to subspecies or variety, can be used as a successful management species in the waters of the Montana life zone.

On the other side of the stunted-population question, in a number of places the increase in fishing pressure in some Montana- and alpine-life zones has resulted in an overharvest with the same result—small fish. This problem is somewhat easier to deal with than the proliferation of fish in waters having low fertility. By and large, however, even with the increased use of the wilderness areas, especially backpacker use, there has been little effect on fish populations, at least at the time of this writing. This does not imply, however, that an interesting population of larger-size trout is not vulnerable to intense fishing pressure.

Stunted populations of trout and those populations that exhibit better growth rates and larger-size fish are governed by the same environmental constraints. Very simply, trout grow slowly when water temperatures seldom exceed 55°F. during the peak of the growing season. And the growing season in many of these waters does not exceed six weeks. No matter how fertile the water, when growth is limited by temperature a fish takes a long while to grow to an interesting size for the angler. In an overpopulated situation a seven to eight-inch fish could be produced in a three-to-four-year period. There are just too many factors to take into consideration to make a broad-brush statement on growth rates of trout in these waters. On a lake by lake basis, however, given the pertinent data a fisheries biologist can prognosticate with a good deal of accuracy the rate of growth for a particular trout species.

The chemistry of these lakes is especially important from the standpoint of the problem of acidification. Though certain lakes in Europe and in the Northeast, especially in the Adirondacks, have suffered from this, and the Rocky Mountain area is certainly vulnerable, the major industrial areas are in the East and the prevailing winds are from the West. We are fortunate so far, but as this planet becomes increasingly industrialized the possibility of this problem occurring in Western waters cannot be discounted. In the data I am familiar with pH readings (a measure of the hydrogen-ion content with readings of less than 7 on the acid side) of the Rocky Mountain lakes range from a low of 5.6 to a high of 7.5, an acceptable range for all the trout fisheries with which I am familiar.

I have already noted that oxygen values are close to saturation, generally ranging from 6 to 12 parts per million. The total hardness—a measure of possible productivity—is usually low. As an example, lakes in Wyoming's Wind River Range seldom have readings over 35 parts per million, and lows of less than seven parts per million are frequently encountered. [More productive lakes with abundant vegetation typically have readings of several times those figures. J. M.]

As if low-nutrient values and cold water weren't enough of a problem, phosphate, an important fish-food producer, is readily precipitated out and lost in the bottom muds by the nutrient-robbing combination of an abundance of oxygen and the presence of iron. There is some consolation, however, that in spite of low nutrients and lack of eutrophication, the lakes are always pretty and are almost always drinkable.

Temperature and chemistry, as I have noted, are the keys to productivity; and productivity in the sky lakes, at least for the purposes of this discussion, is plankton. The make-up of plankton collections from these lakes is fairly predictable. The forms are familiar to all limnologists and consist of Cyclops, Daphnia, Diaptomus, and Rotatoria (made up of *Rotitera, Asterionell,* and *Filinia*), important to the fisherman only from the standpoint of the condition and health of the fish. Of more direct interest are the higher forms of invertebrates, of which Chironomid midge larvae are most abundant. There are about six species of Chironomidae found in these waters. In July the fisherman could be competing with the emergence of one or the other of these species. At this time a red rubberband fly or

Water fleas *(Daphnia pulex)*

calf-hair fly—fishing the fly as it comes to the surface, as a pupa—could result in a day of successful fishing.

The so-called winter stonefly, *Nemoura,* is also found in many of the sky-water lakes. (The little stoneflies of the Nemouridae family are generally brownish gray, and adults may range in length from one-quarter to one inch.) Emergence is generally in early summer, and while the hatch is in progress close imitation of the natural can be used to advantage. Of particular interest to the fly fisherman is that a percentage of food obtained by trout in these waters is the result of the drift of terrestrial insects. Fish-food studies on a number of alpine waters in Colorado have indicated that this drift is an important source of trout food. Leeches are also an important source of food, and a number of effective imitations have been devised by fly fishermen fishing these waters.

From an aesthetic sense, sky-water lakes can provide the fly fisherman with some of the most unique and exciting experiences of his fishing career. These incredibly beautiful lakes even create a distraction to serious fishing, so that the catching of fish sometimes seems irrelevant. On the other hand, the fly fisherman who is backpacking and who is watching the weight of his pack must often rely on his skill to provide an evening or morning meal. The reward of catching and eating high-altitude trout, and experiencing the beauty of this country, where the search for adequate descriptions is often better left to silent sharing, may make these waters the world's finest trout fishery.

FLY-FISHING
THE
SKY WATERS

Earl West

[Because fishing these special waters involves some special tactics not covered in subsequent and more general chapters, I asked Earl West, a friend and neighbor of Fred Eiserman in Wyoming and who fly-fishes these waters frequently, to pass along some suggestions that will help those of us who arrive at this top of the trout's world for the first time. J. M.]

THERE ARE SOME SPECIAL TECHNIQUES USED IN SCOUTING AN ALPINE LAKE. If surface feeding is underway, the job is easy, although this does not often occur in alpine lakes that hold large fish. Surface feeders take long trips in a fairly straight line, detouring a few feet right or left to take a floating insect. The fish are taken by noting their direction of travel—either by actually observing the fish if in close or by noting the recurring rises—then casting your fly about ten feet ahead to intersect the trout's path. These are certainly the easiest fish to catch: opportunistic feeders that will seize anything half-decently presented. This can get boring, even when the fish are sizable, and I'm often inclined to stroll over the next hill looking for something more challenging.

  In the absence of surface activity, put on a weighted fly and polarized sunglasses and take off around the lake, trying to locate hotspots. Inlets usually hold concentrations of trout, but only if the entering stream is of gentle gradient, which means it will carry food. Inlets usually contain fish of various sizes that take up precise feeding stations in the moving water, which may extend one-hundred feet or more into the lake. It should be remembered that the larger, dominant fish occupy the food-rich spots all over the lake, so thoughtful anglers keep moving around the lake searching for the big ones. Outlets are excellent holding spots, and some of the lake's larger residents will almost always be found there. I'm not referring to the outlet stream itself, but the one-hundred feet or so of the lake above the stream where the water is in some motion.

The ideal big-fish lakes have extensive shelves, also called littoral zones: those relatively shallow (fifteen feet or less) and usually boulder-strewn areas along the shoreline. They are the trout's buffet table—the oxygen-rich environment that produces aquatic insect life. The shelves are usually narrow enough so that the outer edges can be reached with medium-length casts. This edge is the real hotspot. The fish lie among the boulders on this breakover point or cruise along it. Their food supply is there, and their protective zone is in the adjacent deep water.

Alpine-lake fishing is shoreline fishing. There is no need to use boats, rafts, float-tubes, or waders (even if you could get them back into the mountains) since most of the fish are right there in front of you. Many fisherman, especially spin-casters, nearly dislocate a shoulder casting as far as possible into the deep black waters out in the center of the lake. It's often some time until they attach some significance to the fact that the strikes are occurring as the lure passes over the shelf edge. I suppose they believe the fish are following the lure from out in the lake, or perhaps they are remembering times when rising fish were feeding all over the lake simply because airborne insects were landing everywhere. But remember, for the large underwater feeders, work the shelf edge. I am constantly on the lookout for points, projections or an outlying boulder from which to cast. From such locations I throw my maximum cast along the shelf edge, usually parallel to the shoreline. The retrieved fly is in trout-favored habitat 100 percent of the time. Without question, I consider this to be the best fly-fishing tactic for alpine lakes.

Excepting the occasional milky hue of some lakes that is produced by glacial flour, the high lakes are of exceptional clarity. On those fortunate days when there is little or no breeze, one can spot the cruising fish and experience the thrill of seeing them take the fly—or suffer the pains of witnessing the rejection of your offering. The cruisers will, often as not, show some interest in the fly; if they don't take, then change flies and change again, alter the speed of the retrieve and the action of the fly until the fish takes or, out of exasperation, you decide to go find some less discerning fish. It's fascinating fishing, challenging and educational, since one can learn the habits of the fish and see the direct results of different flies and fishing methods.

The cruisers will usually be alone or in pairs. Only once have I seen what would amount to a school, but what a spectacular sight it was! My wife, Mary, and I were enjoying an afternoon on a long narrow lake high in the Wind River Mountains. On the south shore a small bright stream tumbled four-hundred feet down into the lake we were fishing. Mary, an inveterate explorer, asked if there might be a lake up there. I checked the map.

"Yes, but it's very small. I doubt that there would be fish in it."

"Well, I'll go up and look around anyway."

Later I looked up in answer to the shouts. Mary was frantically motioning me to climb up. The lake was a mirrored jewel perched in a lovely cirque—less than 10 acres and so clear we could see forever into the depths.

"OK. Here they come now. See?" she pointed, and I looked.

Twelve cutthroats. The smallest was at least four pounds and the largest certainly would have weighed eight. We could easily see the huge black spots on their tails, the crimson underbellies, the deep bodies with shoulders so heavy that their heads in contrast appeared beaklike.

"They followed my fly the first few times," said Mary, "right up to my feet, but wouldn't bite it."

The twelve of them cruised back and forth along 150 feet of shoreline. We tried every fly we had and every conceivable retrieve. At first we'd occasionally get one to follow, but later they showed absolute disinterest. Could we have hooked one fish, I believe that it might have triggered a behavior pattern, and we could have caught several: I've seen it happen before. But it was not to be. Discouraged, we walked around the lake several times, searching for more trout. There were none. The twelve were the only inhabitants and were surely the result of an unauthorized plant, hauled up from the lower lake. We left the mountains the next day without being able to give the giants another try. I never got back. They are dead of old age by now and left no progeny because there were no suitable spawning areas. But I shall never forget the sight of the orderly little group engaged in their lazy, aimless cruising.

Trout of that size would be considered trophies no matter where they were caught, and while I don't suggest that such outsize specimens are exceedingly common in the mountains (except for mackinaw), there are many lakes that hold fish in the two- to five-pound class.

Large fish are always difficult to catch, but without a doubt the most difficult, most perplexing, most exasperating of all are big golden trout, the ultimate trophy. I once spent two full days on a golden-trout lake, finally taking a single fish of three pounds. I was pleased by the accomplishment, but would have been much happier had it been one of the numerous five- and six-pounders that cruised by, never once turning toward my fly. This is their normal behavior; some fishermen believe they have impaired vision; others swear they are totally blind. I have another theory. Most goldens inhabit the highest lakes, the ones called "wall" lakes, with very limited shelf areas. Their diet is primarily minute zooplankton, and an artificial fly is just not imitating their food. They have another aggravating habit that adds to the difficulty of capture. When a golden finally does follow your fly, opens its mouth and takes it, the fish usually does nothing; it just stops. Other trout are apt to turn, hooking themselves in the hinge. When you attempt to set the hook in a golden, you're likely to pull the fly straight out of its mouth—and the fish will not accommodate you with a second effort.

6

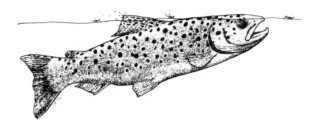

STILLWATERS WEST

Peter Moyle and Donald Baltz

SOME OF THE MOST PRODUCTIVE TROUT WATERS IN THE WORLD ARE THE low- to mid-elevation lakes and reservoirs of the western United States. Not only do many of these stillwaters produce large numbers of trout, but they also produce trout of astonishing size. World-record cutthroat trout, rainbow trout, and Dolly Varden have come from such lakes, and exceptionally large brook trout, brown trout, and kokanee salmon are not uncommon in angler catches. In addition, a number of the natural lakes are of special interest because they contain (or contained) unique native strains of trout, such as the Eagle Lake trout of California, the Lahontan cutthroat of Nevada, and the Henrys Lake cutthroat of Idaho. Despite their fame as trout waters, these stillwaters face formidable management problems, created by increased fishing pressure, the introduction of nonnative fishes and invertebrates, and most of all, competing demands for water in a water-short region. In this chapter therefore, we will first describe the general ecology of these lakes and reservoirs to show why they produce so many trout. Next we'll discuss what has happened to these lakes in recent years, to point out why so many of them are not as productive as they used to be. Finally, we will describe some of the better-known lakes, on a lake-by-lake basis, pointing out some unique aspects of their ecology and management.

GENERAL ECOLOGY

There are only a limited number of generalizations that can be made about the ecology of low- to mid-elevation lakes and reservoirs of the far West, because they are an extremely diverse group of waters. They include mainstream impoundments on rivers, large natural desert sinks such as Pyramid Lake, Nevada, and mountain lakes of various sizes such as Lake Pend Oreille of Idaho. These lakes differ from the high-altitude lakes discussed in the previous chapter by ly-

(74)

ing below 1,700 meters (5,576 feet) in elevation, by being mostly large in size (over 260 hectares; one square mile), and by often lacking the crystalline waters we usually associate with trout. They also differ in being much more productive of fish by any measure one could wish to make.

The high production of fish is caused by a number of interacting factors, but perhaps the most important is that the lakes have large drainage areas from which they receive the nutrients necessary for plant growth. They typically contain fairly high concentrations of dissolved minerals, giving them pH values on the alkaline side (7.2–8.5). They also occur at low enough elevations so that the surface waters can get quite warm in the summer. The warm temperatures and high nutrient levels interact to produce blooms of planktonic algae. As a result, it's not uncommon for the lakes to have a murky green cast to them in summer. While such blooms may offend the aesthetic sensibilities of the trout angler, they are the main source of food for the zooplankton, such as water fleas (such as *Daphnia* and *Bosmina*) and copepods, as well as bottom-dwelling organisms such as Chironomid midge and mayfly larvae, which consume the dead algae that settles to the bottom. These organisms in turn are fed upon by predatory invertebrates, such as damselflies, certain copepods, and chaoborid (phantom) midges. Both the algae-feeding and the predatory invertebrates are consumed in large numbers by fish. They are particularly important in the diet of small trout (under eight inches) of all species, but may also enter the diet of larger trout when some particular kind of invertebrate is unusually abundant. Feeding on invertebrates may cause rapid growth in trout for the first year or so of life, but it is rarely sufficient to continue such growth in later life and to produce the lunker trout for which these western stillwaters are famous. Instead, the larger trout feed on other fish, particularly species specialized for feeding on small invertebrates, such as tui chubs, redside shiners, kokanee salmon, and, in reservoirs, threadfin shad.

The importance of fish in the diet of trout is shown by the spurt of growth trout exhibit when they switch to feeding primarily on fish. This growth slows only when the trout start maturing and divert energy from body growth into the development of gonads. Fisheries managers often take advantage of this growth phenomenon and plant immature trout in reservoirs at sizes large enough so that the trout can begin to feed immediately on fish. Such trout may double their weight in a few months. In California, experimental plants of coho (silver) salmon, six to eight inches long, in reservoirs have been quite successful because the salmon feed voraciously on threadfin shad and reach nineteen to twenty-one inches in less than a year.

The reason feeding on fish is important for trout to achieve rapid growth and large size is related to the amount of energy contained in different kinds of prey. The smaller the prey in relation to the size of the trout, the more energy it takes the trout to capture them and, consequently, the less net energy will be gained by eating them. If a prey organism is too small, a trout will have to expend more energy capturing it than it will get out of it, unless the prey is unusually abundant so that many can be captured with little effort. Forage fish represent large energy packages to predatory trout, so if they are abundant the energy the trout expend in capturing them is more than repaid. The result is rapid growth of the trout and trout of large size.

Partly because of this energetic relationship between prey size and predator size, small trout usually occupy different habitats than large trout, since they have to live where prey of the appropriate size is available. Not just coincidentally, these also tend to be areas where they are not likely to be eaten by big trout. In lakes, small trout are most likely to be found near shore, where they can feed on bottom-dwelling insects and flying insects as well as zooplankton. It is worth noting that, although zooplankton is often found in the stomachs of small trout, it is not a particularly good forage for them because trout and salmon, with the exception of kokanee, lack the mouth and gill-raker structure to feed on it very efficiently. This and the avoidance of predators are presumably the reasons that many lake-dwelling trout spend the first two years of their lives in streams where they feed on insects. This pattern, for example, is characteristic of the rainbow trout of Lake Pend Oreille and of the brown trout of Shasta Reservoir, California.

Another reason why it may be advantageous for small trout to do their initial growing in streams is that by doing so they may avoid competing with the same species of fish the large trout prey upon. Such species, but particularly minnows, are often more efficient at harvesting small invertebrates than the trout. This was demonstrated very nicely by the studies of Dr. Peter Larkin and his students that documented the impact of redside-shiner introductions on rainbow trout in British Columbia lakes. Before the shiners became established, the small trout fed primarily upon a small shrimp (*Hyalella*) that lived in beds of aquatic plants close to shore. The trout captured the shrimp as they emerged from the plants. Once the shiners became established, they quickly depleted the shrimp populations because they would actually penetrate into the plant beds to capture them. The growth and survival of the small trout subsequently declined, although this was at least partly compensated for by the increased growth of larger trout that could now feed on the shiners.

As the previous example indicates, aquatic plant beds may be very important to young trout as sources of food. Such beds contain complex communities of invertebrates, most of which feed on the algae (especially diatoms) that grow attached to the plants or on each other. Not only may the trout feed on the invertebrates, but they may use the plants as cover, to avoid being eaten themselves. If the plant beds are extensive, they may play an important role in the nutrient cycling in the lakes, taking up nutrients in the summer but releasing them in the winter as the dead plants decay. The importance of plant beds in the three roles just described are poorly known for western lakes, but many of the natural lakes have extensive plant beds in their shallow areas. One of the most important food organisms in plant beds is the freshwater shrimp, *Hyalella azteca*. It is a staple food of trout and other fishes in many lakes that exceed 10°C. (50°F.) during the summer. Reproduction of the shrimp is keyed to the spring blooms of algae on soft sediments, upon which they feed, and to the development of the aquatic plant beds in water less than three meters deep, in which they find cover. Egg production begins in the spring and continues through the fall. The maximum population size is reached in late summer, but there is no hatch comparable to that found in many insects. However, freshwater shrimp are frequently important in the diets of trout because they are constantly available, even if not in the numbers characteristic of hatches of aquatic insects and other prey.

In reservoirs, which have fluctuating water levels, aquatic plant beds are notable by their absence. Survival of small trout in reservoirs is notoriously poor, probably because of the absence of plant beds and other appropriate cover as well as of proper food organisms. Reservoirs, of course, also often provide poor habitat for young trout because they stratify in the summer, leaving the shallow waters too warm for the survival of trout. The natural lakes in the region may or may not stratify. Lake Pend Oreille, for example, stratifies but the surface waters are still cool enough to support trout. Pyramid Lake in Nevada, in contrast, does not stratify in many years because strong summer winds keep it well mixed. It remains cool enough to support trout, however.

MANAGEMENT PROBLEMS

The trout fisheries of western stillwaters seem to be in a state of almost perpetual crisis, as one factor after another threatens to change the nature of the fish populations, usually for the worse. These factors fall into three main categories which are, in reverse order of impact on the trout: fishing pressure, introductions of new species, and competing uses for the water.

Fishing pressure, thanks to both more sophisticated fisheries managers and fishermen, is less and less a factor causing the decline of fish populations in western stillwaters, despite a general increase in amount of fishing. Anglers seem to be more willing to accept restrictive regulations that limit the number and size of fish they can keep and managers seem to be more willing to set regulations for individual bodies of water, even though it makes their job much harder. One reason for the change in attitude is the realization that fisheries for trophy-size wild trout (particularly of native strains) can only be maintained if the take is greatly restricted. Tragedies like the extinction of Lahontan cutthroat trout in Pyramid Lake and Lake Tahoe, the result of commercial fishing coupled with other factors, are unlikely to be repeated. For example, the commercial fishery for kokanee in Lake Pend Oreille was halted in 1973 and the sport fishery reduced when it became evident the populations were declining severely.

Another way fish and game departments throughout the West are responding to the increased fishing pressure is to supplement the wild populations with hatchery-reared fish. In some cases, such as Henrys Lake, Lake Pend Oreille, and Eagle Lake, ripe fish coming up from the lake are trapped, spawned, and the eggs and young reared in a hatchery, to be released into the proper lake after a year or so. This strategy avoids the heavy mortality usually characteristic of early life-history stages, recognizing that fishing rather than food is probably the main factor limiting the number of adult fish. The fishery benefits from having many trout planted at a size at which they can take advantage of the large populations of forage fishes, such as threadfin shad, present in many western reservoirs. In these reservoirs, trout, usually subcatchable-size rainbows of a domestic strain, are planted some time prior to the opening of fishing season to give them time to grow on a diet of fish. Usually by the time fishing season opens, such trout are well above catchable size and those remaining from previous years are near-lunkers. One of the most spectacular fisheries of this sort is at Crowley Reservoir on California's Owens River. On opening day, a significant percentage of the population of Los Angeles is either on the lake or on its banks and most of the people are catching fish, using every bait available.

While the addition of hatchery fish to the lakes is still a popular management strategy, the addition of new species is not nearly as popular as it used to be, even though it is still deceptively attractive as a simple panacea for many complex problems. The decline in popularity of species introductions is the result of two factors. First, most of the familiar species, especially of trout, have been tried in most major bodies of water. Second, many of the introductions have failed and many others have created as many problems as they have solved. To begin with, there is no denying that the principal fisheries in most of these lakes are for nonnative species: rainbow trout (from the West Coast), brown trout (from Europe), brook trout (from the eastern United States), and kokanee (from the western United States and Canada). It should be recognized, however, that in many of the natural lakes these fishes have replaced or hybridized with native salmonids, particularly cutthroat trout. Another result of these introductions is that complex communities of four to six species of salmonids have been created in lakes that formerly contained just one to three species. Whether or not such communities can be maintained by other than artificial means is not known. Unfortunately, salmonids are not the only fishes being added to the fish communities of these lakes. Various species of minnows, suckers, and perch have become established, usually as the result of some bait fisherman dumping his leftover bait into the lake (but sometimes the introductions have been made deliberately by managers to provide forage). As the studies in British Columbia have demonstrated, and as experience has proven elsewhere, the establishment of such forage fishes usually results in a trade-off between improved adult growth and decreased growth and survival of the young.

One of the most recent official fads of introduction, however, has not been with fish but with invertebrates, particularly the planktonic oppossum shrimp, *Mysis*. [Oppossum shrimp typically inhabit deeper waters, are of a crustacean order superficially resembling crayfish, and may grow to one inch in length.] *Mysis* is native to the Great Lakes and a few other deep, cold lakes. Since where it is native, it's important in the diet of the salmonids (particularly lake trout), it was assumed that it would also become important in the diets of trout and salmon wherever it became established, resulting in improved growth rates, especially of smaller fish. As a consequence, it has been widely introduced throughout the West into deep lakes and reservoirs, including Lake Pend Oreille and Lake Tahoe. In both lakes, the most dramatic event associated with the establishment of the shrimp has been negative: a decline of the populations of the water flea, *Daphnia*, apparently because of *Mysis* predation on them. *Daphnia* is an important constituent in the diet of kokanee and other plankton-feeding fish, including the young of many gamefishes. In Lake Tahoe, *Daphnia* has nearly disappeared and the growth of kokanee has been reduced. In Lake Pend Oreille, the change in zooplankton following the establishment of *Mysis* has been accompanied by a decline in the kokanee populations. Whether or not the three events are related is not known for sure, but the coincidence is suspicious. Since kokanee are the main food of large trout in the lake, the trophy sport fishery may also be affected eventually.

While both fishing pressure and introductions have affected the fish populations of western stillwaters, their effects are minimal compared to the manipulations of the water itself and its diversion for irrigation, power, and other uses. Perhaps the best-known effect has been the creation of new bodies of water altogether, countless reservoirs of all sizes, shapes, and depths. While many reservoirs have spectacular trout fisheries, almost all have to be artificially maintained by planting hatchery fish. This is partly because of heavy angler demand and partly because there are usually few places for the trout to spawn, nor is there much habitat for the young along the barren shores. Also, water levels tend to rise and fall at the whim of the water users, usually with little regard for the impact on fish populations. A number of the natural lakes, such as Lake Pend Oreille and Henrys Lake, have small dams on their outlets, which increase their average depth and size, but also increase the amount of fluctuation of water level. How this affects the fish populations is poorly known.

While many new reservoirs have been created, in some instances this has been at the expense of natural lakes. Lake Winnemucca in Nevada, once a good producer of cutthroat trout, became dry in 1938 following the diversion of much of the flow of the Truckee River. This same diversion has caused the levels of Pyramid Lake to drop by more than twenty-seven meters. The drop in water level exposed the delta of the Truckee River, making it impossible for the native strain of Lahontan cutthroat, as well as the cui-ui sucker, to make their annual spawning runs up the river. The result was extinction for the already depleted (by fishing) trout populations and a place on the endangered species list for the cui-ui.

SPECIAL STILLWATERS

Every lake and reservoir has its own characteristics and fish populations, the result of its unique combination of history, geological features, location, and manipulation by man. To give an idea of the variety of stillwaters that exist in the

West, the rest of this chapter will describe the characteristics, fisheries, and management problems of some of the better-known stillwaters: Lake Pend Oreille, Henrys Lake, Pyramid and Walker lakes, Eagle Lake, and reservoirs of California's Central Valley. Stillwaters equally deserving attention because of their trout populations but not covered here, include Flathead Lake (Montana), Hungry Horse Reservoir (Montana), Yellowstone Lake (Wyoming), Bear Lake (Utah), Lake Coeur d'Alene (Idaho), and the many reservoirs on the Colorado River and its tributaries.

Lake Pend Oreille covers 38,348 hectares (147 square miles) in the mountains of northern Idaho, at an elevation of 625 meters (2,029 feet). It is a natural lake fed by the waters of the Clark Fork of the Columbia River, although it was enlarged in 1952 by the construction of Albeni Falls Dam on the outlet. The dam created an annual fluctuation of the lake level of 3 to 4 meters, 10 to 13 feet, but otherwise did not change the nature of the lake dramatically since it was already one of the deepest lakes in North America, with a maximum depth of 351 meters (1,152 feet) and an average depth of about 164 meters (538 feet). Limnologists generally classify the lake as oligotrophic, indicated by its coolness (summer surface temperatures of 12 to 14°C, 54 to 57°F) and clarity. However, it is more productive than most such lakes, especially in bays where pollution has resulted in noticeable algae blooms. The natural productivity of the lake, coupled with its size, has always meant that it has contained both large fish populations and large individual fish. Although the lake is home to a number of nongame fishes and a few bass and perch, it is dominated by salmonids, particularly kokanee salmon and its principal predators, rainbow trout and Dolly Varden. Other salmonids in the lake include cutthroat trout, mountain whitefish, and lake whitefish (a species introduced from the Great Lakes).

Kokanee are by far the most abundant gamefish in the lake, thriving on the abundant zooplankton. They spawn both in tributary streams and along certain shorelines at the south end of the lake. The young kokanee join the zooplankton soon after emerging from the gravel. If zooplankton of the appropriate size are abundant, the kokanee grow and survive well and are soon being consumed by predatory trout. By the time they reach their third summer they start to enter the fishery, caught either by trollers or, in the spring, by shore fishermen. The fishery for kokanee has always been spectacular, even in its decline in recent years. Between 1951 and 1965, the average combined catch of the commercial and sport fisheries was about one million fish per year. Since then, the catch has declined to about half that amount and the kokanee populations are apparently still declining, despite the cessation of the commercial fishery in 1973. Alarmed by this decline, which also is likely to affect the populations of predatory trout, in 1974 the Idaho Department of Fish and Game began a major research program on the lake, focusing on the kokanee. These studies indicate that there are three interacting factors that may have contributed to the decline: the fishery, spawning failures, and the introduction of the *Mysis* shrimp. It should be emphasized that the relative role these factors have played in the decline is not really known; other unknown factors may also be important. Nevertheless, the three factors just listed are the most likely candidates. The fishery for kokanee, despite its intensity prior to 1973, probably has not been a major factor in the decline. For one thing, the population decline continued even after the fishing pressure was somewhat relieved. In addition, the fishery declined as the kokanee population declined, so the catch seemed to be a more or less constant percentage of the population (10 to 20 percent if the estimates of the Idaho Department of Fish and Game are correct). In contrast to the fishery, spawning failures may have been playing a major role in the decline. In the 1960s, low populations of kokanee year classes seem to have been related to winter drawdowns of the lake that exposed kokanee spawning beds along the shoreline and to severe winter floods that may have destroyed spawning beds in streams.

If spawning failures were initially responsible for the decline, the establishment of the *Mysis* shrimp in the lake may be at least partly responsible for its continuance. *Mysis* did not become abundant in the lake until 1975. As they became abundant the zooplankton community changed dramatically, mostly toward smaller species. Kokanee feed on these smaller forms less efficiently than on the larger forms and consequently grow slower. In addition, one small zooplankter (*Bosmina*) that used to be abundant in the spring and early summer is not any longer. There is some suspicion that it may be critical for this species to be abundant when the kokanee fry first enter the lake, since *Bosmina* is the right size for them and is easily captured. The kokanee may, in this respect, be like many marine fishes, the larvae of which starve to death in a few days if prey of exactly the right size and nutritional value are not present when the young fish are. One bright side to this picture is that the larger kokanee do feed on *Mysis*, and this appears to increase their growth rates. In recent years, kokanee as large as 49 cm (18.9 inches) have appeared in the spawning runs.

One of the reasons it is important to understand why the kokanee has been declining is that they are the main prey of the famous rainbow trout of Pend Oreille. The largest sport-caught rainbow (37 pounds) was caught there in 1947 and trout in the 22 to 26-pound size range are not uncommon still. These rainbow are all of the Kamloops strain, which originated in Kamloops Lake, British Columbia. Obviously, they adapted beautifully to Lake Pend Oreille, where they have developed a unique life-history strategy. They spawn in the tributary streams, where the young spend the first two years of their lives. Growth in the streams is slow compared to that in the lake and the fish leave the streams when they are about 5.5 to 6 inches long. For the next year, they feed largely on zooplankton and terrestrial insects, gradually switching to fish, but reaching only 10.6 to 11.8 inches at the end of the third year. By the time the fish are in their fourth year and around 17 inches long, they are feeding exclusively on fish, mostly kokanee, and growing at a tremendous rate. They reach exceptionally large sizes in the next three to four years because they rarely spawn before the sixth year and can put all their excess energy into growth. Thus a typical five-year-old fish is about 25 inches long, a six-year-old, 31 inches, and a seven-year-old, 34 inches. The largest fish are those that delay the onset of maturity until their seventh year. Most fish can spawn more than once, and a few live as long as nine years. Starting in 1951, the Idaho Department of Fish and Game has attempted to increase the numbers of Kamloops rainbow in the lake by stocking fish of a domestic strain. Recent studies, however, indicate that almost all the 700 to 1,600 trophy-size rainbows caught each year are the progeny of wild parents.

Another fish that achieves record sizes by feeding on kokanee is the Dolly Varden or bull trout, which is native to the lake. In 1949, the world-record Dolly Varden was taken from the lake, at 32 pounds. This species, unfortunately, is rather uncommon in the lake and seems to be declining in numbers. One of the main reasons for the decline is the construction of Cabinet Gorge Dam on the Clark Fork above Lake Pend Oreille, which has cut off access to the spawning grounds.

Henrys Lake, although located in Idaho, is remarkably different from Lake Pend Oreille. It's less than one-tenth the size (2,632 hectares) and shallower (maximum depth about 6 m), with a bottom that's covered with aquatic plants in the summer and with water that is heavy with algae blooms. It is also a reservoir built on the site of a natural lake. Despite all these unlikely conditions, it is an outstanding trout lake because the temperatures stay cool, the water is well oxygenated by wind, and the production of invertebrates for trout food is high. The fishery is mainly for native cutthroat trout, although brook trout are taken in some numbers. Rainbow trout and rainbow-cutthroat hybrids are also present, as are sculpins and redside-shiners. The trout are extremely numerous and fast growing, even though they are feeding mainly on invertebrates. The cutthroats, for example, are over 15.5 inches long by the end of their third year and fish over 19.5 inches are not uncommon.

Perhaps the most fascinating aspect of Henrys Lake is the famous damselfly migration, which helps to sustain the trout and attracts fly fishermen from all over. The damselfly nymphs occur throughout the lake among the aquatic plants, where they prey on other insects. When the time comes for them to transform into flying adults, there is a general shoreward migration of nymphs seeking emergent vegetation to crawl out on. During this time, late June and early July, the nymphs are unusually vulnerable to the trout and become their main food. It should be pointed out, however, that over the entire year other organisms, but particularly freshwater shrimps (*Hyalella, Gammarus*), are much more important in the diet. At times, prey as small as *Daphnia* or as large as sculpins and shiners are the most important items.

Because of its uniqueness and heavy fishing pressure, Henrys Lake is now managed as a trophy-trout fishery, to the general satisfaction of the anglers who have long used it. The fish populations themselves are largely maintained through the artificial spawning and rearing of trout that move up Hatchery Creek to spawn.

Pyramid and Walker lakes, in contrast to the two previous mountain lakes, are large desert sinks in Nevada. Even though Pyramid Lake is the sink of the Truckee River and Walker Lake is the sink of the Walker River, they are treated to-

Damselfly nymph

gether here because they have similar origins, similar trout populations, and similar problems that cry for immediate solutions before the living lakes become dead seas. Both lakes are remnants of Lake Lahontan, a giant lake that covered much of northwestern Nevada during wetter times. Pyramid Lake is the largest and deepest (over 110 m, 360 feet) of the lakes and supports the richest fish fauna. It contains Lahontan cutthroat trout, Sacramento perch (introduced from California), tui chubs, Tahoe suckers, the endangered cui-ui sucker, and others. Walker Lake contains only the trout and the tui chubs. In both lakes, the fish are very abundant. The reason for this is the rich store of nutrients washed in from the Sierra Nevada and kept constantly stirred up by the wind. For trout lakes, they are quite turbid (underwater visibility of 2 to 4 m) with suspended silt, algae, and zooplankton. The zooplankton provide a rich source of food for the smaller fish, especially the tui chubs, which are fed upon in turn by the trout. The trout consequently grow rapidly and achieve large sizes. The largest cutthroat trout known was taken from Pyramid Lake in 1925; it weighed 41 pounds.

Unfortunately, such monster trout are no longer present in Pyramid Lake, perhaps because the original Pyramid Lake strain of Lahontan cutthroat is apparently extinct. The present trout in the lake are derived from a Walker Lake strain that is maintained in a hatchery and occasionally reaches 11 to 15 pounds. The Walker Lake fishery is also sustained by hatchery plants. This is necessary because both the Truckee and Walker rivers have had much of their flows diverted and are no longer accessible to the trout for spawning. The decrease in flows has also caused the lake levels to drop rapidly. Pyramid Lake has dropped over 27 m (80 feet) since the early 1900s, while Walker Lake is nearly half of what it used to be. Since in such desert sinks the salts tend to become more concentrated as the lakes dry up, both lakes have become more alkaline. In Walker Lake, only the cutthroat and tui chubs still live there because the other species present, including the hardy Sacramento perch, died out a number of years ago as the water became too alkaline for them.

In both Walker and Pyramid lakes, the fishery for cutthroat trout is highly dependent upon water temperatures. During the summer, the trout generally remain fairly deep, where the water is cooler. As temperatures drop in the fall, the trout move inshore to feed on the tui chubs that are so abundant there. During this time (mid-October to January) many fish are caught just offshore, at depths of 3 to 15 m. Trout can also be caught from shore, however, in shallow water, as they move in to feed. Inshore feeding slows down as the waters cool further in January and February, but fishing improves as the water warms up. By April and early May, however, the trout are back in deep waters again.

It is customary, when talking about Pyramid Lake, to lament the loss not only of the native cutthroat strain, but also of the fabled emerald trout and its companion, the royal silver trout of Lake Tahoe. Both trout were described from a few specimens in the early 1900s by J. O. Snyder, an eminent ichthyologist and enthusiastic trout angler, and few have been seen since. The reason for this seems to be that what Snyder described were really rainbow trout that had been planted in the lakes and had grown fat and silvery in response to the good food supply. In recent years, marked rainbows, planted in Lake Tahoe by the department of fish and game, have been captured after a few years in the lake. Their characteristics are nearly identical with those of the royal silver trout.

Eagle Lake in northeastern California is another remnant of Lake Lahontan, but appears to have been an arm that was cut off from the rest of the lake except when the lake was at peak fullness. As a consequence of its isolation, the lake contains its own unique trout, the Eagle Lake trout. This fish is usually listed today as a type of rainbow trout, but it may be more closely related to the golden trout or the still undescribed redband trout of the nearby Pit River drainage. In any case, it is a fish uniquely adapted to the highly alkaline conditions of Eagle Lake (pH 8.4 to 9.6). Eagle Lake is very productive, like Pyramid and Walker lakes, but most of it is quite shallow, less than 3 m deep. However, parts of the south basin of the lake are around 30 m deep, so the average depth is about 14 m. Because so much of the lake is shallow, it supports vast beds of aquatic plants, which provide habitat for numerous invertebrates, upon which feed the abundant small fish, particularly tui chubs and redside shiners. The trout forage in the shallow areas in October through June but move into deep water in the summer when shallow water temperatures exceed 70°F. Only the deep south basin of the lake stratifies, since winds keep the shallow regions well mixed, and the trout there tend to stay below the thermocline in the summer. Eagle Lake trout feed mainly on tui chubs but are not adverse to taking aquatic insects, freshwater shrimp, and snails when chubs are not available. On this diet, they grow rapidly, reaching 45 to 55 cm in three years. Since they are mature at three, growth slows thereafter, and trout larger than 70 cm (27.5 inches) or 3.5 kg are very rare. This is despite the fact that Eagle Lake trout are among the longest lived trout, living up to eleven years.

In the spring the trout are most vulnerable to angling because they seem to move inshore, perhaps as part of a general movement toward Pine Creek, the lake's only tributary. Formerly, they migrated some 45 km upstream to spawn but today all the trout are stopped by a weir and spawned artificially. This is necessary because diversions and damage to the watershed have made the creek unsuitable for spawning. The trout are reared in the hatchery for a year before being released in the lake at 15 to 20 cm. Eagle Lake trout are now being planted in alkaline reservoirs around California because of their predatory habits and ability to live under adverse (for trout) conditions.

The Eagle Lake trout is one of a number of kinds of trout and salmon that have been planted in California reservoirs on an experimental basis, by the California Department of Fish and Game, to find out what type is best suited for the particular conditions of each reservoir. Reservoirs present a major management problem throughout the West because they are, in terms of area, the most extensive flatwaters, replacing free-flowing streams. Like natural lakes, reservoirs vary tremendously in their characteristics, such as size, depth, temperature regime, and productivity. All share the characteristic, however, of fluctuating on an irregular basis, with large differences on an annual basis between the size of the minimum and maximum pools. Such fluctuations create barren and often muddy shorelines, so there is little cover for small trout, and often deny trout access to what spawning grounds might be available. Thus the trout populations have to be maintained artificially by planting 15 to 20 cm long fish. Fortunately for the trout and the trout angler, the larger mid-elevation reservoirs support large populations of threadfin shad, a small planktivorous fish that lives in the open waters. These shad are usually the principal food of the trout.

A good example of such a trout-shad reservoir is Lake Berryessa in Napa County, California, which covers 8,084 hectares (32 square miles) and has a maximum depth of 84 m. It stratifies in the summer and so supports good fisheries for bass and sunfish, as well as for trout. The distribution of planted rainbow trout and coho salmon in the lake is fairly predictable on the basis of temperatures, since they tend to avoid water warmer than 70°F. Thus, in the summer, they are found below the thermocline. Although the shad are found mainly above the thermocline, the main summer food of the trout and salmon is still shad, so presumably they make forays into the upper waters to feed. As the water cools in the fall, the trout enter the surface waters in nearly fulltime pursuit of shad and become quite vulnerable to fishing. On the shad diet, rainbow trout planted in May at 140 to 159 gm ($\frac{1}{3}$ pound) triple in size in about six months, and if they manage to avoid being caught for another year, will weigh well over 1 kg. (2 $\frac{1}{2}$ pounds). Growth of coho salmon planted in May is similar to that of trout for the first six months but may be even faster thereafter. The reason for this is that the salmon continue to feed heavily in the winter, when trout feeding apparently slows down. Interestingly enough, there is some indication that this winter predation of salmon may improve the summer fisheries for largemouth bass. Juvenile largemouth bass have to compete for plankton with shad and may starve to death or fail to grow rapidly enough to avoid being eaten by other bass if the shad populations are too large in the spring. Therefore, reduction of shad by salmon may increase largemouth bass survival by increasing zooplankton populations. On the other hand, such predation may also reduce the spring surge in growth frequently experienced by trout and salmon when shad are abundant. The impact of salmon on shad populations is likely to be particularly severe if a cold winter has also caused heavy shad mortalities.

The interactions between salmon, shad, largemouth bass, and water temperatures are but one example of the complexity of interactions present in western stillwaters. Obviously, the angler is also a major part of the equation, since not only were the fish placed in the reservoirs (and many lakes) for the benefit of anglers in the first place, but the intensity of harvest may be reflected in the abundance of everything from trout to forage fishes to zooplankton. Good fishing in the future is going to depend upon our understanding these interactions and upon our ability to manage the waters accordingly.

Part Three

TACKLE

AND

TACTICS

If you already are fly-fishing for trout in streams, it's quite possible to go to a local trout pond with no changes in your gear and to start catching fish right away. I have done that often—with the possible exception of the catching-fish part—and you may have, also. Let us not so encumber our fishing with theory that it ceases to be fun.

But it's also fun to catch fish, and not always easy. And in the following chapters, I and some angling friends relate some of the problems we've had and some of the solutions we're found in a wide variety of stillwater situations. We look at specialized equipment and the ways in which it can best be used. The ways in which the various basic categories of common fly patterns can be applied to stillwaters are explored, along with some uncommon patterns that are the stillwater angler's miscellaneous bestiary. It's a wide-ranging tour of fly-fishing ideas that ends with a look at the biggest stillwater-trout fishery in the world—the Great Lakes, where yes, dear reader, the big ones do take flies.

7

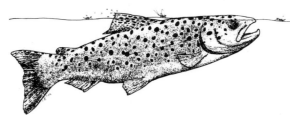

THE
BASIC
NECESSITIES

Hal Janssen

IN HIS FINE BOOK, *Loch Fishing in Theory and Practice,* R. C. BRIDGETT WROTE that it was beyond the power of anyone to prescribe for another the correct or adequate equipment for fishing, since so much depends on the angler and the type of loch he's fishing. There have been almost unbelievable developments in fly-fishing tackle and tactics since his book was published in 1924, yet his words still hold true. And even without consideration of an individual angler's capabilities, the many different sorts of stillwater situations constantly demand different techniques and tackle.

Even on the sole basis of techniques and appropriate tackle, there's no real formula, but consideration must be given to such things as whether you'll be wading, fishing from a boat, or using a float tube to get within casting range of the fish. The general type of water must also be considered: a large deep lake with no weeds or a broad bay that's shallow and weedy, a small pond that's well sheltered from the wind, or a wide lake over which the wind howls unabated. Each stillwater situation will dictate equipment choices.

I'll use Nevada's Pyramid Lake as an example, to show how such a situation can be thought through beforehand. This is a large, deep lake in the western Nevada desert; there are no trees along the edges, nor are there steep banks to shelter anglers from the stiff wind that invariably whips over the dunes and miles of flatlands along the shore. The lake is also home for some of the largest cutthroat trout in the world, some attaining weights well over twenty pounds. These enormous fish come within range of shoreline fly casters at certain times of the year when the fish are cruising within fifty to one hundred feet of the banks. At the same time—late fall and early spring—weather conditions are the most severe. When the wind is blowing from twenty to thirty miles an hour and the temperature approaches freezing, the cutthroat move into the shallows to feed on schools of tui chubs and such aquatic insects as damselflies, dragonflies, and freshwater shrimp in areas from ten to thirty feet deep.

The windy conditions and size of the fish dictate a fly rod from eight-and-a-half to ten-feet long coupled with an eight- or nine-weight sinking line to allow fishing at the required depths. The long rod and heavy line help to overcome the wind, which could make casting a lighter line almost impossible. The fish are large, so the reel must hold about two hundred yards of backing in addition to the large sinking line. My own choice of an outfit for this situation is as follows: a glass or graphite medium-action nine-foot rod that will perform well with a 250-grain line (nine-weight), an extra-fast-sinking shooting-taper line backed by twenty-pound-test Dacron backing, all on a smooth-running single-action reel (preferably with a rim control that can be palmed to provide additional drag against a powerful fish). My leader would be eight- to twelve-feet long, tapered to eight-pound-test at the tip, and I'd start by using a #6 Olive Woolly Worm to suggest both the dragonfly nymphs and the freshwater shrimp on which the cutthroats will be feeding. Pyramid Lake, remember, is an extreme situation, but it does illustrate exactly how conditions on your particular lake might govern the equipment you choose.

In general, a rod between eight-and-a-half and ten feet is ideal when wading or fishing from a float tube. In both instances, the fisherman is low in the water, and the longer rod will make a high backcast more easily and will also allow more line control when fishing. When fishing from a boat, both these problems are lessened, and a rod might well be as short as eight feet. On a lake in flat terrain where wind is apt to be a factor, a longer rod and a heavier line (seven-weight or more) will be most helpful. On more sheltered lakes where wind is usually less severe, rods down to eight feet for lines of from three- to six-weight will most often be fine, although line size will also be partly determined by the sizes of the flies to be cast.

For most stillwater trout fishing, the ideal fly rod is one that's flexible throughout its entire length and capable of handling a long, light leader and line without having to be forced in casting. These softer-actioned rods will better absorb what shocks are given the leader when playing a fish. In situations where large flies and heavier leaders are required, a stiffer rod will be more suitable, one with enough power to push heavier line sizes into a wind. I have found there are two types of rods that have no place in the stillwater angler's collection: very short

A fine brown, caught on a long fly rod *John Merwin*

rods and those with very stiff actions. A very short rod doesn't allow the angler to keep his line from tangling in the weeds, nor does it allow for an easy and high backcast. A stiff rod makes fishing with a long, light leader difficult and doesn't act as an effective shock absorber when playing fish of any consequence.

Contrary to the common belief that a fly reel simply stores line, I've found that after the rod and a good leader, the reel is probably the most important piece of equipment you can own. If you don't realize that already, you'll find out just how important the reel is the first time you hook a fish strong enough to pull line from it. Naturally, the size of your reel should be matched to the rod you're fish-

The Hardy Sunbeam, one of the newer single-action fly reels on the American market and superlative in stillwater *Hal Janssen*

ing. You should also consider the size of the fish you might encounter. For example, you shouldn't fish a lake that holds large trout with only a two-inch diameter fly reel and its correspondingly small line capacity. Nor should you consider using a three-and-half-inch reel on a very lightweight rod for a three-weight line; its weight would be awkward. The most important concern, however, is in choosing a reel that is absolutely smooth when both giving and retrieving line; a jerky reel mechanism spells disaster with a big fish. A reel with a rim control (spool flange exposed on one side, such as are sold by Scientific Anglers, Orvis, Berkley, Martin, and others) is a definite advantage when playing a large fish, because it gives the fisherman the ability to apply anything from a minimum to a maximum amount of tension on the spool simply by pressing on the flange. You'll want to choose one that's as light as possible yet which will still carry an ample supply of backing.

Finally, your reel should have interchangeable spools so you can make quick line changes. As you'll see, you need a variety of fly lines, and interchangeable spools are one means of carrying them. One reel without interchangeable spools, and one that shouldn't normally be considered by stillwater anglers, is the automatic. Not only are automatics heavy and cumbersome but they hold insufficient backing for most of my fishing. Such reels have many moving parts to attract sand and dirt, and when compared to the single-action reel, are much more apt to become almost inoperable in very cold weather. Single-action reels are of consistently simple function; automatics aren't.

Once you've selected your rod and reel, you'll be choosing the proper fly lines. The stillwater fly fisherman should be armed with a complete selection of lines ranging from floaters to those that sink to various depths, all balanced to his choice of rod. The choice of any fly-line type, as was the case with rods, is dictated by the type and depth of water you're going to fish—also, in some instances, by the type of fly that you feel will work best. As a rule of thumb, the floating line is effective from the surface to about three-feet deep (unless a long leader and weighted fly are used, in which case the depth is greater), an intermediate

The Orvis CFO single-action fly reel, this model customized by the addition of a counter-weight opposite the handle to insure perfect rotational balance when a fish makes a high-speed run. Unquestionably, one of the finest trout reels ever produced. *Hal Janssen*

line from two down to five feet, a medium-sinking line from four down to about ten feet, and an extra-fast-sinking line in a depth range of seven to fifteen feet. Depths greater than fifteen feet require some sort of lead-core sinking line. There are a number of sinking fly lines with sinking qualities that fall in between these ranges, but the types just mentioned are the basic set you'll need to handle just about any stillwater situation.

Under most conditions, whether fishing from a boat or wading, the use of a full line is a definite advantage over the use of a shooting-taper line backed by monofilament. For example, when fishing a sinking line in short quick pulls as is done to imitate damselfly nymphs in Henrys Lake, you must be in total control of the line at all times. In many cases, the very light strikes can only be detected with the help of the larger-diameter finish of the plastic fly line, certainly much better than with fine-diameter monofilament shooting line. I also find that early in the morning and at other times when my hands may be cold, the larger diameter and texture of the line's plastic coating allows for much more consistent manipulation of the line, very necessary when imitating shrimp, damsel or dragonflies, as well as quickly emerging caddis. Naturally, when using a full line, distance shouldn't be considered a primary factor. If it is, a sinking shooting-taper with monofilament shooting-line should be used. In general, I'm firmly convinced that any beginning stillwater fly fisherman will quickly find that a medium- or slow-sinking weight-forward line will quickly contribute to success.

I do use shooting tapers when using line weights of seven or more and when long casts are a necessity, such as on Pyramid Lake. The use of shooting-tapers can add greatly to your versatility: most are about thirty feet long and can be easily coiled and carried in your wader pocket or fishing shirt. It's more convenient than the extra reel spools you need when using a series of full fly lines. In situations such as Pyramid, I like to carry six or seven shooting tapers of different densities. In the course of a day and as conditions require, I'll change quickly and easily from one line to another without having to change reel spools or re-string the rod, simply by clipping off one shooting taper, coiling it up, uncoiling another and tying it to the shooting line just as I tie on a fly.

One of the lines I mentioned isn't really new, but seems generally unknown among anglers: the intermediate line. This line has the same sinking qualities as the old silk lines that were in general use years ago. It floats low on the surface until the surface tension has been broken by pulling the line quickly through the water with a tug or two, which causes it to sink ever so slowly. As you'll see in subsequent chapters on various techniques, drag on the line at the surface can be caused by wind and can be a real problem with a floating line. Intermediate lines can be used to great advantage by stillwater anglers, partly because they help to solve this problem.

The leader is the last of the important tackle items. So much has already been written on basic leader construction that there's little need for me to rehash it, and leader lengths appropriate for a variety of situations are treated in subsequent chapters. I do want here to handle questions of leader materials, knots, and the question of knotless versus knotted tapered leaders.

Since almost all commercial tapered, one-piece leaders are no more than nine-feet long, and since you'll often need a longer leader, you're often forced to build your own, either from scratch or by adding on to a ready-made nine-footer. Even commercial leaders come in various butt diameters, so as a rule of thumb, choose a butt section that is about .010 smaller than the tip of the fly line, which usually amounts to about two-thirds of the line's diameter. This will help to turn the leader over when casting. I've found, by the way, that the knots used in constructing hand-tied leaders—the blood knot or the double surgeon's knot—add some mass to the leader and help in turning the leader over.

Since knots decrease a leader's strength, one can't argue the fact that a knotless tapered leader is stronger than one with knots in it, other things being equal. But a knotted leader does have a couple of advantages: small amounts of moss and weeds hang up on the knots instead of sliding down onto the fly, and by using a maximum length of tippet material, the sink of the fly can be gauged more effectively than with a knotless leader. If your knots are tied properly, the strength of your knotted, tapered leader shouldn't be a determining factor in your choice.

Even if you're using a knotless leader, you will usually be adding one or more sections of tippet material. In recent years, the introduction of smaller-diameter leader materials has given stillwater anglers a big boost. I have often advocated using the smallest diameter tippet material possible for the conditions being fished. My reason for this is not to keep the fish from seeing the leader, but to allow the fly freedom to move in a natural manner, unrestricted by stiffer, larger-diameter material. One example is that the smaller the tippet size, the more unrestricted will be the sinking of your nymph, a definite plus.

Whether you're building a leader from scratch or just adding tippet sections, making good knots with the newer, stronger fine-diameter materials is a problem. Some traditional knots don't seem to work as well as they did with the older nylon monofilaments, and I've tried some modifications that seem to work better. I use, for example, a triple surgeon's knot instead of a double when joining two sections together. And instead of a five- or six-turn blood knot, a double blood or a seven-turn blood knot seems to be more effective. When tying on a fly, the use of an improved clinch knot seems to decrease leader strength too much. I've found in both tests and in fishing that by taking the leader through the hook eye *twice,* and then tying a regular six- or seven-turn clinch knot that I get better knot strength. This has become the same knot I use when tying on flies for salmon and steelhead, even when using light four- or six-pound-test material.

Of the newer generation of leader material, there's only one being marketed as a knotless tapered leader in nine and twelve-foot lengths, a copolymer nylon leader sold by both Creative Sports in Walnut Creek, California, and the Mill-pond in Los Gatos, California.

The single most important thing in your choice of a leader, whether it's knotted or knotless, is that you have total confidence in your choice. This will come with experience and the trial-and-error process that we all go through.

So far, I've taken you through the basic tackle requirements—rods, reels, lines and leaders—in essence, the necessities. There's also a whole series of items that I call convenience equipment and that must be considered when laying out your basic tackle. The function of each has to be carefully determined, according to the job it is expected to do.

Your first consideration should be a clothing item that's not only comfortable but also capable of carrying all those little conveniences that are so essential to the fly fisherman. In England, many stillwater fishermen prefer something on the order of a haversack, a small bag that holds everything from fish hooks to lunch and a bottle of wine. Unfortunately this type of bag isn't practical for most of us here because we move around a lot more. So we've turned our attention to the only alternative on the market—the fishing vest.

Fly-fishing vests have long been a part of the fly fisherman's traditional uniform, along with waders or hip boots and a fishing hat, but I've found that for the really active fly fisherman, even the best-designed vests leave a lot to be desired. For one thing, they're cumbersome, and no matter how short they are cut, they seem always to be hanging in the water when you wade or fish from a float tube. To make matters worse, the fly-box pockets are positioned at the bottom, so as soon as the vest touches the water, the fly boxes get wet. When wearing one of the shorter models packed with all the necessary items, you may also find that comfort was not a consideration when the garment was designed. Most vests have zippered pockets in the back to provide extra storage, but they can never be reached without taking the whole thing off. And though all sorts of small pockets stick out, in which things are stored, you can hardly ever find anything when you need it. The pockets are usually filled to bulging with everything you can cram into them, to the point that your arms can never be comfortable because they're so far from your body. And almost every pocket seems designed to stick out and catch your line during casting and may also get in the way when you're landing a fish.

I've managed to come up with a solution that works well for me and involves

Hal Janssen with the fishing shirt he designed for easy equipment access when fishing from a float tube or wading. *Photo courtesy of Hal Janssen*

little effort to make: a fishing shirt. Start out with a basic short-sleeved army-type shirt to which you can add box-shaped pockets placed according to your needs. Four roomy pockets accommodate most of my gear, but you may want to make variations of your own. A khaki color works out nicely because it blends well with most backgrounds. Because you'll wear it inside your waders, it will never be hanging in the water, and there's plenty of room on the front for all the pockets you'll need. I found the first shirt that I designed to be so comfortable that after coming off the lake I continued wearing it even while traveling from one place to another. Another nice feature about the army shirt is the epaulets on the shoulders, which handily accommodate the straps of your waders. I now have several variations of the original shirt. One is just for steelhead, and another has long sleeves for winter use. I even designed one with an extra-large pocket to hold my saltwater fly box.

If you're convinced that you should build yourself a shirt, the next step is to make a list of the things you'll want to have with you so you can plan the size and positions of your pockets.

You'll want to include a thermometer for checking the water temperature. My preference is the Hardy Angler's Thermometer, which is enclosed in a strong metal frame and fitted with a spring clip to hold it securely inside a pocket. You should have a fingernail clipper for trimming your knots; I carry the smallest one I can find, which I attach to a button on my fishing shirt with a lanyard. I prefer a lanyard to the spring-loaded retractable units because the latter is just one more thing on which the line can get caught. By using a long cord, you'll find the clippers easy to slide in and out of your pocket at a moment's notice. Dry-fly dressing is also an important item, which can also be used on a portion of your leader, and this is easiest with one of the paste-type preparations. One of the newer types of leader-sink materials will be useful for keeping your leader free of grit and grease, which can accumulate from the surface and retard the sinking ability of the fly.

You'll need one pocket large enough to hold spools of different-size leader material. I like to carry about seven different sizes of tippet material on small spools; I keep these tied together on a cord, arranged according to size; this way they are readily available when I need to change tippets. This method has been

Sundries from the well-stocked fishing shirt: cement, spools of tippet material, a file set for sharpening hooks, lip balm, and small tools for equipment repairs. *Hal Janssen*

convenient for me down through the years, but many stillwater fishermen prefer the Dennison leader dispenser now on the market, which holds six small spools of leader from which the material is dispensed through six small holes in the sides. It is a convenient arrangement, but the spools are so small that the leader material takes a set and must be straightened before use. Although there are several different types of commercially produced leader straighteners, I don't like to carry them. Instead, I straighten the material by stretching it between my hands.

Hook hones are another item you will want to have room for in your shirt, and there are many different types on the market, ranging from small sharpening steels to carborundum stones. My preference is a small set of diamond-tooth files, which come in a handy plastic case small enough to fit conveniently into my pocket. I've found it necessary when fishing small nymphs and dry flies to carry a pair of forceps with me so the hook can be removed from the fish as gently as possible; when the hook can't be removed without hurting the fish, I cut the leader and allow the fish and fly to go free. The hook will eventually rust away, and the fish can go about his affairs wiser for the experience.

Whenever you are near the water, you'll find mosquitos, so it's wise to carry a small tube of insect repellent. The one-ounce tube of Cutter brand repellent serves my needs—and it's the only brand I know that will not harm the finish on the fly line.

When fly-fishing any stillwater situation, it's a good idea to wear some type of eyeglasses for protection, as wind is a normal occurrence on most lakes, and a change in wind direction coupled with an errant cast can force the fly directly back into your face. During my twenty-five years of fly-fishing I have never been badly hooked while casting, but this is due to the type of clothing I wear to reduce the risk. I have dug many a hook out of the collar of my shirt, which was turned up against the wind, and on several occasions I've had my glasses deflect the hook.

The final, and perhaps most important item to keep in your shirt pocket is your fly box, and there are many types from which to choose. Over the years I've tried almost every type, including boxes with foam fillings, unbreakable plastic boxes, metal coil-spring and clip-type boxes, aluminum boxes with individual compartment lids, and little single-compartment plastic boxes. The type that proved to be the most effective for my needs was the Perrine No. 92 wet-fly and nymph box. Contrary to some people's concern about the coils causing hooks to dull, I found this not to be the case. And the size ($7/8$" x 3 $3/4$" x 6") is ideal for holding 140 to 200 nymphs and wet flies, keeping even the tiny #18 hooks securely held.

For carrying dry flies when stillwater fishing I found that the DeWitt fly box always worked best in the past; but I recently had the opportunity to try out a box sent to me by a fishing friend, John Goddard of England, who owns the Eeffeco Company. The Eeffeco box proved to be very satisfactory; it is manufactured of unbreakable plastic and lined with foam that has been cut so it will hold large quantities of dry flies without crushing the hackles. Unlike foam found in boxes that have been previously introduced on the market, the foam in the Eeffeco fly

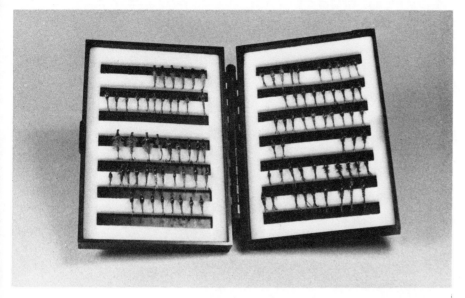

The Effeco fly box features foam inserts that don't absorb water, thereby retarding rust on your hooks. *Hal Janssen*

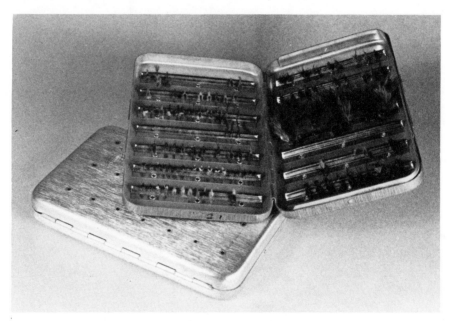

The Perrine coil-spring fly box, which the author of this chapter suggests for carrying wet flies and nymphs *Hal Janssen*

box seems to resist rather than retain water. It is lightweight, durable, and of a convenient size. In my estimation it will be around for a long time.

That covers the items you'll want to keep in your shirt, but there are some other items that might accompany you on your trips. If you're among the fast-growing group of fly fishermen who enjoy fishing from float tubes, you'll find that a small collapsible net can save you a lot of hassle by helping to prevent the fish from taking a nose-dive and tangling the line around your feet. Of the many nets on the market, I've found that the little Northfork pocket net sold by the Orvis Company works well in this instance. It folds to a convenient nine-inch size, and

Hal Janssen in a California lake about to release a trout that he took on a small nymph
Photo courtesy of Hal Janssen

can be sprung open with one hand to an eight- by thirteen-inch size with a twenty-four-inch-deep bag. It's made of stainless steel and anodized aluminum, and it's rugged and well engineered. The size of this little net allows it to fit nicely into any of the pouches that are normally found on float tubes. When you're wading, it will also fit into the pouch on the inside of your waders.

In describing what works best for me, I hope I've provided you with a guide for establishing your own needs, thereby eliminating some of the trial and error that most people encounter when investing both time and money in a new sport or hobby.

8

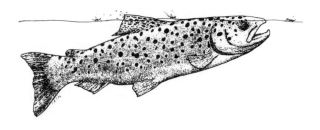

GETTING
AROUND

John Merwin

BOG SHOES. THE IDEA OF GLIDING EASILY OVER THE MUCKY CHANNELS between the hummocks with a miniature john boat strapped to each foot is a lingering dream from long-ago frog hunts. Days spent exploring the boggy edges of a pond after school; nights spent reading the Herter's catalog. They were too expensive, but with them I could reach the unreachable: bigger frogs, bird's nests, and the brook trout that rose in the open water beyond the cattails and muck. I could get them now, I suppose, but unfortunate lapses of better judgment have allowed the fantasy to fade—too much like trying to ski uphill. Subsequent years have proved at least part of that fantasy to be rooted in fact: if trout are rising in a stillwater situation, the odds are nine in ten that they'll be doing so outside of your immediate casting range. Fly-fishing for stillwater trout is one of the few instances in which the grass really is greener on the other side of the fence—lake— and this chapter deals with the various means you can use to get there.

Fishing from shore, wading, a belly boat, portable craft such as prams and canoes, and even larger boats on bigger waters all can solve special problems while sometimes creating a few of their own. We'll explore many of them in this chapter, but first I want to reinforce an important point also made earlier: you can go down to the lake with the gear you use for stream trout, rent a wooden rowboat for a few bucks, row out in the lake and start catching fish. Simple as that. But when you start wondering about how to catch more fish, about how better to fish a particular dropoff, about what to do on a lake with no rentals, or a backpacking proposition, then you're looking at many of the situations and alternatives offered in the following pages.

For many people, fishing from shore, without getting into the water, is often the only game in town. In some ways, this is the ideal stillwater approach, since the fisherman is not disturbing the water or bottom in any way. I once stood on the shore of Wyoming's Yellowstone Lake watching several schools of cutthroat cruise back and forth a few feet out from the open gravel point that was our casting platform. A friend and I had simply grabbed fly rods from the back of the car and walked out on the point to fish. The trout were schooled there because it was spawning time, and there wasn't enough flow in their spawning tributary to allow them to swim up it. The area immediately adjacent to the tributary was posted against shoreline fishing, but the cruising range of the schools extended farther. One angler was fishing within the posted zone while wearing waders and standing up to his knees in water. I had no waders, so walked farther down the beach where fishing was apparently legal and started casting.

"Hey!" The fellow in waders had turned and hollered at me.

"What's the matter?"

He pointed to one of the signs. "There's no fishing from shore. You'd better get out of here." He turned and resumed fishing.

"What do you think you're doing?" I asked, trying to be not-quite polite.

"I'm in the water. That's not the same thing." He ignored me thereafter.

The cutthroat, their normal wariness completely dispelled by the frustrated spawning urge, were easy to catch; it was only necessary to drop a nymph a simple rod's length away from the beach. My friend and I had each released one fish when I walked over and asked him if he was sufficiently embarrassed. He was, and we left. I still feel that way, and even more so for the people who ran down the bank to fish the place as we were leaving. I hope they read this.

Such instances of pathetically easy shoreline fishing are rare. In the first place, trout are usually much selective, and questions of pattern selection and presentation as discussed in other chapters become much more important. Trout feeding close to shore are also apt to be extra wary, just like brown trout in the very shallow water of a stream. The most immediate security available to trout in lakes is deep water. When fish cruise the shoreline shallows where most of their food is likely to be, they are doing so at the expense of their own safety. Instinctively, they become more wary and are easily spooked. The shoreline fisherman who neglects to keep a low profile or who moves too quickly may see nothing more than a heavy wake heading for deeper water. Take your time, or you won't take your fish.

Well-stocked trout ponds surrounded by immaculate grounds. No backcast obstacles. An easy cast to the middle of the pond. Yes, there are such places, most within private clubs or estates in this country and perhaps characteristic of some commercial stillwater fisheries in Britain. If you've fished much at all, you'll recognize immediately that aside from the trout's selectivity as to fly pattern, such a situation is a piece of cake. With respect to open and public waters in this county, it's also very rare. The real world is one of trees that prevent a backcast or trout that rise beyond reach, either or both conspiring to make the shore-based angler wish for wings. The first and most obvious answer is to walk out into the water.

WADERS AND WADING

By the simple expedient of wading instead of fishing from shore, you have given yourself room to backcast where there may have been none before. You have gained that extra twenty or thirty feet you might have needed to reach those rising fish that were once just out of range. You have lowered your own height with respect to that of the fish and may thus be more successful at not spooking them.

On the other hand, you may also have spooked every fish within several hundred yards by clumsily getting into the water. Or have slipped and fallen in. Or torn your waders on a log. Or feel like you'll freeze to death after standing up to your waist in water for two hours. Or gotten horribly stuck in the bottom muck. Or at worst, all of the previous, and you *still* can't reach the fish you were after.

Most stream fisherman who start working trout lakes will do so by wading simply because that's the equipment most of them have. And in a few instances— usually when fish are close enough to shore—it's the best way. You can, of course, simply wade wet; many people do, either with long pants or shorts and with a wide variety of footgear—usually none of it designed for the purpose. Since warm water over a shallow, sandy bottom is rare in a trout lake, and since driving home while sopping wet on a chilly evening is uncomfortable as hell, I don't wade wet. Hip boots are most often a waste of time; you'll want to wade more deeply. You need chest waders.

About a year ago, I and some others were involved in a wader-testing project for a magazine article we were producing. We obtained a sample of every brand of nationally distributed chest wader, and tested and rated them on various performance points. For sheer durability when bushwhacking around the edge of a brushy pond or through snags in the water, Graylites are tops. They are extremely tough, but also heavy and with a boot foot of only fair quality. The only place I know that sells them is Buz's Fly Shop in Visalia, California, for about $90 at this writing. Boot-foot waders by Royal Red Ball (Cahill model) and Hodgman (deluxe model) are also quite tough and are less expensive. Boot-foot waders by Marathon offer one unique advantage to stillwater fly fishermen; they are the only boot-foot wader with fitted ankles. This means that when you take a step after your foot's been embedded in muck, as often happens, your foot won't slide out of the boot. It's a brilliant design concept for chest waders and solves a problem that's both serious and all too common.

Unlike the stream fisherman who does most of his walking on current-polished rocks, you probably don't need felt soles and may sometimes be better off without them. Felt soles on mud are useless. Worse than useless, actually, because they can turn into skis when the flat felt obtains no traction on soft footing. Cleated soles are the answer, and, happily, most manufacturers offer a cleated-sole option for less money. The exception will be when you're wading on a rocky bottom—unusual in many lakes—in which case you'll need felt if the rocks are clean or metal-studded wading sandals if they're covered with algae or moss.

Wading a trout lake often means standing still in cold water—waist deep or deeper, and often for long periods; keeping warm is a problem. Almost all chest waders are cut sufficiently full to allow some sort of warm clothing underneath. Longjohns are okay, but warm-up pants are much warmer, hence better. Stay away from the down-filled versions. Down loses its insulating value when wet and won't be much help if your waders start to leak. The various synthetic fillers now used in sleeping bags and some outdoor clothing are much better.

One other way to solve the problem is to use one of the new neoprene-type stocking-foot waders. There are now two coming into general distribution: O'Neill waders from Creative Sports in Walnut Creek, California, and the Polar Bear Wader from the Archer and Angler Pro Shop in Seattle. These are made of the same foam-type material used for divers' wet suits, except these are designed to keep the wearer dry. I have worn them for several hours at a crack in water of about 50°F. with nothing but street clothes underneath and found them to be both warm and extremely comfortable. I could have stood the same temperatures in conventional waders for no more than a half hour or so. If they should get holed while you're wading, they then function exactly like a wet suit, which means you'll be wet but still warm. I did find one drawback late this spring: if you have to hike on land wearing these things in warm weather, you'll fry. I wore mine for a quarter-mile hike in 80° weather and was as sweat-soaked as if I'd been swimming. If you have to hike in, carry them.

Two other stocking-foot waders are also often used now by stillwater fishermen: SealDri by Cantex Supply, Wichita, Kansas, and the Flyweights by Uniroyal. SealDri waders are seamless latex, comfortable because they stretch when you do, and have been around for a long time. The Flyweights are tough but ultralight, only twelve ounces per pair, and are made of a nylon fabric backed by a waterproof polyurethane coating. Neither of these are any warmer than conventional boot-foot types.

If you're using stocking-foot waders, you'll need wading shoes. As far as I've been able to discover, there's only one generally distributed wading shoe that doesn't have a felt sole: the Stream-Sure by Royal Red Ball, which comes in both rubber-studded and felt-soled versions for less than $30. Present models have a nylon upper, which means they won't rot. I've used these ankle-high shoes in both fresh and saltwater for the past several months, and they've worn well, the single exception being that the laces rotted and broke. I replaced them with nylon laces.

Finally, some of you may be tempted by one of the several types of insulated waders offered by a variety of manufacturers. These will keep your feet warm and little else. Most have insulation molded into the boot foot; a couple of others offer pressed felt "boots" that fit inside the outer boot. In either case, protection is offered no higher than slightly below the knee, and when you're freezing from the waist down, that's small consolation.

Last on the list of wading gear is a stripping basket, helpful most of the time, and almost essential if you're making long tosses with a shooting-taper system. One of the most commonly used types is also the least expensive: a two-dollar plastic dishpan and about a dollar's worth of elastic, nylon shock cord. Cut a small hole at the upper corner of each end of the pan, thread the quarter-inch cord through the holes and tie it around your waist. When you strip line into it on a retrieve, the line will coil nicely and shoot freely on the next cast. Otherwise it's apt to tangle in snags or around your feet, or possibly just sink below the surface, all of which will make a clean shoot difficult on the next cast. You might be tempted to cut small holes in the bottom of the pan to let accumulated water drain out. Don't. When you wade deeply, the pan will float on the surface right in front of you; if you put holes in it, water will enter and hinder your casting.

The only real key to stillwater wading technique is to do it slowly. You are, after all, sneaking up on wild creatures that will run for cover if they get a hint of your movements. Don't grind your feet on the bottom gravel; fish are especially sensitive to underwater noise. And don't step in and wade heavily out from shore until you've determined whether or not the fish you're after are close to the shore. It's a simple matter of taking the time to look first. If you've waded toward some rising or subsurface-feeding fish, you may often find the fish working closer to you after things have calmed down. It's better to wait them out as they come in rather than run the chance of spooking them by moving. Also, as the fish approach, change the attitude of your casting from vertical to near horizontal; this will usually keep your casting motions out of the fish's view.

Wading in order to fly-fish a lake is a nuisance. If the fish are concentrated in a wadable spot with a solid bottom, it's great, but that's often not the case. Even in the course of an evening's fishing, conditions will change, fish will cruise out of reach, bigger fish will rise on the other side of the cove, and the wading angler will be frustrated since he can't move around well enough to cover the fish. And wading in soft ooze is never pleasant. The only real answer is some sort of watercraft, the exact type depending on the waters you fish, the amount you travel, and your own finances.

FLOAT TUBES

It was a little like looking over your shoulder on a dark night or whistling while you went by the cemetery. I suddenly realized how a mayfly on the surface might feel while waiting to get gobbled up—absolutely unnerved. It was my first time in a float tube, or belly boat as they're often called. My feet hung down in the water from my seat in the middle of the canvas-covered inner tube, swim fins over the feet of my stocking-foot waders. Just as I always made it home past the cemetery, so I convinced myself that there wasn't anything big enough in here to take me in a head-and-tail rise and flipped the fins a couple of times. I glided quietly backward for a few feet. A slow, steady kicking produced a slow, steady glide. There was no noise and only a slight wake that spread to shore and disappeared. I changed the angle of my kicks and changed direction easily. A kick with one foot only turned me half way around. It was a revelation.

Float tubes in stillwaters are a relatively recent and largely western phenomenon. Although they've been manufactured since the 1940s, when they were mostly used by southern bass fishermen, they didn't really catch on with trout anglers in the West until the early 1960s. Essentially, they are a fabric covering inside of which is a small truck-type inner tube. The covering allows for the attachment of pockets and other accessories, but most importantly holds the seat or sling in which the fisherman sits. Chest waders are usually worn. Propulsion is either by swim fins or paddle-pushers, hinged "paddles" that buckle to your feet. The paddle swings back as you bring a foot forward, then extends outward as you bring your foot back. You can thus propell yourself forward with a gentle walking motion. Operation of the whole affair is essentially noiseless if done with care, and that in combination with the angler's low profile in the water makes the device ideal for quiet water and wary fish. Since float tubes are also easily portable, they can be carried into a lake over considerable distances and inflated with a small manual air pump once you get there.

Gary Strodtz, a fishing friend from Sumner, Washington, has used belly boats on the lakes of his area for several years. I asked Gary for some advice I could pass along, and the following are his comments.

"Conventional swim fins offer the fastest propulsion and are the most efficient in terms of energy expended. This is quite an advantage on large lakes, especially when bucking a strong wind. There are many different types of fins on the market, but the best kind for the float tuber are lightweight and adjustable with some positive means of attaching to the foot (e.g. a strap or buckle). It's also advisable to buy a pair that float, since one may occasionally come off. Swim fins are worn over stocking-foot waders, so it's also important to buy a pair of sufficient foot size.

"In using either paddle pushers or swim fins, the fisherman must practice to gain good control. This isn't difficult and only requires the angler to relax; working too hard will not increase your speed, but it might induce leg cramps. Cramps are painful, but can generally be remedied by straightening out the leg and relaxing.

"The first concern in using a float tube should be safety; and float tubes *are* safe when used within their limitations. Accidents happen as a result of poor judgment, lack of knowledge, or overstepping one's own limitations. Watch for hidden obstacles when entering and leaving the water; these can often trip an

Backpacking this gear to a remote Vermont pond solved the problem of reaching brook trout that cruised beyond reach of a caster on foot. *John Merwin*

angler and lead to a dunking. Waders should be worn completely pulled up, not folded down to the waist, and a life jacket should be worn. Water skiers' safety belts have proved to be comfortable back supports when in a float tube as well as holding your waders in around your middle and providing flotation if need be. Fish with a buddy or at least make sure there's someone around who can help if you get in trouble. All the manufacturers I know, by the way, agree that the most dangerous use of float tubes is in floating or crossing a river. The float tube was designed for stillwaters and should only be used there.

"Tipping over in a float tube is possible, although difficult in stillwater. The combination of float tube and angler produces an iceberg effect in which most of the weight is below the waterline. With the center of gravity so low, it's hard to flip. If you do spill, you can slip out of the tube and then use it for support while you work your way to shore. The newer float-tube models come with a quick-release strap on the seat, which assists in a quick exit. Once again, the most likely time for spills is when entering and leaving the water, and it helps to remember that your feet are encumbered by paddle pushers or fins.

"Float tubes are made of tough, puncture-resistant fabrics, and it's highly unlikely that foul-hooking the tube while casting would pierce the fabric and puncture the tube. Even if this should happen, it's unlikely that more than a small leak would develop. Unlike a car tire, the float tube carries a volume of air at low pressure. The various float-tube makers all admonish against overinflation, but neglect to say just what that means. Air expands with increasing temperature, causing the possibility of damage to the tube and covering as they become warmer. It's best to inflate the float tube so the inner tube just fills out the cover. If the tube is left in a hot car trunk or in the sun, air should be released to compensate for expansion. As the air cools or when the tube is in cooler water, air should be added with a hand pump.

"Maintenance of a float tube is a simple matter of an occasional cleaning. A seam may become loose once in a while, and they're easily fixed on a home sewing machine. When storing a float tube after the season, it's best to reduce the air pressure and to make sure that everything's dry to prevent rotting and mildew."

Gary also told me that he's experimented with a variety of the brighter colors offered by various manufacturers and has found that none seem to spook fish. It makes sense, since from below the tube will be seen as darkly opaque and from the side is viewed at such a low angle by the fish as to make color inconsequential. Also, since movement is most often what spooks fish, the angler is usually the culprit and not his tube.

Float tubes aren't best-suited for long-distance cruising in a lake. Don't forget that as far as you paddle yourself from shore, you're going to have to get back. Warmth is more of a problem for the float tuber than for the wading angler who can, if need be, step on land periodically to warm up. As before, wear warm clothing under your waders, use one of the newer neoprene-type waders, or both.

Float tubes in sheltered, quiet waters may be the ideal craft with which to approach and catch wary fish. But you can't move easily over substantial distances either to follow cruising schools or to search for rising fish. Some bottom types may not be appropriate for their use, either. If you want to switch quickly from a deeper bay where you float with ease to the bottomless muck of the shallows, you're going to have trouble. It's time for another step up on our list of watercraft and into a small boat.

CANOES AND PRAMS

The trout pond I most often fish involves a half-mile trip by water from the landing to the most productive bay. I'm fishing water that's a few inches deep over the delta of the inlet stream for a while, and then switching to the ten-foot depths in the old stream channel amid standing timber. It's a small pond, sheltered, and holds mostly brown trout and largemouth bass. The trout often cruise quietly near the surface, softly taking the midges that emerge morning and evening throughout the season. It is ideally suited to fishing from a canoe.

The same canoe takes me easily through the swamp channels where I once floundered wait-deep in muck through the cattail bogs in search of scattered spring-hole brookies. It is a friend saving me the aching shoulder of hauling casts out from the shoreline. Instead, I now drift with sinking line and nymph extended behind, carried by the wind over the surface, noting exactly where the hits come and then anchoring there to cast. The canoe travels easily on top of the car and I can lift it on and off and carry it on my back for short distances without too much strain. Perhaps most important, its graceful lines, silence, and a long wilderness tradition of canoeing make it a part of the very essence of fly-fishing.

Of the multitudes of small craft available to anglers, the two in most common use by fly fishermen seem to be canoes and small aluminum prams, both of which are easily car-topped and gotten in and out of the water with little difficulty. A canoe will get you from place to place with less effort than is spent rowing a blunt-nosed pram. A pram is more stable; you can stand (with caution) in it to cast, and although I've done the same in a canoe and never tipped, it makes me too nervous. I stay seated. If a pram has oarlocks attached to the oars, and it should, when you sneak up on the fish you can simply let go the oars and pick up the rod. In a canoe, the paddle must be quietly set down out of the way before the rod is taken up. It's a matter of only a few seconds, but can make a difference when you're trying to intercept a cruising fish.

Most prams are aluminum, and there's no better material for transmitting noise into the water. You should no more bang around in an aluminum pram or canoe then you should splash in the water when approaching fish. Be careful. Fiberglass and the ABS or Royalex foam-sandwich materials dampen noise to a greater extent and I prefer them for that reason.

Remember that in either craft, you are in a higher position with respect to the fish than was the case when wading or in a float tube, which means fish will be more easily spooked. When fish are working nearby, I keep movement to an absolute minimum and cast sidearm, away from the fish. I change the direction of the cast for the final delivery, but still sometimes spook fish, particularly when they've worked in close to where I'm anchored. I've had better luck by waiting until they've worked a little farther away, but it's a tough wait.

It's almost axiomatic that if your line can tangle on something in the boat it will do so. Keep the bottom in front of you absolutely clear of anything at all so you can strip line and then cast without fouling. Once again, a stripping basket may be helpful, particularly with a shooting-taper system and its long, light shooting line. Instead of a dishpan, though, use a large round plastic-mesh laundry basket on the bottom of the boat. The plastic mesh means a wind will blow through it instead of tipping it over.

Roger Keim, who uses a canoe to chase brookies around assorted Maine ponds near his Bangor home, once pointed out to me the potential problems in the relative positions of sun, angler, and fish in clear-water situations. Our conversation was a little theoretical, but intriguing and may have some implications for your own fishing. In essence, if you're fishing over twenty feet of clear water and the sun is forty-five degrees above the horizon and behind you, then your boat's shadow is being projected on the bottom about twenty feet away. It's a surprising thought, because like most people I had assumed that because I couldn't see my shadow it didn't exist. It does, obviously, and it may be spooking fish. Conventional wisdom often has the angler with the sun at his back, a shadowy figure to

Canoeing remains an idyllic way to fish
a small pond. *John Merwin*

Barney Rushton of British Columbia prepares to fish from his small pram for trout in one of the cool lakes of the area. *Lefty Kreh*

the fish instead of being brightly illuminated. Perhaps the better approach when fishing at some depth is the opposite. I really don't know, nor have I encountered anyone who will say one way or another with certainty. Perhaps I would be suspicious of anyone who did, there being no such thing as a sure thing in any of our stillwaters.

Given the added mobility of a canoe or pram, it becomes a real temptation to chase fish, paddling or rowing in frustrated haste from one sporadic rise to another. A few unsuccessful casts and off to the next rise a hundred yards away. On one occasion I stood in a canoe and watched a rainbow make an unbroken string of rises every ten feet or so for almost a quarter of a mile. But more often trout, especially brown and brook trout, will be working a well-defined beat in a relatively small area. Sporadic rises most often mean that most of the feeding activity is going on under the surface. Pick an area and work it carefully. Unfortunately,

The larger the craft the more stable the landing platform *Engerbretson/Dvorak*

those rises are tempting and I've often been suckered into paddling all over a lake in pursuit. It has never worked as well as concentration.

When those rises fall into the definite pattern of cruising fish, your small craft does give you the ease of movement necessary to intercept them. Early fall means flights of minute flying ants on one pond I fish, and on calm days the cruising rainbows string their riseforms in a straight line for hundreds of yards. I can see them coming at considerable distance, paddle slowly over near their line of travel, and wait for the fish. It often works and is certainly most easily done in a small boat.

Two anglers fly casting from the same pram or canoe can become a comedy of tangled lines and foul-hooked friends. Most problems are alleviated by casting alternately instead of at the same time. One other suggestion that has helped many people is to practice casting while sitting on the ground. You'll start to see immediately the problems you'll later encounter in a small boat: keep your backcast fairly high. Don't use too much body English (unless you're a good swimmer). Paying attention to where your backcast goes when there are two anglers in a boat is the key to a lasting friendship.

If you've fly-fished for stream trout, you know that a hooked fish heads for some sort of cover, stumps, rocks, or whatever. Your task in playing the fish is to keep it away from such obstructions. One of the curious twists that obtains in stillwaters is that instead of keeping a fish away from cover, you're pulling it toward a place where it can hide: under your boat. A struggling fish near the boat will often run underneath, so you must be ready. Extend the rod and follow the fish with it, even sticking the tip underwater if necessary. The only danger here is that the fish is apt to do this quite suddenly; you must simply keep the possibility in mind and be ready.

Finally, rowing and paddling can be enjoyable exercise up to a point, after which it becomes work, especially in the wind. For quietly fishing a small pond for a few hours and for effortlessly sneaking up on trout, an electric trolling motor is ideal. Also, many small trout ponds in populated areas are surrounded by cottages, and the rules of the lake may prohibit gasoline motors entirely. Small gasoline outboards are lightweight and suitable for both canoes or small prams. They're fine for getting from place to place, but can't compete with the slow crawl and relative silence of an electric for approaching wary fish.

Choice of a boat becomes a question of appropriateness and a knowledge of the waters you'll be fishing most often. A canoe isn't approapiate for Lake Michigan, and a bass boat would be out of place on a beaver pond. In thinking of trout, lakes, and watercraft, I'm reminded of a conversation I once had with Bill Riviere, who wrote the fine canoeing book, *Pole, Paddle, and Portage.* The two keys to a long and fruitful life, he told me then, are a fly rod and a canoe. A quiet pond and rising trout were implicit in his statement.

9

THE
NYMPH
IN STILLWATER

Hal Janssen

WHEN FISHING IN STILLWATER ONE SHOULD ALWAYS BEAR IN MIND THAT the lake or pond is an aquatic ecosystem all its own. Everything contained therein is part of a fragile chain: each link plays its role in the sustaining of life. The more the stillwater fly fisherman knows about this aquatic world, the greater are his chances for success. The serious fly fisherman should personally investigate what goes on beneath the surface of a pond. Once he becomes aware of the world and habits of the trout, he'll become more conscious of his techniques and their application. He will find his interest stimulated by observation, and those observations will open his mind to what fly-fishing is all about.

Not every fly fisherman can take the time to go out on aquatic field trips before fishing; but, in addition to reading, he can study the more common aquatic insects in a home aquarium. Setting up an aquarium can become a fascinating project for the entire family; the creatures can be collected on a picnic outing, and then taken home and cared for. Subsequent observation of the daily activities of these temporary pets will not only stimulate your interest in fishing but increase your stillwater awareness and help you to become a more successful fisherman.

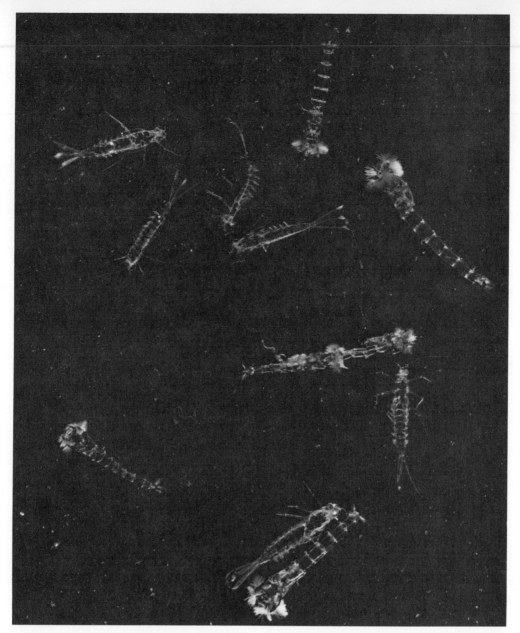

Clues to the hatch: midge and mayfly shucks on the surface *John Merwin*

MAYFLY NYMPHS

Due to their sheer abundance in some areas, mayfly nymphs may be a staple part of the trout's daily diet in the spring, summer, and sometimes well into fall if the weather remains warm. The nymphs of various stillwater species range in size from practically microscopic to two or two-and-a-half inches in length. They are essentially defenseless, depending upon their protective coloration and, for various species, the ability to reproduce in massive quantities as a means of insuring their continuation.

The nymphs of some species mature within months (*Callibaetis* and others) and may have more than one population cycle in a single year. Some require up to two years, but most undergo one life cycle in stillwater in one year. In hatching, most nymphs will rise to the surface film, break the nymphal shuck along their backs, and pull themselves free to fly away as winged adults. The amount of time it takes for this emergence depends on weather conditions and the time of day. Each species has a typical time of emergence, which will vary from month to month in the course of a season, both in terms of time of day and the required time for actual emergence. During June and July, for example, when middays are warm, the mornings can remain quite cold until the sun rises high enough to warm the water and air. In these cold-morning conditions, nymphal emergence can take up to twenty seconds in comparison to warmer periods when emergence is sometimes quicker than the eye can detect. Also, since actual hatching times are at least partly keyed to temperature, and since the time of day at which a particular temperature is reached changes with the season, so will the hatching activity of a particular species change with the calendar.

Mayflies prefer to emerge in calm-water conditions; a slight breeze is not a deterrent, but strong winds will often postpone the hatch. If wind becomes a factor when you're fishing during an emergence period, look for a sheltered area where the emergence will not be affected by rough-water conditions. Various genera of nymphs are also highly selective in the types of habitat they utilize and in stillwater particular attention should be given to areas sheltered from direct wind and to the aquatic vegetation present. If you find a habitat suited to the nymphs, you can almost always assume this will also suit the feeding habits of the trout. Once you find the ideal environment and can consistently recognize it, your chances of success will increase accordingly.

When using a mayfly nymph in stillwater, several different techniques can be applied, the majority of which revolve around the conditions prevailing on the lake you're fishing. In general, I've found mayfly nymphs to be most successfully fished with a floating line, long leader, and a weighted fly. As with any imitation, the best way to determine the correct presentation is to know how the real thing behaves beneath the surface. By becoming aware of the movements of a mayfly nymph from first daylight through actual emergence, you'll begin to see the development of a nymph-fishing system.

Mayfly nymph *(Callibaetis species)*

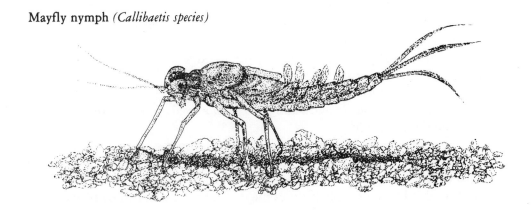

Burrowing mayfly nymph (*Hexagenia species*)

On a lake in early morning, you'll sometimes find surface conditions to be calm, with little, if any, surface activity on the part of the trout. The reason is the trout's main food source is not on the surface, but below it, where the fish are feeding on the food that is most easily available to them at this time of day. I call this early-morning fishing period the pre-emergence. During this stage, the nymphs are actively moving about in the weeds along the bottom in preparation for their emergence, somewhat like an athlete's limbering-up exercises in preparation for a race. In this case, the mayfly nymph is moving about, lifting ever so gently off the weed beds and exercising its body. It lifts slowly up, and then settles back into the weeds again, repeating the process erratically, In some instances, the nymphs may be migrating upward through the weeds that border deep-water channels, or they may be moving from deep water to shallow water where their emergence will be less impeded by adverse weather conditions. The sheltered side of the lake shoreline or the leeward side of a bed of weeds are the ideal places for the fisherman to be at the time of the hatch.

Visualize a large brown trout cruising slowly over the top of the weed beds. Large numbers of nymphs are moving erratically off the weed beds and settling back down again as they prepare to emerge. The trout can take these nymphs without expending the energy it would have to use in chasing a faster-moving prey, such as a minnow, dragonfly nymph, or an emerging caddis. The trout takes the nymphs casually, almost without effort, as they lack the mobility to get away. This is the way you'll want your imitation to look, so work your retrieve accordingly: slow, erratic, pausing at regular intervals.

When fishing during this time of pre-emergence, often between eight and ten in the morning, I choose a mayfly-nymph imitation with a dark, shiny wing case tied on a #14 or 16 long-shanked hook and weighted with six to ten turns of one-amp lead fuse wire. My leader is twenty to twenty-five feet in length, divided into three equal parts: a butt section of fairly heavy material, a middle section made up of tapered sections to allow the joining of a small-diameter tippet, which comprises the third section.

There's a simple tippet-length formula that will allow a weighted nymph to sink to the bottom as quickly as possible. I have found that by using the smallest-diameter material that will still maintain a safe breaking-strength, and by using a tippet section that is one-and-a-half times the depth of the water to be fished, I am able to sink a weighted fly easily to the appropriate depth. A long, light tippet also stretches like a shock absorber when striking and playing a fish.

For best results, make a cast over the edges of the submerged weeds and allow the fly to sink about to their depth, then slowly retrieve about six to eight inches of fly line, repeating the process until you feel that your nymph has covered the productive water. Then make another cast and repeat the process. By using this method, your weighted fly on the long leader will be suspended somewhat vertically while sinking and while being retrieved upward. The floating line and the heavier leader sections stay afloat. As you retrieve, the fly will make six- to eight-inch vertical movements up from the weeds and will settle back down during the pause, much the same as its living counterpart.

It's important to remember that while fishing this particular method, you must be alert. The fish will take your nymph very casually, and you won't be able to feel any kind of a tug. Rely on your eyesight, keeping your eyes trained directly on the area where the leader enters the water. Having made a cast or two, you will have noted the speed with which the nymph is drawing the leader down through the surface. If the leader stops drawing or its speed of draw increases from the norm, you should quickly lift the rod and tighten the line without hesitation. This may seem difficult at first, but remember that the fish is leisurely feeding on small, slow-moving food; the take will be slow. The fish will also have the opportunity to eject your nymph unless you act quickly, so always remain alert.

A second phase of pre-emergence activity—the middle pre-emergence period—occurs between ten and noon. During this time the nymphs move farther up in the water and become even more vulnerable. Some of the nymphs will have started to emerge at the surface, but the larger trout's attention is still in the mid-

Mayfly nymphs *(Caenis species) John Merwin*

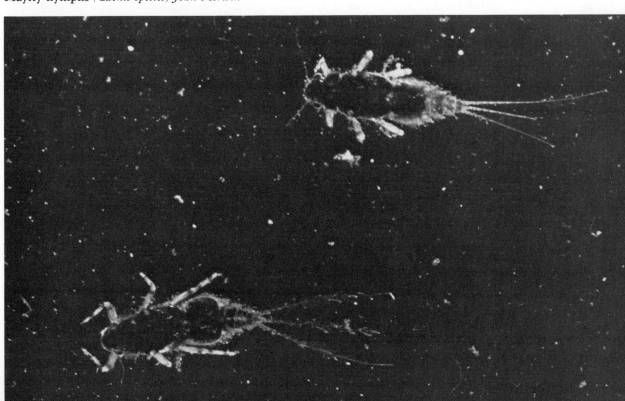

dle zone through which the majority of nymphs are now ascending. They aren't settling all the way back into the weeds at this point, just starting up, stopping, drifting back down a bit and then starting upward again. The fisherman, aware of this, will continue with the same type and size of nymph imitation, except now weighted with three to six turns of wire instead of six to ten. And instead of having a leader tippet that is six-feet long, for example, the tippet length can be reduced to three feet, which will keep the nymph from sinking all the way to the weeds and allow it to stay within the middle zone.

The take is going to be a little more definite in this middle zone, but will not be so definite as to be violent. The fish is now moving up and back and forth over the top of the weed beds, not quite as slowly as before. This increased activity on the fish's part will produce a firmer take or draw on the leader than when the nymph was deeper in the water. Still, you must continue to focus attention on the leader's point of entry below the surface and be ready to cushion a violent reaction from the fish when the rod is lifted and the line tightened. At this time a softer, slow-action rod is an advantage, because it will help to absorb the shock to the light-strength leader material.

Later in the day, often from about noon until two, is essentially the emergence period when the stillwater fly fisherman who's interested in success can do one of two things: change to a dry fly imitating the emerged adults that are now in abundance on the surface, or tie on a mayfly nymph designed to float just under the surface. My own preference is to stay with the same type of nymph that was used in the previous two stages, but tied without any lead whatsoever, and to increase my leader size to three pound test, which will hold the unweighted fly close to the surface. Cast the fly just ahead of any fish that shows itself on the surface, and retrieve it six to eight inches at a time in very slow, steady pulls. This will cause the fly to move up to the surface film and then to sink slightly on the pause. Watch for a swirl in the water where you imagine your fly to be, and be on the alert for any movements out of the ordinary within that immediate area. You may also keep your eye glued to the point where your leader enters the water. In either case, strikes at this time are more apt to be violent, as the fish tries to get the nymph before it escapes through the surface.

Visibilty is often hindered at this time of day as the cooler water can become slightly ruffled by currents of the now-warmer air. As the sun moves higher in the sky and farther into the west, more surface disturbance will occur, this stopping most hatching of the mayflies, but usually not interfering with the emergence of caddis and midges.

I have found that when the day is bright and the lake surface remains calm, the use of an unweighted, rough-bodied mayfly nymph will work. Grease this fly and cast well ahead of a feeding fish; allow the fly to lay motionless on the surface as if hatching. This is an excellent technique, but a rather limited one, as conditions must be almost perfect for it to be fished successfully.

When windy conditions retard periods of emergence, fish concentrate their efforts by cruising in channels along the edges of the weed beds, and feeding not on nymphs that are getting ready for emergence but on nymphs that are actively moving from one weed bed to another. During a heavy wind large numbers of mayfly nymphs may also be shaken loose from their positions within the weeds that are hanging over the edge of drop-offs and channels, so fish will move slowly along this area, which is protected from the wind but which still affords good visibility and an excellent feeding advantage. At this time I prefer to use the same long, leader tippet that was used in the early-morning hours of pre-emergence. The wind will ruffle the surface and create drag on the fly line, which will move the fly slowly along the edge of or across the channel, depending on your position. It's always best, though not easiest, to make your cast directly into the wind so the nymph either comes back toward you or at an angle to one side or the other. The strike indication will be movement in the line as it's drifting along. It will suddenly quit drifting and start to tighten. Occasionally a smash take will occur during windy conditions when the hook is actually set by the wind causing a drag on the line. In these cases the tippet usually breaks when the fish bolts unless you quickly allow the line to slip through your stripping finger.

When the wind becomes extremely strong, you may experience difficulty in detecting the strike until it's too late. When this is the case you may wish to change to a medium- or slow-sinking line, which will quickly break the surface—and also solve the problem of too much drag. With these lines, you can fish the mayfly nymph slowly along the edges of the weeds without being bothered by wind. I cast the sinking line directly over the weeds and retrieve it to the edge of the weeds, into the channel, and back up the side from which I am casting. This is also an excellent time to get up-wind from the edges of the weeds and cast down along the edges of a drop-off, slowly working your mayfly nymph back to you.

The methods I've outlined work quite well to imitate the nymphs of such mayfly genera as *Callibaetis, Tricorythodes,* and *Siphlonurus.* A little faster retrieve of the fly, followed by a brief pause, may work better for the more active *Siphlonurus* nymphs during the times mentioned. Toward evening, just as the sun is starting to set, a *Hexagenia* nymph can either be fished on a floating line and long leader with the weighted imitation (which is my favorite method), or fished slowly with the sinking line and unweighted fly. The *Hexagenia* is probably one of the hardest of the mayfly nymphs to imitate, both because of its large size and because it is prevalent only at certain times of the year and late in the evening. For consistent success in searching stillwater with a nymph, your best choices are probably the *Callibaetis* and the *Siphlonurus* nymphs, which are prevalent across the country and during the day from April through October.

CADDISFLIES

Although trout may at times pick caddis larva from the weeds or off the bottom, these larva are so sedentary or slow moving as to be impractical to imitate. In stillwater, the most intense feeding activity takes place when the caddis have completed pupation on the bottom and the free-swimming pupae are heading rapidly to the surface to hatch.

The shape of the caddis pupa bears a certain resemblance to its adult form. The thorax and abdomen are distinctly formed, and the wings are readily visible on the inside of the skin of the pupa. The antennae and legs lie along the edge of the body, extending past the last abdominal segment. Heavy fringing on the legs allows the pupa maneuverability, permitting it to swim rapidly toward the surface. In stillwaters, the pupa will emerge in open water while hanging in the surface film; the pupal skin splits, and the adult rapidly emerges. The pupa, at times and in some lakes, displays such maneuverability that it can be seen moving just under the surface prior to emergence.

The large traveling sedge, best known in the lakes of British Columbia, emerges at midday, offering the fisherman the opportunity to match this type of hatch. But I have mostly seen sedges hatch right at dark, when the adults can be seen moving rapidly across the surface, heading for the nearest bank or stationary object. Limited daily emergence is probably one of the main reasons that caddis pupae aren't more widely used by stillwater fishermen.

It's worth noting that some of the damselfly imitations that are currently used throughout the Northwest and British Columbia, as well as some shrimp and dragonfly patterns, are no doubt taken for emerging caddis rather than for what they were originally intended. When you use any of these patterns with the normal short, choppy, fast stillwater retrieve, or a constant retrieve of eight- to twenty-inch pulls, or a combination of both, your fly is actually simulating the emergence of the caddis as well as if you were doing so deliberately. Remember that you may have the best imitation possible of a particular insect, but you should never assume that it is being taken by the trout as such if you are not manipulating the fly in the proper manner.

In fishing a caddis pupa in stillwater, the use of a medium-sinking fly line and a leader of nine to fifteen feet coupled with a slightly weighted caddis pupa will keep the fly suspended below the leader and the line. When the retrieve is begun, the pupa will start to climb in an arc much like a natural making its way to the surface. I normally like to work a caddis pupa from the latter part of the afternoon until dusk, and use a retrieve that's fairly fast and consistent. If you choose this method, use a leader tippet with at least a four-pound-test breaking strength; the speed of your nymph as you retrieve will often induce a violent strike. When trout are feeding on emerging caddis they really don't have time to take a long look at the fly. They'll normally react immediately and aggressively to head off the pupa before it can make it to the surface and emerge.

An indication that trout have started feeding on caddis is a splashy and sloppy surface rise that means the fish is after escaping food. When feeding on these emergers, the trout sometimes comes out of the water ten to twelve inches from the actual target and is able to change the attitude of its body on the downward turn to trap the adult caddis against the surface. When the trout attempts to take the adult from directly underneath, the caddis will usually get away, since the

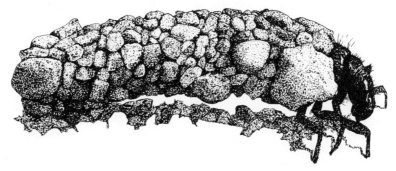

Caddis larva in case

trout's quick rise creates a catapult effect pushing the caddis into flight. The splashy rise is the fly fisherman's cue to change to the sinking-line technique. In fairly shallow water, however, the use of a floating line and a leader of approximately twelve feet, with the caddis pupa weighted to keep the fly below the leader, will allow presentation suggestive of the emerging caddis.

The force with which the trout takes the caddis actually will set the hook for you, so your main concern in the event of a strike will be to allow the line to slip through your stripping finger promptly. The force of the strike could otherwise break your leader.

Right at dark, the use of an unweighted caddis-pupa pattern on a floating line is an excellent method. You should keep the caddis pupa moving at a steady and constant pace just under the surface. Watch for a humping or swirling indication in the area where the fly should be, even though the strike will most often be readily felt.

The caddis-pupa method is not the most popular technique employed by still-water fly fishermen, but the excitement and force of the strike and the late-evening time of the hatch can make it a dramatic experience—one that is definitely worth the effort.

DAMSELFLIES

Damselflies are those metallic blue, brown, or green insects with long, slim bodies that can be seen hovering or rapidly moving above the surface of lakes and ponds on hot, lazy summer days. When at rest, the damselfly holds its finely veined wings in a folded off-vertical position like a butterfly, rather than horizontally like a dragonfly. Both insects belong to the order Odonata, with the damselfly in the suborder Zygoptera. Damselflies are a favorite food of trout, especially in their aquatic nymphal stage.

The full-grown damsel nymph will reach a length of five-sixteenths up to one-and-three-quarter inches, depending upon the species. It has a fierce appetite and has been known to consume small fish as well as other large aquatic nymphs. The nymphs have a somewhat flattened head with widely spaced eyes, a rather slim body, and three oarlike gills located at the rear of its abdomen. Most damsel nymphs have a life span of one year; some of the larger species, however, may spend up to two years in the aquatic stage.

To hatch, damsel nymphs normally migrate to shore, where they will climb on some object above the surface to emerge. The timing of the migration is to a certain extent dependent upon weather conditions and often starts for the day between nine in the morning and two in the afternoon. During this time some nymphs will travel just under the surface, while others will swim along the bottom. They swim with a distinctive motion, actually a side-to-side wiggle, using their paddlelike gills in a sculling motion. On some lakes you could almost set your watch by the emergence of the damsels while in other locations, emergence will take place over a space of several months. On Henrys Lake in Idaho, for example, peak emergence time is usually right around the first of July. This emergence has become as popular with fly fishermen throughout the country as the famous green-drake mayfly hatch on the Henrys Fork of the Snake River.

In Henrys Lake, the damsel migration will occur daily over approximately a three-week period. During this time large numbers of damselflies will be consumed, and the trout's feeding will actually be keyed upon their emergence. During peak migration the surface may come alive with slashing trout, and although the number of damsels visible to the fisherman will be great, this mass of insects may actually represent less than ten percent of the total migrating population. The largest concentration of nymphs will be traveling close to the bottom, and it's here that the biggest trout will concentrate their feeding efforts, because of the quantities available to them at these safe depths.

Your damsel imitation should be fished in a small, shallow lake that has a good growth of weed beds, for this is prime damsel habitat. Fishing small lakes is an advantage, because they afford you the opportunity to observe the total surface of the lake, which will give you an idea of where the majority of damselfly activity is taking place.

When fishing damsel nymphs, I've found that different types of fish will respond differently to various types of retrieves. This is due to slight variations in their feeding habits. Cutthroat trout prefer a long, steady retrieve with occasional pauses to allow the fish to catch up with the fly. Although the cutthroat is a lazy feeder, it is also quite curious, and the movement of the fly will cause it to investigate. It is during your pause that the fish will normally overtake the fly and leisurely swim away with it. The rainbow prefers almost a medium retrieve, but not one that is actually faster than the damselfly is capable of swimming. Whatever retrieve you use for the rainbow, make sure that it is steady and that there is no variation in movement. Brown trout prefer a series of medium-fast pulls of six to eight inches each, with a pause between each series of pulls; during this pause the brown should be expected to take. The brook trout, which is a deep feeder, will seldom be taken in a damselfly environment on anything but an extra-fast-sinking line. The brook trout does not move much off the bottom to get its food, except when in pursuit of the damselfly. This fish prefers a very slow, short retrieve with extra-long pauses between a series of twenty to twenty-five one- to one-and-a-half-inch pulls.

It's important to position yourself in such a manner that your fly is traveling toward the shore, the same as the natural insect's migratory pattern. When using a float tube or boat, you should have your back to the nearest bank.

In trying to determine the best place on the lake to make your presentation, you should look for areas of large surface weed beds that either are surrounded by deeper water or flanked on either side by deep channels. Obstructions, such as old snags, deadfalls in the water, or boat docks make excellent places for the damselfly to crawl up on and hatch, so look for these, also. Again, consider the position from which you're casting and retrieving with regard to these objects.

If you're wading, you are naturally in a good position to make your cast and draw the fly toward shore. It is when wading that you should consider the use of a floating line and a leader of approximately ten to fifteen feet. This type of equipment is best used on an eight- to an eight-and-a-half-foot fly rod of fairly soft action, as extra-long casts are really not important when fishing a damselfly nymph. The rod should be soft so it will absorb shock, since trout normally move at a fairly fast pace when in pursuit of migrating damsels. This strong, quick, positive strike will rule out the use of light leader tippets, so you must seek a happy medium, selecting a tippet that is small enough to allow your fly to move freely, but strong enough to hold. I normally use a four-pound-test tippet section, using at least three feet of tippet to absorb shock.

I like to use my boat when fishing damsel nymphs, so the weed beds and channels are visible at all times. I can use either a medium-sinking fly line or an extra-fast-sinking fly line to put my nymph down to the same depth as the subsurface damsels. Always keep in mind that you should be alert as your damsel is crossing over the top of the weeds and when it is just starting to come up in the water as you guide it back to the boat, because these are the most likely times for a strike.

When first beginning your retrieve immediately after your cast, you should remember to pull the slack out of the belly of the line, which normally sinks faster than the tip. Then, about halfway back to the boat, your fly should be swinging directly over the top of the weeds and starting its upward curve, a movement similar to that of the natural. Remember also to keep your rod tip low and pointed at the fly to get the best feel for a strike.

As you experiment with various manipulations of your damselfly, you should visualize the movement of the natural as it swims along with its side-to-side movements. It actually carries its head above its tail and swims at an angle. It will swim for a short distance and then pause, which causes it to sink for a few seconds, before continuing on its undulating way. The only way to come close to imitating the natural movement is to use an unweighted damsel nymph, whether fishing with a floating or a sinking line. You will find that the weight of the hook and materials are sufficient to sink the fly, even when using a floating line.

In tying my flies I prefer a #10 3XL hook, although there are times when the trout don't seem to be interested in anything but patterns tied on a 3XL #6. Most small-pond damselflies range in size from #10 to #12 3XL. During the early part of the season, immature damsel nymphs are approximately the length of a #14 or #16 3 XL hook. They are very active and quite abundant just off the bottom, and are often consumed by the trout feeding on mayfly nymphs. Most of these immature damsel nymphs are similar to the more mature damsel nymph, with the exception that their colors are usually more pale, almost white with a tint of pale green, pale yellow, or pale tan. The gills of the mature nymph appear as small paddles but on the immature damsel they look like three little hackle fibers sticking out at right angles.

Like the mayfly nymph, the mature damselfly nymph is often the same general color as the weeds that form its habitat. It's important to note that when you hold a live nymph in the palm of your hand, it has different color characteristics than when submerged in water. Pale-olive damsels in the hand appear tannish-olive in the water. The damsel that appears dark-olive in your hand is rusty-olive in the water. And it seems that no two lakes contain damsels of the same color, so you might want to take your fly-tying materials with you in the boat or lakeside.

Although I don't believe that the precise color of the fly is as important as the shape of the imitation, it's always good to know that you have come as close as possible to the natural insect. For those who want to be more precise with regard to color, the best method is to wet a small sample of the colors of furs that you plan to use so you can see how they will look when submerged and in comparison to the natural damsel's coloration.

The two most important things to remember for successful damselfly fishing are to make sure you are in the proper position when you retrieve, and to manipulate the fly in a lifelike manner. Always keep in mind that although the damselfly nymph looks as if it is traveling at a high rate of speed, it's actually moving quite slowly and covering little distance for the amount of movement it's going through.

DRAGONFLIES

Like the damselfly, the dragonfly is in the order Odonata, but is in its own suborder: Anisoptera. The dragonfly is a powerful and graceful flyer and has the ability to pursue and catch almost all adult insects on the wing. The nymphs are strikingly different in physical appearance from the adults, generally corpulent and grotesque, with spindly legs and heads smaller than the adults. The nymph is a hunter, equipped with a long and jointed labium (lower lip), which can be rapidly extended, seizing prey in pincers at its end. The dragonfly nymph is attracted to its prey by sight, and catches it either by quiet waiting or slow stalking.

The nymphs take from one to five years (depending on species) to become fully grown, at which time they crawl out of the water and attach to a suitable ob-

Dragonfly nymph—burrowing type *(Gomphus species)*

ject. The adult then emerges through a slit in the dorsal area just behind the head.

Unlike the damselfly, the dragonfly nymph exerts relatively little visible movement. Depending on the genus, they may bury themselves superficially in the lake bottom to wait for food; others hunt food as they clamber about the weeds. When it's time for the nymph to migrate, they actually walk ashore rather than swim, so there is no great excitement on the part of the trout as there is when the damsels migrate. Because of this, the dragonfly is not considered to be a primary food item, and is usually considered an alternative choice of fly pattern, to be used when other types of nymphs are not available to trout.

I would guess that quite a few of the patterns fished to imitate a dragonfly nymph are taken as traveling caddis pupae rather than dragonflies, or in some instances because they resemble a small sculpin or minnow. When fishing the dragonfly nymph, I seem to have the best luck with a medium- or extra-fast-sinking line and an unweighted, large, flat-bodied nymph or woolly worm fished on a nine- to twelve-foot leader. After my cast is made, I allow the line to take the fly down to an appropriate depth before starting my retrieve. The retrieve used is a series of deliberate two- to three-inch pulls of medium speed with an occasional long, fast, steady pull of two to three feet, a slight pause, and then the two to three-inch medium pulls repeated. The movement of the fly should be relatively even or perhaps slightly angled up from the bottom, which would be similar to the natural movements of the dragonfly nymph rather than the emerging movements of mayflies or caddis arcing their way to the surface to emerge.

I find it best to fish a fairly large-size dragonfly nymph as deeply as possible and as close to the edges of the weed beds as possible. Many times the trout's feeding instinct will be triggered by the movements of a fly near the edge of a weed bed. If the same type of fly movement were to occur in open water, the chances of rejection by the trout would be much greater. It is almost impossible to imitate the side-to-side waddling movement of the dragonfly nymph on the bottom or to imitate the sometimes darting movement of the natural. More often than not, perhaps, the imitation catches the trout by surprise and triggers the feeding reflex that occurs when an insect is trying to avoid capture.

The speed with which the dragonfly nymph is being retrieved to simulate the natural insect is indicative of the type of violent strike that will often take place. As when fishing the caddis imitation, you must be alert so you can slip line through your stripping finger in order to counter the shock of the strike.

The reason for the success of the woolly worm pattern and the large, roughly tied fur nymphs in use today is probably because of their resemblance to a dragonfly nymph. A large, shaggily tied suggestive pattern of the nymph is a far more effective imitation than that offered by the woolly worm.

When in doubt on any new water to be fished or during rough-weather conditions, you just might try fishing a dragonfly nymph on a sinking line. Its size and the appropriate type of retrieve will allow you to cover a lot of water and increase your chance of success while learning and observing a new stillwater situation.

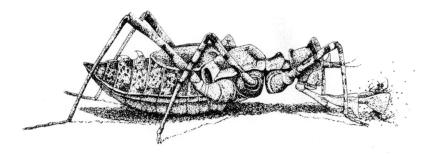

Dragonfly nymph capturing food with its hinged lower lip

10

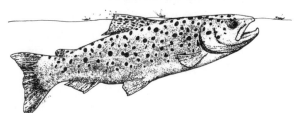

FISHING
THE
DRY FLY

Dave Engerbretson

MY INITIAL IMPRESSION OF LAKE FISHING, AS IS OFTEN THE CASE WITH those who learned trout fishing in streams, was of a sport for heavy tackle, sinking lines, and long periods of waiting for the fly to reach the desired depth. The wait was followed by a quick retrieve, an ultra-long cast, and another wait. Like most first impressions, this one was not at all accurate. Virtually every idea I had concerning stillwater fly-fishing proved to be wrong, and none was more incorrect than the belief that my dry flies would find little use in the lakes.

I should have known better. Bugs hatch in lakes, and they land on lakes. Bugs on top of the water mean fish feeding on the surface, and that means dry-fly fishing. So simple—but it took a while for the thought to occur to me.

The fact, of course, is that most of the insects of importance to stream anglers—mayflies, caddis, midges, and terrestrials—are also important to stillwater fly fishers. In addition, some species such as damselflies and dragonflies, are of greater significance in lakes. Though most stillwater fly-fishing situations require subsurface patterns, many opportunities exist for absolutely spectacular action on the surface.

While the majority of insects of importance to anglers and the basic techniques for fishing surface flies are similar in streams and stillwater, there are some obvious differences between the two types of fly-fishing. And the most important difference is the most obvious one—in streams the water moves and in stillwater it doesn't. Thus in steams, food is carried to the trout, while in stillwater, the trout usually must move to find food on the surface.

Though the basic difference between stillwater and stream fishing is obvious, I vividly recall the many frustrating hours I spent before its significance occurred to me. My first encounter with stillwater trout came on a small lake nestled deep in the mountains of New Hampshire. Though still a novice trout fisherman, I had wandered into the hills in search of a little pond reputed to contain large brookies.

I was frustrated from the very beginning. Though trout were rising fairly regularly, I could not reach them with my puny casts, and the muddy bottom near the edge of the pond prevented my wading any closer to the fish. As I circled the small pond, though, I discovered a dilapidated, half-rotten wooden pram hidden in the weeds. Now, I thought, things would surely improve.

They didn't. Poling with a broken stick and bailing with a rusty can, I managed to work my way to the center of the lake where even *my* casts could reach the rising fish. A light breeze ruffled the surface, and I couldn't actually see the fish, but the splashy rises left no doubt as to where they were—or so I thought. As the fish continued to rise all around me, I became a wild man. There's a rise! Cast to it! Nothing. There's another—quick, another cast! And so it went, like a broken record. With all of that practice, I even became quite accurate at hitting the spreading rings left by a rising fish. But I caught nothing. Now, of course, at least one reason for my failure is obvious. I was casting to where the fish had been, not to where they were going to be. Had I been shooting ducks I'd have been behind every one of them.

The first rule for fishing the dry fly in stillwater, then, is to realize that the fish are cruising in search of food in most situations. They rise to take a fly and then move on in search of another. Therefore, the angler must attempt to establish the fish's line by observing several rises in succession, and then place the fly along that line. Often, when surface flies are abundant, individual fish will establish a regular rise pattern. They'll take a fly every six feet, or every eight or ten feet, or at some specific interval. If such a pattern can be observed, your odds of taking the fish improve considerably. I well remember one such fish—a brown trout of about four pounds—that was working the water in a perfect circle in front of my

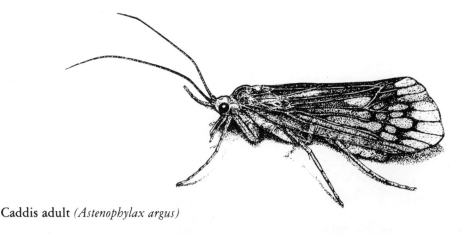

Caddis adult *(Astenophylax argus)*

Speckled mayfly spinners *(Callibaetis species)*

canoe on a Montana lake a few years ago. He took a floating dun at the 1:00 position, another at 11:00, another at 9:00, and one at 7:00. When he reached 5:00, he took my dry fly with a vengence.

Such a situation, though, can lead to another problem. How do you keep your cool when you're watching a large cruising fish glide ever closer to your fly? As you wait, your muscles tighten until your arm is fairly twitching. And when he finally opens his mouth and rolls at your fly, you strike—and miss him completely. Stiking too soon or too fast are problems that often plague the beginning dry-fly fisherman on stillwater. Part of the problem occurs as a result of the excitement that is generated when you can see the approaching fish, but part of it, I believe, is the result of a more deliberate take from the fish. For some reason, fish rising to a dry in stillwater rarely seem to require a rapid strike. When fish are missed, it's almost always the result of striking too quickly.

I found a possible solution to the problem while fishing the "gulpers" on Hebgen Lake in Montana with Art Rourke. Art had missed quite a few nice fish and was just short of being frustrated enough to start throwing rocks. He'd already started cussing. My suggestion that maybe he was striking a little too fast didn't slow him down, so finally I said, "Next time, before you strike, why don't you just say, 'He's got it,' then strike. Say it right out loud so I can hear you." I'll admit that it did sound silly, but Art was getting desperate.

We watched the next fish work its way toward us, and as it rose to Art's fly, I heard Art mutter, "He's . . ." Bang—he struck the fish and missed. The scene repeated itself several times with the same result. Art would begin to say the magic phrase, but in his excitement would strike the fish too soon. I had returned to my own fishing and wasn't looking at Art when I heard him exclaim, "He's got it,

Mayfly spinners *(Callibaetis species) John Merwin*

damn it!" I turned just in time to see him lift his rod and make his first hook-up of the day. Once he tasted success, he became a believer, and from that time on he took fish with regularity.

Yes, it sounds silly, but if you find yourself missing fish on the strike, just make sure that "he's got it" before you set the hook. If all else fails, it's worth a try.

Unless you live in southwestern Montana, or have had an opportunity to fish the area, the term "gulper fishing" may be a new one to you. It is a regional term used to describe a phenomenon that occurs near the end of August on Hebgen Lake. However, it's a situation that takes place on many lakes at various times, and is one that produces spectacular and exciting action wherever it's encountered.

In late August and early September, tremendous hatches of *Tricorythodes* and

Speckled mayfly dun *(Callibaetis species)*

Callibaetis mayflies occur on Hebgen Lake, usually between nine in the morning and noon. On a still day with the water like glass, big browns and rainbows cruise just below the surface, taking the emerging duns and fallen spinners with great enthusiasm. The water literally boils with feeding fish. They rise to single flies, or they wallow across the surface, chomping on as many insects as they can gather. The sounds of the orgy have to be heard to be believed; the fish slurp, smack, burble, and gulp. It's an incredible sight to a fly fisherman in a float tube.

In the midst of such a feeding spree, it might be expected that catching fish is a simple matter, but that's not necessarily the case. One problem facing the angler is the sheer number of insects on the water. Thousands of naturals are not being eaten either, and the odds are generally against the fish even finding your artificial. Thus, while many anglers waste time by frantically changing flies in search of the correct pattern, you will usually be better off to stick with the fly you've selected as a good match and keep on fishing. Of course, if you receive some obvious refusals, it would be well to try either the same pattern in a different size (usually smaller) or a different pattern.

Occasionally in the midst of a heavy hatch, I've had excellent results by changing to a fly that is completely different from those on the water. For example, I may put on a #12 or #14 Adams when the fish are taking something much smaller. My reasoning is that the fish are obviously in a feeding mood, but a perfect match for the natural fly would not be seen. Therefore, the fly that's different (but still reasonable) may attract attention to itself and be taken. It works often enough to deserve a place in your bag of tricks.

It should be remembered, too, that the size of the hatch affects the width of the fish's feeding or cruising lane. While the hatch is sparse and building, the fish may go well out of its way to pick up insects. In effect, its cruising lane may be several feet wide. But as the hatch builds and the number of insects on the water increases, it's not necessary for the fish to wander all over seeking the food that's right in front of him. In such a case, the cruising lane may be only inches wide, and casting accuracy becomes extremely important. The artificial that lands on the line may be taken, while one that lands only a few inches off the target will be completely ignored.

In almost all stillwater surface fishing, presentation of the fly can be critical. Although there are exceptions, the fly that lands with a slap, drops too close to a cruising fish, or has unnatural drag will generally not take fish. Fortunately, all three of these problems are quite easily remedied or avoided.

As in any fly-fishing, the fly can be dropped delicately to the surface if you aim several feet above the target, stop the rod high, and allow the line to straighten in the air before the fly lands. Shooting a short length of line at the end of your forward cast will also help to dissipate the energy of the cast and allow the fly to drop lightly to the water.

To avoid spooking a fish with a fly that lands too close to it, it is only necessary to remember to lead the fish by a few feet when presenting the fly. This distance will vary, of course, with the speed and depth of the cruising fish, the clarity of the water, the amount of wind, and so on. You will only have to watch fish dart out of range a couple of times to show you whether or not you are leading them enough.

Most fly fishermen assume, and perhaps rightly, that drag on the fly is more often a problem of stream fishing than of stillwater fishing. Don't be lulled into a false sense of security: drag can be extremely critical in many stillwater situations. Trout in stillwater usually have plenty of time to drift under a floating fly and inspect it carefully before deciding whether they should take it. For all practical purposes, the situation is almost like that in a spring creek; trout become persnickity, and drag can be the deciding factor in a refusal to take. Drag can be caused by many factors: wind, motion of the boat, waves and ripples on the water, or the angler. Whatever the cause, the vast majority of problems with drag can be avoided with the proper cast and a correctly designed leader.

Starting with our first casting lesson, we've all been taught how to make a nice straight cast, a goal we've worked hard to achieve. We've also tried our best to buy or tie leaders that will turn over and straighten out with ease. Now I suppose these are both worthy objectives, but in most dry-fly fishing, a straight line and leader are the last things I want. If the leader and line are perfectly straight and if any part of that system is pulled, the fly will move unnaturally. The solution to many of our drag problems, then, is to learn to cast with a controlled amount of slack in the line and the leader.

Almost any book on fly-casting will illustrate a variety of methods for making a slack-line cast. The one I use most often for stillwater fishing is the technique in which the rod is moved from side-to-side on the forward cast. After the power has been applied to the forward cast and the rod tip stopped, simply waggle the rod laterally as the line is unrolling before you. With this method the amount of

Remember that while standing in a boat and casting is easier then casting while wading or in a float tube, additional caution is needed to avoid spooking the fish. *Engerbretson/Dvorak*

slack can be controlled precisely, and it can be placed exactly where you want it depending on the timing of your waggle. A few small wrinkles near the line tip, a lot of big waves near the middle of the line, or any combination is possible. Check a casting manual and practice the method on the grass before your next fishing trip. You'll like the results.

The cast is only half of the solution, though. The other half is the leader design. It's true that a slack-line cast can also put slack into the leader, but there is also a leader design that will help the cause considerably. I call it the Harvey Leader, since it was develped by George Harvey, the dean of the Pennsylvania limestone fishermen. Contrary to popular tradition, George does not build his spring-creek leaders with heavy butt sections and the classic 60/20/20 formula. Instead, his leader butt consists of a ten-inch section of stiff nylon .017 inches in diameter. This is permanently attached to the line, and his basic leader is attached to this section. The leader itself tapers from .015 inches down to the desired tippet size. At the .011-inch section, he changes from a stiff to a soft nylon. The taper for a typical Harvey leader is shown in the following table.

9' 4X Harvey Leader*

.015"	18–20" (stiff)
.013"	18–20" (stiff)
.011"	18–20" (stiff)
.009" (2X)	12" (soft)
.008" (3X)	18" (soft)
.007" (4X)	22" (soft)

*To taper to smaller tippet sizes, the .009" section should be stiff nylon, and the remainder soft. The 3X and 4X sections should be shortened to 12" and 18" respectively and the 22" tippet of 5X or 6X added.

George fine tunes this leader to make it perform properly with the specific fly he is using. A large, bushy fly may require a shortening of the tippet, while a small or sparsely tied fly will require a longer tippet. This will be determined by how the leader performs on the first few casts after a change of flies.

This leader is not for large hairwing patterns or blustery days, and it will require slightly more punch from the caster to turn the fly over. But when used properly, the fly will settle to the water as softly as a tuft of thistle down, and the leader will lie in a series of gentle wiggles. And that is what avoiding drag is all about.

Some anglers attempt to solve the drag problem by using inordinately long leaders and tippets, and this will work, too. However, I find the Harvey style of leader considerably easier to handle and control. You might give both methods a try, and make your own choice. Should the leader float or sink when fishing dry flies in stillwater? There are those who insist that the leader sink, and just as

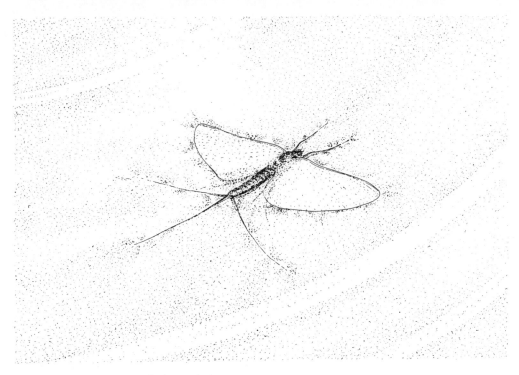

Mayfly spinner *(Tricorythodes species)*

many who say it doesn't really matter as long as there's no drag. I suppose I'm in the latter category but I'm going to continue to experiment with both methods until I can make up my mind.

There is one other important consideration that many anglers miss when trying to avoid drag, and that is your anchor when fishing from a boat. Or I should say, your anchors. When there is any significant wind, two anchors—one at the bow and one at the stern—will hold your boat in postion and prevent it from swinging and dragging the fly. A minor point, but it can be significant.

Avoiding drag may be the rule, but like all rules, there are exceptions. In lakes, it's often necessary to create drag. Or more correctly, it's necessary to add lifelike action to your artificial fly. Some flies—caddis, for example—create quite a disturbance on the water when taking off or when laying their eggs. They skit-

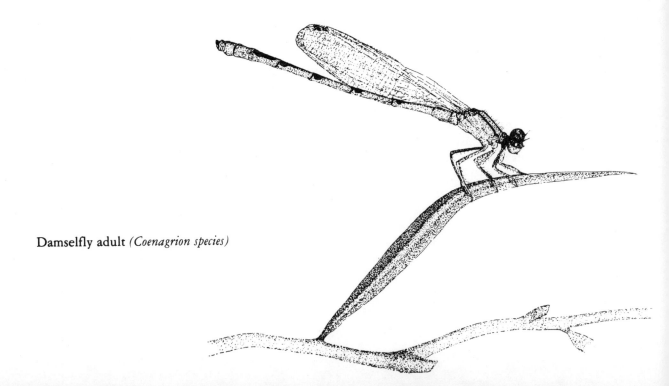

Damselfly adult *(Coenagrion species)*

ter and skate, and even make little wakes as they dart about their business. In such cases, we should attempt to make our flies act precisely the same way. Watch the flies on the water and see how they behave. Be especially alert to how the flies are acting that are being taken by the fish. Maybe a slight occasional twitch of your artificial is all that will be needed. Or maybe short, slow strips of the line, or short, quick strips and a stop. Possibly a long, skittering skate that leaves a wake is called for. The key to solving this problem is observation, imitation, and experimentation.

I recall one particular day on one of Washington's desert seep lakes where the solution to the problem provided spectacular action. Despite the rather strong wind that often blows across these lakes, a heavy flight of caddis was bringing many good fish to the surface. The rises were splashy and savage as the fish chased the elusive bugs that were being blown across the surface. I had taken a few fish, but nothing like I should have in view of the activity all around me. Out of frustration, I tied on a big skater-type fly of a color to match the caddis, and the problem was solved. After making a short cast, I held the rod high above my head until the wind picked up the bushy fly and sent it skimming across the water. The rise that immediately followed took me by such surprise that I missed the fish completely, but I had the answer, and the rest of the afternoon was one to remember.

Intentionally creating motion with a surface pattern is also an effective technique to use occasionally when fishing terrestrial imitations, land insects such as bees, ants, beetles, grasshoppers, and crickets. Though they live their entire life cycles on land, many of these insects will fall, jump, land, or be blown into the water, and trout take them with great relish. Depending upon the species of insect and the circumstances that deposited it into the water, many of the terrestrials literally kick up a fuss in their attempts to reach the safety of dry land. When fishing a grasshopper or a cricket, for example, it's a good idea to cause your artificial to act as naturally as possible. Since many of these large insects fall into the water with a rather heavy plop, make your artificial do the same. This isn't the time for delicacy; give your forward cast a bit more power and allow the fly to land with a splat. Don't overdo it; just make it sound as natural as possible. Let the hopper lie quietly for a short time as if stunned, and then give it a series of twitches. Let it stop, then twitch it again. If there's a trout in the area, that's probably all it will take to bring a strike that'll knock your socks off.

Not all terrestrials behave in this manner, of course. An ant, beetle, or inchworm may wiggle vigorously in the water or it may float quietly. Even the big hoppers and crickets are not always active. Again, the key is to observe the naturals, imitate their actions, and experiment with your presentation.

Almost any place on a lake is potential dry-fly water at some time. When a hatch of insects is coming off a small lake, the entire pond may be covered with rising fish. On the other hand, much of the time certain areas will be considerably more productive than others. This is especially true if the lake is large. Trout feed on the surface when that's the place they find their food. In scouting a lake,

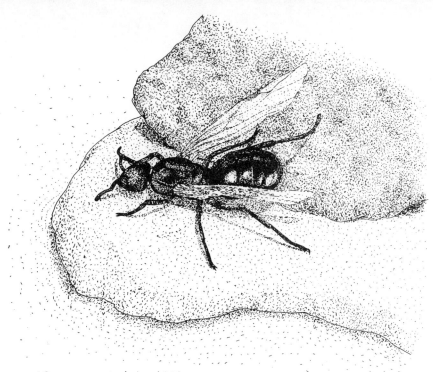

Flying ant *(Camponotus species)*

it makes sense to look for areas where insects could conceivably be on the surface. Look for shallow bays, weed beds at various depths and drift lines. Shallow bays—sometimes as shallow as a foot or two—will often harbor huge populations of mayflies and midges in a rather muddy bottom, and while trout may not live in these areas, they move in to feed when the insects emerge. In such cases, the fishing is very much like that in a spring creek. The low, clear water makes the fish extremely wary and selective, and fine leaders attached to artificial flies that closely match the naturals are in order. This can be stillwater dry-fly fishing at its best. Many times in such a location, clouds of midges will be seen dancing in the air, and fish will be rising every place you look. The obvious conclusion is that you should catch a natural adult insect, match it with an artificial, and start fishing. Unfortunately, this may not produce the hoped-for results. Midges often emerge quickly, and almost literally come out of the case flying. Thus the adults are in the air and not on the water where they can be eaten by the trout. The rises seen in this situation are almost certain to be fish taking the pupal form of the insect from the surface tension, especially if the riseforms are gentle.

Fishing midge pupae in the surface film is discussed in the chapter on midges. You should, however, be aware that there are times when the fish will be taking the adults off the top and be prepared to fish dry-fly patterns in those instances. Cold weather, for example, usually will delay the emergence from the pupal case, and rain or wind may either prevent the adults from taking flight or may knock them to the water after they are airborn. When the hatch is sparse, the adult pattern may also be effective, as the feeding fish may be inclined to take whatever is available.

Weed beds, either completely or partly submerged, are often rich in insect life and are good places to expect hatching insects to produce dry-fly activity. In the case of exposed vegetation, pay particular attention to the little depressions

You'll need sharp eyes to spot the often-subtle feeding of stillwater trout . . .

. . . and sharp reflexes to hook them! *Photo sequence by Valentine Atkinson*

that exist along the margin of the bed and even to the small pockets of open water within the bed. Such places may be difficult to hit with a fly, and the fish will certainly be difficult to land if hooked but the potential for locating large fish with a probing dry-fly is excellent.

Drift lines offer great potential. As a result of the combined action of wind and waves, material on the surface of a lake—including hatching, dead, and dying insects—is often collected into long lines of debris that can be found almost anywhere. Varying from several inches to several feet in width, these lines literally sweep the water's surface and provide a concentrated food supply for cruising fish. Always be on the look out for drift lines as you move about a lake, and when one is observed, look closely for the presence of feeding fish. Fish will often cruise along just under the scum patch and rise deliberately to pluck an insect gently from the surface. The riseform may be difficult to see, so scrutinize the area carefully.

Drift lines are not always so obvious, and at times the only thing to indicate their presence will be feeding fish. When you see fish that appear to be feeding along a relatively narrow area, you should suspect the presence of a drift line and place your casts accurately along it. Look for a pattern to the rises, as the line will most likely not be perfectly straight but will curve and wander all over the surface. Unless you locate the line, random casts are likely to be futile. Quite often drift lines will be found along the windward shore of a lake as the result of the backwash from a fairly steep shoreline, and the fact that much of the material on the lake's surface will eventually be blown to that location. The location of these lines will vary from right at the shoreline in the case of a gradually sloping bank to many yards away from one that is steeply sloped. Since all manner of insect life may become trapped in a drift line the pattern of choice may not be particularly important. Stillborn duns, duns, spinners, and terrestrials are all well suited to drift-line fishing. Of course, if some particular insect is observed in great numbers, that is obviously the pattern to try.

The stillwater angler should also be alert to the presence of currents in a lake; currents *do* often exist in lakes. They may be found where streams enter the lake, near the outflow from a lake, or around islands and points of land as the result of wind action. When present, currents can provide a ready flow of food to the fish, and in such cases the fish may not cruise but will take up feeding stations similar to trout in streams. Again, it sometimes takes careful observation to determine that the currents exist, but it's important to take note of the condition since your fly will be presented differently to a fish on a station than to one that is cruising.

Some lakes have conditions that are unique to that body of water, and which can produce excellent dry-fly fishing at certain times. There are, for example, a number of lakes in the state of Washington that are bordered in places by sheer rocky cliffs. On very windy days, it's not unusual to find hatching mayflies being battered into these cliffs and falling to the water like rain. Needless to say, when this happens, the knowledgeable dry-fly angler who seeks out the cliffs in search of the phenomenon has a field day.

Currents will exist in stillwater where streams can be found entering the lake. *Engerbretson/Dvorak*

If you think, as I once did, that lake fishing is a subsurface game, take another look at it. Opportunities for excellent top-water activity abound on almost every body of stillwater, and the angler who takes advantage of them is in for a treat.

11

FISHING
THE
STREAMER

Lefty Kreh

THE ANGLER WHO TRIES TO ENTICE TROUT TO FLIES IS OFTEN AT A DISAD-
vantage with most of the patterns he casts if he's seeking bigger fish. Large fish
need more food than small ones; and when given a choice, they don't want to
pursue scores of small insects to obtain what they need for nourishment. Baitfish
are bigger and better groceries, and streamer flies can be constructed large
enough to appeal to the biggest fish in the lake or small enough to entice any particular age or size of trout.

Streamers come in two basic forms: those that imitate a prevalent species of
forage or baitfish, and those that don't resemble anything in nature. An example
of the first is the alewife or smelt imitation; the naturals can be the main source
of food supply for trout in particular lakes and many standard patterns have been
developed over the years to imitate these and other baitfishes. Streamers that
don't imitate particular species are often called attractors, which can be a misnomer. The inference is that these flies are so bright, colorful, or attractive that they
draw the fish to them, hopefully making it strike. But many attractor-type flies
are dull and drab, lacking in fine designs or fancy colors. Some of my best attractor patterns for lakes are all olive, brown, or black, certainly not what are commonly considered attractors, but they do draw fish.

There is one outstanding difference between streamers used in rivers and those used in lakes. Rivers have currents that will undulate and manipulate the feathers, even if the angler does nothing more than hold the fly in the flow. This gives life and motion to the fly, and is perhaps one reason why so many novice anglers use streamers; the current is a constantly working ally that helps the angler deceive the fish. But the angler who fishes lakes must realize as he ties or purchases his streamers that they will have to be of different materials than many of the patterns used in a river or stream. The wings, especially, must be built from soft feathers or hair that works with the slightest twitch, vital in lakes where there's little or no current. Marabou is one of the best materials for lake streamers. If you're going to use bucktail, it will have to be the fine, soft type; and if that can't be found, you may look for substitutes, such as arctic foxtail, which bend under the slightest twitch.

Trout in lakes also get a better look at a streamer. The current isn't pulling it away, and the fish doesn't have to fight the flow to examine the fly. The fish can approach and follow your pattern for some time before it decides whether or not to strike, which means that you must give more attention to tying the fly. Many streamers used in swift water have crude bodies made from chenille or wrapped tinsel. But if you're building imitative flies, bodies constructed of appropriately colored dubbed fur give a fat, transluscent appearance that will draw more strikes.

Each is a mystery; each offers a slightly different environment, although lakes in general fall into certain patterns. You should familiarize yourself with the lakes you fish. Not only do you want to know the bottom contours, dropoffs, spring holes, weedbeds, and rocks, but you also need to know what are on the grocery shelves down there. You must know your lake, even if you're using streamers that match the color, size, shape, and swimming characteristics of its baitfish.

Any trout you keep should have its stomach examined to determine what type of forage fish have been eaten. Wading softly along a shoreline and peering into the shallows will give you indications of the types of bait that live there. And there's nothing wrong with taking a minnow net and seining or dipping baitfish to obtain samples (where legal). Remember, however, that samples in alcohol or formaldehyde will fade in color, even though they will retain total length and body shape.

Also stir around in the weeds, along logs, under rocks. Some of the baitfish, such as sculpins, are often hidden during the brighter hours of the day, coming out to feed at dawn and dusk. Your stick will flush them from hiding so you can study them. Be aware, also, that you'll find certain types of baitfish in specific locales. Alewives are free-roamers and will travel throughout the lake in large schools, but sculpin and many of the killifish are often solitary. Some baitfish prefer at least a flow of water and may be found only where a stream enters a lake, while other species may prefer shaded areas. Still others will live in or near weeds. Whatever the habitat, it pays to match the imitative pattern to the habitat

A nice rainbow that fell for a big marabou streamer fished deep *Lefty Kreh*

where that baitfish lives. No experienced bass fisherman would think of going on a strange lake, or even one he fishes often, without using his depth finder. For some strange reason, trout fishermen are often repelled by the idea of using depth finders. But trout often lie around submerged objects, such as large boulders, aquatic grassbeds, or in underwater channels. If you want to learn a lake and find the fish, then learn to use a depth finder.

There's also a last imitative trick that sometimes works. I've often found that if there are many alewives in an area that average, say, three inches, a fly that is four inches long but which still resembles the baitfish will often be singled out and draw more strikes than a fly that is an exact-size copy. What I'm suggesting is that you should certainly tie flies that are faithful copies, but don't hesitate to make a few magnums, just in case.

When I tie streamer flies, and if the pattern will allow, I use Mustad model 34007 stainless-steel hooks. These are exceedingly well made, have a rather thin wire for a stainless hook, and hold a point well. More important, they don't rust. Many of the imitative lake patterns are light in color, and after a few sessions, they may become discolored with rust, losing some of the realistic appearance that appeals to the trout.

Because streamers are frequently accepted by the fish after the fly darts forward and stops—while the line is a bit slack between fly and angler—the hooks on streamers need to be extremely sharp. I think this is one of the major reasons for failure to hook trout that take in deep water, where the pulse of the strike is often barely felt by the angler. There are also many cases in lakes when the fish

(145)

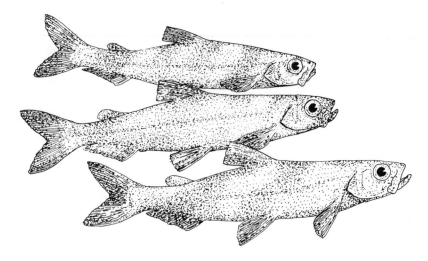

Delta smelt *(Hypomesus transpacificus)*

slips up behind and nips at the fly. I use 12- or 15-pound-test monofilament to attach a small hook at the rear of the wing, fastening the other end to the hook shank when tying the fly. Marabous frequently produce short strikes, and the stinger hook has paid off handsomely when used with them.

Once you've determined the patterns, you will need the equipment to get the fly out there, retrieve it, and fight the fish successfully. As in any specialized area, some tackle and gear is best suited to the task. The normal floating fly line is okay in many situations, but the shooting-taper system is particularly suited to fishing on lakes with streamers. The basic problem in lake fishing, unless there is visible surface activity, is to search the likely waters with your fly, meaning it must travel a great deal to pass in front of enough fish to make the casting worthwhile. No other fly-line system can so easily permit this. If you're not familiar with the shooting-taper setup, it's simply a thin, long running line tied to a heavier, 25- to 32-foot tapered fly-line head of a weight to balance the rod. The head is able to maintain momentum in the air, and the shooting line is dragged along behind to distances far greater than those obtainable with standard weight-forward or double-tapered lines. The original shooting lines were monofilament, and with this thin, slick line, tournament casters were able to wipe all previous distance-casting records from the books.

Some special monofilament lines have been developed just for shooting purposes with heads. Cortland Line Company makes Cobra, and Sunset Line Company offers Unifilament; both are oval monofilaments especially suited to shooting-taper work. One of the outstanding advantages of oval lines is that if they develop twisting, it becomes immediately noticeable. Twisting restricts the cast and can cause serious tangles. Almost every angler knows that nylon monofilament lines have a memory factor: the characteristic of remaining in the shape in which it was stored. A monofilament line that's been curled tightly on a reel spool tends to lie in coils the size of the reel spool when stripped to the ground. The caster must do whatever he can, including stretching the line, to remove those line-tangling coils before he can effectively fish. Sunset Line Company introduced several years ago a memory-free line called, appropriately, Amnesia. Strip this line from the reel and it has the coiled appearance of any other monofilament, but just one stretch between the hands and the coils disappear. One objection some people have to oval mono is that it tends to resist sinking; because of its oval cross-section it may plane in the water. Amnesia is round, and the manufacturer states that it sinks faster. Any monofilament, including this one, has a relatively short life. I'm not sure what causes it, but the more the line is used, the less efficient it performs. Offsetting that characteristic is its low price.

Scientific Anglers and Cortland both make a shooting line that is a one- or two-weight level fly line. Braided line of about 12- to 15-pound-test has a vinyl sheath laid over it, so that what you have is simply a very thin, level fly line. This is attached to the rear of the shooting taper. Monofilament's greatest drawback is it's light weight. When you release the shooting taper, it travels forward with tremendous speed, jerking on the light pile of shooting line at your feet, and sometimes lifting all of it from the deck so it crashes in a tangle against the first rod guide. The regular shooting line (resembling the fly line) is rather stiff by comparison and comes off the floor in more open standing waves, so it tangles less frequently. Such shooting line is also much easier to handle on the retrieve than the thinner monofilament. You have to decide which line you want to use. The monofilament will allow you to cast a little farther and to sink the head a bit quicker. The fly-line shooting line will eliminate casting tangles and will sink more slowly, but it is easier to work with.

There are many sinking rates of heads, from those that barely sink, such as the Wet Cel I of Scientific Anglers, through their Hi-Speed Hi-D (the fastest of all sinking fly lines), and the ultimate sinking line at present: lead core. For almost all lake situations, I either opt for a floating head or standard floating weight-forward, or a Hi-Speed Hi-D or lead-core type. I either want a line that floats or that sinks rapidly. By using the countdown method (I'll explain later) and the rapid sinker, I can obtain any depth I want.

In most lakes, something between a seven-weight and a nine-weight line is all you need, and most of the time a seven- or eight-weight line, matched to the rod and reel, is perfect. Generally you'll be casting a good distance, and lines lighter than seven-weight are tough tossing with a bulky streamer, while those larger than eight-weight can be tiring and often mismatched to the fish.

When you're using the shooting lines it helps to mark them every twenty-five feet, beginning from the connection of the shooting taper to the shooting line. Nylon, such as Amnesia, as well as the shooting fly line, can be easily marked with a permanent marking pen; use a dark one on light lines. Make the mark about six inches long, since smaller marks are easily missed. This gives you an indication of how far you've cast and how deeply you've fished.

As others have indicated in their chapters, trout in lakes occupy specific depths at certain times. Light-sensitive plankton, for example, may be nearer the surface in morning and evening, retreating deeper during the day. Baitfish in the food chain that feed on plankton will sometimes follow, and the trout do the same. This means you often have to search vertically for the trout with your flies. The countdown method is invaluable for this reconnoitering. Here's how it works. Make your long cast; then, the moment the cast is finished, begin counting: 1001, 1002, 1003, and so on. At, say 1010, you stopped counting, began your retrieve, and failed to get a strike. Count the next cast to 1014 and begin another retrieve. If this is where you get a strike, you have now determined at what depth the fish are lying. It sounds like a crude system, but with the countdown method you can put that same fly and line back within a foot of the previous cast. It's a vital technique for any deep-water work where a specific depth must be fished.

Fishing British Columbia with Barney Rushton for Kamloops trout, I was directed as to how I should slowly retrieve the imitation of a leech that he handed me. I had trouble making the line flow smoothly over my finger and had missed several strikes. I rubbed a small amount of line dressing in the groove of my finger. The line slid across the slick surface so well on the retrieve that I was able to feel every tap on the end of the line. Since that time I've made it a habit to grease that finger when using nymphs or streamers in lakes where a long, slow retrieve in the depths is required and I need to have my senses tuned for a subtle take by the trout.

Whenever I'm fishing in deep water, where I am *not* casting close to the trout, I never use a leader longer than three feet, often one only eighteen inches long. I'm certain, first of all, that trout see *all* leaders, so I don't believe that leader length is important in that regard. Trout certainly don't swim up leaders to see how long they are. Lake fishermen using seven- to twelve-foot leaders and fishing a fast-sinking line will find on examination that the fly may be riding a yard or two higher than the line, since the fly—especially an unweighted version—may be bouyed up by the leader. But with an eighteen-inch to three-foot leader, where the line is, so will be the fly. It's worth a try, and you'll find that you'll outfish those around you who are using longer leaders. However, if you're fishing in shallow water—where the impact of the line on the water near the fish will frighten it—you will want a longer leader, maybe even a ten-footer.

Trout frequently cruise the shallows, especially in the early and late hours of the day. Where certain baitfish or nymphs are in the shallows, trout will come in to feed. These cruisers may often be seen along the shoreline, fleeing at your approach, but there is a way to catch these super-wary fish. While regular streamers will work, those tied upside down are better, and the Keel-Hook streamer is the best and my favorite for this work. Toss the Keel-Hook streamer out on the bottom where the trout is expected to pass by. Hide behind a bush, boulder, or other obstruction where you won't be seen by the trout. Then, when the fish is within a few feet of the fly, flip the rod tip and make the fly leap off the bottom. The trout will often spin on its fins to get over there and gulp it down. One of my favorite patterns for this is Dave Whitlock's Sculpin.

There's another good streamer in lakes, where at times you'll need a float-

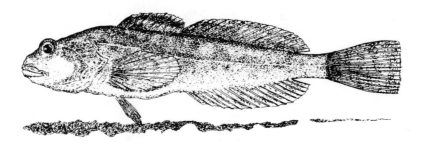

Sculpin

ing line and at others a fast sinker. Locate where a cool stream comes in to a lake; usually a few yards out from the mouth, which has been silted in from the dirt carried by the stream, there will be a dropoff. Trout will hide against that dropoff and wait for all sorts of food to come tumbling to them. A streamer that is fished through, just as the food would approach the fish, can often be deadly.

Another trick that works best with conventional floating lines, although a fly-line shooting line will also be satisfactory, is to mend line to govern the path of your retrieve. Let's say that you want the fly to come straight back to you for some distance, but then you want it to pass by a large rock, possibly holding a big trout, that's off to the right. Make the cast and mend the line well to the right on the water. The fly will follow the path of the line as it was mended, and you can fish several spots that are to one side or the other on the same retrieve.

Casting a streamer to the shoreline and bringing it back out is the method used by most when fly-fishing but if you examine what you're doing, you'll find it is perhaps the most inefficient of all techniques. The fly goes to the shore, and pointing directly at the angler (sometimes giving no profile to the fish), the fly comes immediately back to the caster. Anyone who knows how to make a curve to the left or right, as you do in dry-fly fishing, can present the fly much better to the fish. Make a cast, curving the fly and leader to the left. On the retrieve, the streamer will travel parallel to the shoreline for the length of the curve before it leaves the bank and starts back to the angler.

One last thought about lake fishing with streamers. If your lake harbors brown trout, as so many do, then you're missing a real bet if you don't use some 1/0 or 2/0 big, weighted, bulky streamers after dark. Big browns in lakes often feed at night, just as they do in streams. If night fishing for trout is legal in your state, you surely should investigate this kind of fishing, which almost no one practices.

12

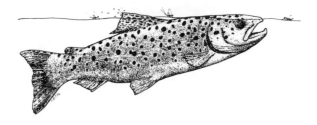

THE
MIDGES

John Merwin

A HIGH-MEADOW BASIN CUPS THE POND GENTLY IN THE MONTANA ROCK-ies, many bumpy miles in four-wheel-drive from the nearest pavement. Sooner or later, the name and exact location will find their way into print. The onslaught will be inevitable, and the pond will die. It is delicate, fragile, and it holds huge trout.

I lay on my back in a warm envelope of meadow grasses, alternately watching the water surface below and a red-tailed hawk that hunted high over the eastern slope. Various small rodents should be plentiful there; the open grasses and thick brush of the slope would offer shelter and food. Yet the same slope also gave the hawk the afternoon thermals, its means to hunt the animals the slope protected. The bird folded its wings and started to plummet, then braked and soared once more. Its shrill whistle could be heard for miles on that windless afternoon, and I smiled at its disappointment.

A dimple. The surface had been so still for so long that the quiet riseform was startling. There was another and then another. The fish were rising sporadically at the far end of the pond, less than half a mile away, and I picked up my rod to hike down. Walking slowly and well back from the pond's edge, I could see the

rises start to fall into a pattern. Several fish were apparently cruising back and forth a few feet off the reeds in water shallow enough for the warming sun to have stimulated some insects into hatching. As I got closer, I started to circle well behind the reeds. Then I walked on my knees, then on hands and knees, and finally I held the rod in one hand and let it trail behind as I did the last few yards on my stomach so the thick reeds concealed me entirely from the fish. So far, so good.

I inched around slowly to get my knees underneath and then slowly peeped over the top. The water was about two feet deep and very clear. A fish was rising about twenty yards down along the shore. Another rise a few feet closer, then another closer still; the fish apparently was working my way. I could see the rise-forms well, but not the fish, which was still hidden by the reflected sky. The trout wasn't taking something from the top, for nothing broke the surface and there were no bubbles. Only a bumping of the water followed by a sudden and large depression in the surface as the fish turned back down, then quiet ripples. The trout was obviously big. I licked my lips and waited what seemed like ten years for the fish to come ten yards.

The fish cruised by just under the surface. I bit my lip and sat down quietly behind the reeds. It was a rainbow, far bigger that any trout I'd caught—or even *seen* caught—and it was a perfect setup. From what I'd read and heard and seen, the fish was apparently taking midge pupae just under the surface. There were a few tan adult midges in the air, small ones. The box of midges. I started feeling around in my vest, wondering where I'd put them and muttering about shaking hands and the buck fever that was at once so annoying and deliciously exciting.

The box of midges was now in hand. I'd come prepared with about a hundred assorted pupal and adult imitations, all the way down to some #26s. I stuck my head up again to check on the fish. It was cruising and rising as before, now heading toward me from the opposite direction along the reeds. I watched and started to think about timing and presentation, fumbling to open the fly box at the same time. I got another good look at the fish as it went by; it would easily weigh ten pounds. The box came open upside down.

It was probably the greatest crisis of my life, and so absolutely ludicrous that I laughed while fishing around in the grass for the right fly. It also broke the tension, and I tied a little pupa to the 6X point without too much trouble.

The naturals are just under the surface. Grease the leader, but not the fly. Soak the fly so it'll sink right away. Don't scare the fish. No false casting, just a flip. The required drill went quickly then, and a few feet of line and the long leader floated on the water. The fish was now thirty feet away and coming. Perfect.

I could see the spots on its broad tail clearly as it swam under my floating leader and six feet away from the fly. I had badly misjudged its line of travel. It was impossible; I was too good, too careful. The fish rose again, ten feet down the shore. I panicked, lifted, and cast ahead of the riseform. The fish panicked, too, and boiled out of the shallows. My nerves were shot, and I sat in the grass to pick up my flies. Midge fishing is like that.

Midges are the single most important group of insects in American stillwaters, both from the angler's viewpoint and that of the trout. They are also the most diverse, complex, and least known. The few anglers who unravel their secrets on a local basis are rewarded with extraordinary fishing. For the majority, a midge hatch is a time of frustration, a time when really large fish wallow on the surface, within easy reach but oblivious to a standard array of dry flies.

It has been a frustrating topic for angling writers, too. Midges, and especially the important Chironomidea subfamily, are the greatest single void in the literature of fly-fishing. In his fine work, *An Angler's Entomology* (Barnes, 1956), the British angler/entomologist J. R. Harris expressed the common feeling: "It has always seemed to me that these Chironomids have not received as much attention as their importance warrants. This is perhaps because they are of more importance to lake than to river anglers, and little has been written yet about the entomology of lakes. Of all the flies which occur on lakes, these are the most widely distributed and the most prolific. They will be found on every unpolluted lake in Britain and Ireland, and during the periods of their emergence they are among the most valuable of the natural species which constitute food for trout."

The volume of conventional angling wisdom about midges in this country is slight. In the United Kingdom, where anglers have taken more note of them, the situation is slightly better.

Midges form a substantial portion of the insect order Diptera, the two-winged flies. A listing by common name of some better-known members of that order may give you a better idea of its size and diversity: mosquitos, blackflies, no-see-ums, deer flies, craneflies, midges, mothflies (not moths), net-veined midges, soldier flies, horseflies, shore flies, beach flies, marsh flies, and many others. The list of common names is almost endless. Happily, we can dispense with a large portion of this order quickly. Only about half of the approximately 10,000 Dipteran species are reported to have aquatic larvae and pupae. Those that do, encompass every conceivable sort of freshwater habitat, with a few forms even utilizing salt water.

Having neatly eliminated half the order as being unavailable to trout, a major snag is now encountered: the various aquatic larvae of the rest of the order are clearly the most diverse of all aquatic insect orders in terms of specific structure and choice of habitat. Some can still be eliminated on the basis of unavailability to trout; one example is the horsefly (family Tabanidae), since most species undergo pupation in damp ground. And since this chapter doesn't deal with midges in flowing waters, such groups as the net-veined midges (family Blephariceridea) and blackflies (family Simuliidae), which are specifically adapted to stream life and important to trout, can also be eliminated.

The elimination process extends further and on the following basis: using the identification and descriptive keys from Willis Worth and Allan Stone's "Aquatic Diptera" (included in *Aquatic Insects of California,* 1956), which is itself largely a compilation of past work, together with descriptive keys from other references in combination with such little has appeared in popular print, I whittled the list down to those few Dipteran families of general significance to stillwater anglers in this country. It is a curious and frustrating process in many ways; numerous references center on the taxonomy and classification of various genera with mentions of habitat preferences and life histories often being secondary and occasional. Collections that form the basis for such references are often from scattered sources and geographically incomplete. The various researchers who have investigated some portions of these groups have at times used or developed different identification keys for the same groupings. The entomologists themselves become speculative at times when faced with occasional broken threads, and for a lay reader with a cursory knowledge of entomology, it can be staggering.

The various aquatic midges, like all Diptera, have a complete life cycle, which is a significant key to an angler's appreciation of them. Egg, larva, pupa, and adult are the midge's phases, unlike the better-known mayfly and its incomplete life cycle of egg, nymph, and adult. Since most of the more important forms to anglers either dwell on the bottom or frequent vegetation in lakes, the most significant phase in the life cycle is the time of pupal migration to the surface for emergence as adults. It is a time when the insect is most vulnerable to fish, and the fish respond accordingly.

Worth and Stone list twenty-nine families of aquatic Diptera, but among those only two are of primary significance here: the family Tendipedidae, which includes the best-known Chironomid midges, and the mosquito family Culicidae, of which the bizzare phantom midges (subfamily Chaoboridae) are of primary importance to fly fishermen. Various forms within these groups are widely distributed in trout lakes accross the country, and their sheer numbers in a given body of water make them significant not only in their role as trout food, but also in the gross ecology of the lake. There are also a handful of families of lesser importance that I'll discuss briefly at the end of this section.

The Chironomid midges are the real stars of the stillwater world, a status they attain by sheer number and diversity. They are typically regarded as one of a series of closely related subfamilies, and are by far the largest group in a family that numbers some 3,000 known species world wide. Their numbers can be awesome. I once stood near a series of three trout ponds in the Rockies during an evening when there was no wind and the air was oppressively hot. I finally became aware of a steady low-pitched hum and swatted around my ear. It took me a minute or so to realize that it wasn't a mosquito at hand, but vast numbers of swarming adult midges that were filling the entire basin with the sound of their wings. The individual flies in the swarms over my head were quite small, and the fact of their swarms filling miles of space with noise was astonishing. Several years later I read a description of the same thing by Samuel Williston, a late-nineteenth-century American entomologist, who likened their noise to that produced by a distant waterfall.

Adult midges rarely have a body longer than a half inch, often much less. There are no tails of any sort. Wings are often clear, occasionally light shades of

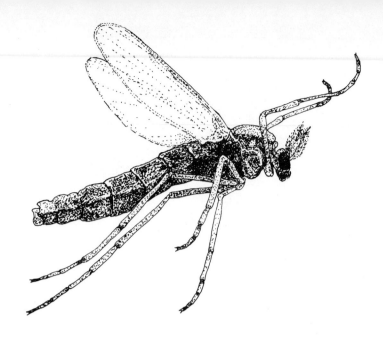

Midge adult *(Chironomus species)*

gray, and when viewed from above are typically held at an angle from the body when at rest, although some forms carry their wings folded straight back over the body. The males are generally more slender than females and feature rather plumose, feathery antennae. The legs of both sexes are spindly and surprisingly long in proportion to their body length. Unlike the various biting midges that may be prevalent over the same waters, the true midges don't have a well-developed proboscis, and that's one way to tell at a quick glance what general sort of flies you're encountering. The mating swarms often seen around lake and pond margins are typically males, into which a female will fly to get a mate. Eggs are typically laid in the calm shallows, and because females usually head for land afterward, falls of spent flies don't usually occur in quantities significant to anglers. One folk tale that's based in fact has adult midge swarms as indicators of good weather; they won't swarm in a wind.

Adults are occasionally important to fly fishermen in a variety of circumstances. The most important is during the spring and fall seasons, when the emergence may be sparse and the air cool enough to keep the adults on the water for a few seconds before flying off. At these times, there aren't sufficient pupae at the surface film to cause the trout to concentrate solely on them, and the fish may slash hurriedly at the adults before they can escape. It's an exciting time of hard strikes on fine tippets and small flies, and a time when a small imitation skated on the surface may work best of all. It's important at other times of the year, too, although in warmer weather the adults depart the water almost instantaneously. Generally, the degree to which an adult imitation will work is in direct proportion to the intensity of the hatch. Trout invariably prefer pupae if they are available in sufficient quantity.

The larvae are wormlike and without true legs. The various Chironomid larvae are all of uniform diameter throughout their body length; larvae of closely related forms may show some swelling in the thorax. There are a pair of stubby prolegs near the head, and another pair at the end of the abdomen. The larvae are distinctly segmented. Some are free-living grazers in littoral vegetation, others ei-

(154)

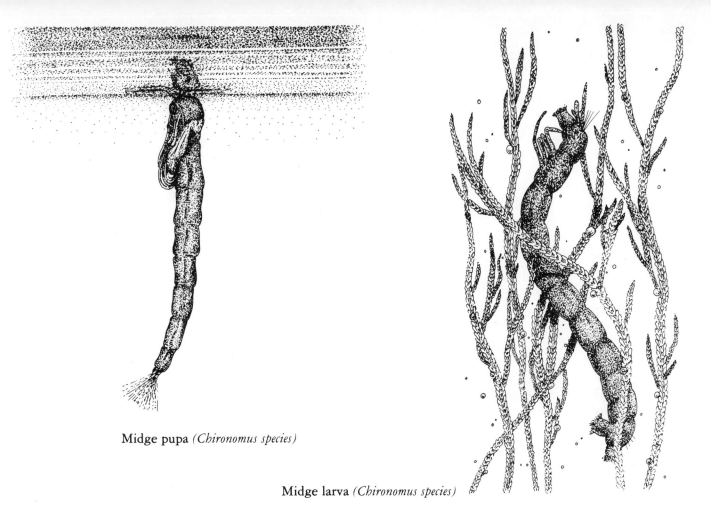

Midge pupa *(Chironomus species)*

Midge larva *(Chironomus species)*

ther burrow into plant stems or make a small tube within the rolled portion of a leaf, spinning a net at one end and filtering water through it with rhythmic undulations of their body as a means of collecting food. Still other members of the diverse Tendipedidae are predacious, crawling or swimming about the bottom and among the plants, eating, among other things, smaller midge larvae.

The range of their habitat is greater than that of any other aquatic insect, extending from the shallowest of waters all the way down to the profundal zone, as deep as 1,000 feet, where they can occur in vast quantities and are typically the only insect form found at such depths. Deep-water populations in excess of 250 individuals in a square foot of bottom have been reported. These forms typically build small tubes extending down into the bottom ooze, and their typically scarlet coloration shows a fascinating modification for life in regions of very low dissolved-oxygen concentrations. The color is derived from a hemoglobin-like pigment, which increases the efficiency with which such oxygen as is available can be utilized. Such depths are typically oxygen deficient, since they are an area of organic decomposition and rarely mixed with the surface waters except (in some lakes) in spring and fall.

The mature larvae are at the greatest depths, while newly hatched forms may occupy more shallow areas in the spring, apparently migrating deeper in somewhat random fashion in the course of their larval growth. The fully grown larva constructs a tube extending as far as six centimeters into the ooze and as much as three millimeters in diameter. The larva apparently never leaves its tube, although it may extend its body outward to scavenge over the surface, pulling itself quickly back in with its rear prolegs if disturbed.

They are a primary key in the ecology of a lake. Dead algae and plankton that formerly occupied the open waters of the lake drift slowly down to the soft, benthic ooze, and the lake nutrients they've utilized might otherwise be lost were it not for their conversion by scavenging Chironomids. In 1950, the entomologist B. M. Walshe described the simple efficiency of their larval feeding as follows: "The principle method of feeding is the filtering of planktonic organisms and particles from a stream of water passing through the tube. The larva spins a cone of salivary secretion across the lumen of the tube, the apex of the cone sometimes being connected to the mouth by a thread. After filtering for some time (by undulating its body within the tube), the larva eats the net, with its enclosed particles, and starts again. The entire process takes less than two minutes, of which half is spent in irrigating the tube, and half in eating and spinning the net. It may be repeated many times, and feeding is sometimes continuous for many hours."

It's important to note that while Tendipidid midge larvae may occupy a wide variety of habits within a single lake, various species will occupy specific and often quite limited areas of bottom or weeds. I have watched pods of gently rolling rainbows as they took emerging pupae in an area of a few square yards while the rest of the calm lake surface remained still. It was not, I know, because all the lake's fish were in that spot, but rather because some were, and hatching activity was keyed for some reason to this particular location. As a hypothesis, it seems reasonable to assume, for example, that a certain midge species might well have developed a preference for living in growths of one aquatic plant species, shallow-water elodea, for instance, and that surface activity when it hatches will be keyed to those locations. It has been demonstrated that some midge species display limited ranges of water temperature preferences, while others may show similar restrictions in terms of depth distribution. The stereotyping of midge habitat with respect to its impact on trout activity in lakes is a broad and important question, the answers to which we are only beginning to learn.

The color of the various larvae is a similar puzzle, especially since it is virtually never used as a criterion in taxonomy, and its mention is infrequent in most technical sources. The red-pigmented larvae typical of low-oxygen areas are distinctive, earning them the common name bloodworms. J. R. Harris noted that many of the forms from the shallower waters of British lakes were a pale olive. The various shades of olive and yellow-green are typical of the many invertebrates that inhabit the shallow weed zones of lakes, and it's a safe bet that those colors predominate in shallow-water midge larvae here as well. As far as fly-fishing in stillwaters is concerned, attempts to imitate and fish midge larvae are a waste of time. The shallow-water forms most often share the same habitat with caddis, mayfly, damsel, and dragonfly nymphs, all of which are more easily imitated in fishing and just as readily taken by randomly cruising trout below the surface. I would much prefer to fish larger subsurface imitations, with which I can readily imitate the movement of the naturals, than fish deep with a tiny larva whose bottom-crawling or open-water wriggling motions are impossible to emulate. The pupae are another matter.

Emerging midge pupae are the form most often taken by trout in stillwaters, sometimes with maddening selectivity. Surface activity may take place anywhere in a lake, although rarely over the whole lake at once. In larger waters, such activity most frequently occurs in bays and coves sheltered from the wind. It may also occur, however, over the greatest depths. I have encountered midges hatching at first light and just at dark and at every time inbetween. Although emergence will apparently still take place when the surface is ruffled by a breeze, I have never had good fishing at such times. Rising fish, hatching flies, and the number of strikes all seem to be at a maximum when the surface is flat calm.

The riseforms of the trout are a significant clue, especially when fishing on a strange lake. Some writers have said that one could tell if trout were midging if there were both rising fish and no insects visible in the air. I once spent a frustrating evening tossing a variety of pupal imitations to some delicately sipping rainbows on the basis of that advice, only to discover finally that the surface was covered with minute black flying ants. The rainbows gobbled them in the quiet head-and-tail rises that I associated with emerging midges, and the wrong answer seemed so obviously right that it was a long time before I bothered to look. Such surface behavior is also typical of mayfly spinner falls and other instances in which small insects are pinned to the surface film and unable to escape. The solution is to look first; the answer will be on the surface. Both mayfly spinners and flying ants are readily seen on the surface; both are apt to fall randomly, and you should be able to see them even if the fish are rising some distance away. You may also be able to see the empty pupal shucks of midges floating on the surface and, if you look carefully, an occasional adult popping off the surface and flying away.

If there is nothing either in the air *or* on the surface, and the trout are cruising with quiet, sporadic sipping rises, then the answer is often a relatively sparse hatch of midges. Although the adults fly quickly away when they emerge, the pupa hang and wiggle near the surface for several minutes or more before emergence actually takes place. It's vital to realize the trout have plenty of time to take these trapped pupae, and that their riseforms may almost be imperceptible, even in flat calm. Both caddis and mayflies emerge much more quickly, and even during a sparse emergence of those flies, they are most often taken with a more violent swirl than is associated with emerging midges.

As the numbers of pupae available at the surface increase, the feeding behavior of the trout changes dramatically. Riseforms become more frequent and usually more closely spaced, either as quiet rings from gentle sips or sometimes as an almost continuous string of rolling, head-and-tail rises—heads, dorsals, and waving tails showing quietly above the surface. It is a fairly common sight on many lakes, and I fish those situations with a fair degree of success now, but it wasn't always the case. The problem is classic. You may well have encountered it, so we can commiserate together.

The bass-bugging was slow that June morning as I worked along the old creek bed still visible as an open path through the flooded trees. I watched a downy woodpecker hop-scotching up a dead spruce until a small wink on the surface caught my eye. Within minutes, a half-dozen rainbows were rolling in absolute silence on the surface in a tight group about twenty feet away. I could see a little dark midge pop off the water here and there, and fished around for some lighter tippet and the smallest thing in my bass-fishing vest, a #16 Adams. The fly rested in their midst. They pushed the leader in the air with their rolling backs and twice a tail fin brushed the fly. They touched it with everything except their mouths for about fifteen minutes, and then they were gone. It was an incredible performance.

"They're like sharks," Dave Whitlock told me this spring as we fished the Battenkill River for little fish and talked about big fish in lakes. The quiet little Arlington Inn along the river is thousands of miles from the Rockies, but over dinner we were both more in Montana than in Vermont, talking about the behavior of big fish on heavy midge hatches. "I've seen rainbows stay right on top, swimming with their noses, backs and tails out of the water, and their mouths open. Just cramming themselves with midges. Four of us only took one trout that afternoon. We guessed it weighed about nine pounds."

Most midge forms pupate in their tubes; free-living forms apparently do so in cocoonlike structures made for the purpose. The pupa break the sealed tube end after metamorphosis and make their way to the surface slowly, totally unlike the mad dash of a caddis. The last abdominal segment has now become a cleft swimming paddle, often with a delicate, light-colored fringing. The slender abdomen is markedly segmented, and in many forms is held in a well-defined curve. The thorax is considerably swollen, and legs, wing cases, head, and antennae all contribute to the anterior mass. A tuft of strikingly white respiratory filaments are at the anterior end. The most apt description I've ever read was by English angler Brian Clarke, who likens the pupa to an elongated comma.

The ascent is marked by a thrashing series of wiggles, in which the modified paddle of a tail propels the pupa upward. A brief rest and slight descent, and then another series of wiggles upward. The pupae in midwater are helpless, easy prey for leisurely feeding trout. They become even easier prey when they reach the surface, where they become concentrated, hanging still, occasionally wiggling, and very vulnerable for many minutes prior to actual emergence. As is common with other emerging insects, the thorax of the pupal shell splits along the back, and the adult crawls out on the surface, flying off immediately or remaining for a second or two, largely depending on the air temperature.

Black, light tan, medium brown, olive, and red are all colors that have been successful for me as imitations. It's tempting to reduce the variety of pupal imitations to three or four general shades in a range of sizes: black, a medium brownish olive, a very light tan, and perhaps red. It is almost certainly an instance in which shape, size, and manipulation are all much more significant than precise color imitation.

Fishing pupal imitations is remarkably simple. A long leader tippet, as Hal Janssen described in his earlier chapter on fishing nymphs, is essential. A floating line is used, and since this most often is an instance of fish taking small flies at the surface in calm weather, a lighter-weight line is most appropriate. One possibility is to grease most of the leader but not the pupa, so the imitation hangs motionless just under the surface. Another is to leave some length of the tippet undressed, allow the pupa to sink, and then make a series of short, slow draws. The following two instances will illustrate what I mean.

I had anchored the canoe in the middle of a narrow neck that was the boundary between a wide cove behind and the main lake beyond. It was midday and midsummer, sunny and relatively cool with no wind at all. Little tan midges were emerging occasionally, and the trout cruised widely and in plain sight, taking the pupae just under the surface. Traveling in and out of the cove, they were forced within casting range by the narrowness of the passage. They held a swimming depth of about three feet, and I could see them angle to the surface, open their mouths, and then go back to cruising level without a change in swimming speed.

I used a nine-foot knotless leader that I'd cut back slightly and had added about four feet of 6X tippet. I tied on a #18 tan pupa and soaked it in my mouth while I watched for fish and greased all but the last two feet of leader. I cast about thirty feet away to where I expected a fish would pass. The long tippet landed in lazy waves, and the fly sank slowly until it hung downward from the still-floating leader. I waited. There was a dimple about sixty feet away, then another still closer. I drew in a little line to straighten the leader on the water, then drew in a few inches more to lift the pupa slightly. I stopped and it sank, then suspended. Suddenly the leader darted sideways. I lifted the rod gently and smiled as a foot-long rainbow cleared the water. It was one of those textbook afternoons when everything worked as it was supposed to work, the half dozen or so that we remember from the season past while forgetting the missed fish, wind knots, and tangled lines of other more characteristic days.

The movement of the fly upward on a gentle draw attracts the fish's attention. It can be practiced in a variety of depths, but depends on at least a portion of the leader remaining on the surface as a strike indicator. It is absolutely essential that the leader be straight throughout its length; the coils of a typically kinked butt section will act as a giant spring to ruin the effect of a slow draw on the line. The tippet should be fine, 5X or 6X for #12 to 18 imitations, and finer for smaller flies. Unweighted imitations are almost always best; the pupa must sink slowly to appear natural. Too much false-casting will dry these tiny flies quickly; casting with a lazy, open loop will help prevent that and will also mean fewer tangles with a very light, long leader. A fly-sinking preparation, such as the Xink marketed by George Gerkhe, has also helped at times; a spare application is more than sufficient.

It is a technique that has worked well numerous times, and the primary ingredient seems to be patience. I have fished hatches on a small Vermont pond as late as early October when incoming flocks of southbound geese came over the ridge and then turned in noisy surprise at the sight of my canoe. On those quiet evenings, brown trout subtly take midge pupa in the bays and coves, and a series of slow draws with a submerged pupa usually accounts for more fish than does chasing after widely scattered rises. It is also a technique most suited to a sparse hatches or the beginning and end of a more intense hatch or when there is no hatch at all. A heavy hatch is more of a problem.

When masses of pupae are collecting at the surface, it becomes more difficult to get a fish to single out your artificial. The problem increases in direct proportion to the number of naturals available. Most often, the trout's selectivity will increase with the intensity of the hatch. When fish are almost continuously rolling and working a small area, it's sometimes a matter of greasing everything except the fly and letting it sit in the melee. The leader will hold the pupa right at the surface, where it's likely to be seen and taken by the fish. It should not be necessary for you to move the fly at all, but you'll still have to watch your leader for movement, because with so many rises right around your fly, it's hard to tell otherwise which rise is yours. When the fish are hog-wallowing on the surface, open mouths engulfing masses of insects, they obviously aren't going to chase after your fly. You'll have to hit the fish's feeding path right on the button and within a couple of inches of its nose. It's frustrating and demands much casting and casting again. Fortunately, the fish are often so preoccupied that opportunities are plentiful, however difficult. It's also fortunate that this phase doesn't last long, at least judging from what I've heard and the couple of times I've seen it, and the fish will continue to pick up stragglers after the main wave of the hatch is over. A pupa, adult, or even a stillborn imitation, will then attract more attention.

I want to leave the Chironomids and get to other things before ending this chapter, but I also want to leave you with this thought: one key to understanding the midges, which have been written about only a little, is an understanding of the caddis, which have been written about a lot. Of course, they are radically different insect groups, but there are also some remarkable similarities. A few midge species for example, build portable cases in lakes, just as some caddis do. We've seen that many midges are net-spinning, just as is a large group of caddis. Although the pupae are rather different in behavior, it is the pupal stage of each that offers them in quantity to stillwater trout. It's an intriguing thought, for which I fully expect to have my wrist slapped by a professional taxonomist.

The phantom midge is a rather macabre little creature whose melodramatic name is an apt description: it's almost invisible. With the exception of a few internal organs, these half-inch larvae are transparent and are typically the only insect inhabiting the open waters of lakes and ponds. They are of the mosquito family Culicidae, but are of the nonbiting subfamily Chaoborinae, a small group within which the genus *Chaoborus* is of most significance to anglers. It occurs in trout lakes (and others) across the country, occasionally in large numbers. The most famous incidence was probably in Clear Lake, California, during the 1940s. The so-called Clear Lake gnat (a *Chaoborus* species) was described by Robert L. Usinger in his introduction to *Aquatic Insects of California:* "In 1940, it was estimated that the total seasonal emergence in the upper part of Clear Lake (44 square miles) was 712 billion gnats or 356 tons, and the phantom larvae were estimated on the basis of adequate samples to number 800 billion. Eggs at a density of ten million per square foot occured near shore in drifts twenty feet wide and several miles long." The fly was a pest gnat in that remarkable instance, and then-contemporary mosquito-control measures reduced the population substantially.

Obviously, that was an exceptional example, but it does help to illustrate that the larvae can occur in sufficient numbers to be an important food source for those creatures living in the open waters of lakes, including forage fishes such as alewives and smelt, and rainbow trout. The larvae themselves are capable of fairly rapid movement, thrashing their bodies to move through the water and capturing various zooplankters with their prehensile antennae. The phantom midges are frequently reported to undergo diurnal vertical migration, apparently following migrating zooplankton toward the surface at night and descending with them during the day. According to some reports, the larvae may actually burrow into the bottom ooze during the daylight hours.

The transformation into a pupa takes place within the last larval skin, although the pupa itself becomes free-swimming. The pupa is air breathing, with a pair of distinctive respiratory "horns" on its thorax, and remains quietly at the surface. At this stage, the pupae are sitting ducks for cruising fish, which may take them intermittently. Although Chaoborid midges are present on some trout lakes that I have fished consistently, I haven't seen them hatch in substantial numbers. I

Phantom larva *(Chaobours species)*

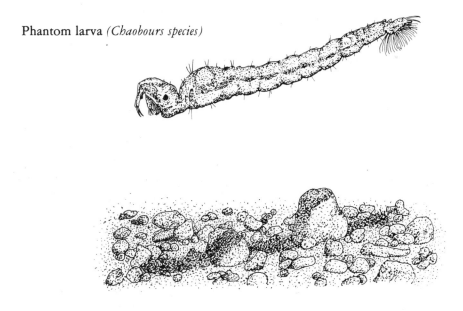

have found their pupal shucks scattered with seeming randomness over these lakes all season long. Because the larvae are hardy and can apparently overwinter in many areas, my most immediate suspicion is that adult emergence may occur intermittently all season long. I have tied imitations of adults on #18 fine-wire hooks and of a general light tan coloration that have worked on the two brief occasions when I was able to see pupal shucks, emergent adults, and rising trout all at the same time. Those same adults, as one might expect, resembled a pale-tan mosquito except for the lack of well-developed biting mouthparts. Their bodies were darkly spotted along the sides, and the wings were distinctly spotted.

There are a handful of other Dipteran families of occasional importance to stillwater fly fishermen. In most instances the location and/or behavior of their larvae and pupae mean they will only occasionaly be available to trout, although adults in some instances may be more important. I will describe a few of them briefly; if you want to pursue any further, a good place to start is with Pennak's *Freshwater Invertebrates of the United States.*

Tipulidae: the craneflies. The fat, wormlike larvae of these spindly, well-known flies are found in the bottom trash of the quiet margins of both streams and lakes. The larvae of some species may be as long as two inches and widely used as an effective bait for trout. In streams, trout may take them in the bottoms of eddies, but in lakes the larvae generally occupy shallow water while the trout are foraging at greater depths.

Adult flies are important to lake anglers because of their size and occasional habit of falling on the water. Their bodies may be as long as two inches, in some forms much smaller. Long, occasionally spotted, wings are held at an angle from the body, and the legs are long, fragile and spindly. At various locations in the United Kingdom, anglers call them "daddy long-legs," not to be confused with our own spider of the same name. A single adult, or even a mating pair, will sometimes hit the water in the general vicinity of a trout. Their flopping on the surface often brings a predictable splash. My friend Dud Soper has a fine cranefly pattern that was included in a recent fly-tying book by Dick Talleur, and I've included it in the subsequent fly-tying section.

Dixidae: The Dixa midges. Small, abundant midges with disproportionately long legs and transparent wings. The larvae inhabiting lake and pond margins superficially resemble mosquito larvae and are typically associated with the surface film in the shallows. Some forms assume a dramatic U-shape when at rest, and in some cases remain in moist areas above but immediately adjacent to the waterline. Pupation takes place on land. Females are reported to lay their eggs while flying over the water with the abdomen breaking the surface, and such activity doubtless causes an occasional chase by trout. The same adult imitations as used for midge adults will suffice, in sizes #16 to 18 and in black or tan, but more heavily hackled than is perhaps normal so the flies can be skated on the surface in imitation of egg-laying adults.

A few other aquatic forms are often found in the shallows and mudflats that are rarely if ever visited by foraging trout: soldier flies (Stratiomyidae), the everpresent no-see-ums and other very small, biting midges (Heleidae), a group of minute mothlike midges, sometimes called mothflies (Psychodidae), and still a few others. Unless you deliberately look for the immature forms, it's doubtful you'll ever encounter them. Adults will occasionally find their way onto the water surface within range of cruising fish, but rarely in quantity sufficient to promote more than a single and rare rise.

There is as yet no catalog—dates, times, and places—of our important midge hatches. And it's only been in recent years that the right tackle has been available to fish them. It is one of the most obvious frontiers in American fly-fishing, and I hope what's been presented here will encourage you in its exploration.

13

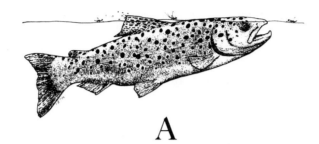

A
MISCELLANEOUS
BESTIARY

Steve Raymond

IT WAS THE LATTER HALF OF SEPTEMBER AND THE THIRD WEEK OF A GLORI-
ous Indian summer. The nights were clear and cold and ablaze with tiny diamond
lights, and the sun came up late in the mornings to cast long shadows across the
frosty meadows. Along toward noon, as the day warmed, the Kamloops trout
would shyly seek the edges of the shoal at the far end of Roche Lake and begin to
feed.

The caddis hatch, when the surface had been covered with fat flies and the
trout had risen eagerly to take them, was filed away with memories of June. The
damselflies and dragonflies also had come and gone, and of the midges only
sparse, sporadic hatches remained until the winter ice would shut them off till
spring. Yet the trout were feeding actively, sometimes briefly visible as fleeting
shapes over the cream-colored bottom marl. They cruised a regular pattern, following the semicircular lip of the shoal to the point where it merged with the
base of a stone cliff that reared vertically from the water.

And that was where we took them, along the face of the cliff, with a little scud
pattern, well sunk and fished with a slow, patient retrieve. The strikes, when they
came, were swift and strong; the line was snatched suddenly from the fingers to

go flashing out through the guides, and the reel shrilled a sudden protest. And then, far out, the trout would leap, high and tumbling, with its bright sides gleaming in the soft September sunlight. They were all good fish, none less than a pound-and-a-half, and occasionally there would be one that would pull the scale down to the four-pound mark when we weighed it in the net.

We were not alone on this British Columbia lake; the weather was much too good for that. All along the shoal, anglers had taken station in their boats, and the cruising trout were forced to run a gauntlet of their flies. Yet only rarely did any of the others hook a fish, and as we released our fifth or sixth we could hear the whispers start across the water: "Wonder whatinhell those guys are using."

The scud pattern was the answer. It was simply a case of having found the right fly at the right time in the right place. The others were using various nymph or pupa imitations at a time when none were hatching. And when they finally overcame their pride enough to ask us what we were using, and we hollered back the answer, they went searching in their fly boxes for scud imitations of their own. But the trout were selective, as they had been for some days past, and those anglers without imitations of the proper size or color, or without the knowledge to fish them properly, ended up fishless and frustrated.

There was nothing particularly unusual about this incident; I have had similar experiences on many lakes. But it does illustrate a point: once the spring and early-summer hatches are over, many otherwise competent fly fishermen are at a loss to know what patterns to use or how to use them. The spring hatches of caddis, mayflies, and damselflies are spectacularly visible, and so is the trout's response to them, so it's not unusual that they have received most of the attention from anglers and fly tiers. But when the feast of the spring hatches is over, stillwater trout return to their traditional basic diet for the remainder of the year: a miscellaneous bestiary of scuds, leeches, water bugs, beetles, and snails.

This creates both problems and opportunities for the angler. The problem is a familiar one: you reach the lake you're planning to fish and look out at a smooth expanse of unbroken water. Not a rise anywhere. You *know* the trout are there, foraging somewhere beneath the surface, but you don't know what they're feeding on. So you can do one of two things: open your fly box and choose the first pattern that catches your fancy, or search for a clue to what the trout may be taking. If you do the former, the odds are stacked against you unless you're mighty lucky. But if you look around for some evidence of organisms that may be present in the water, you reduce the odds considerably. This is especially true on an unfamiliar lake where you have no prior experience to indicate what the trout may be taking.

A search of the shallows will reveal a lot of things. By turning over stones or uprooting water weeds, you may disclose the presence of scuds or sowbugs or snails or other organisms, and if any of these are apparent in great numbers, chances are the trout will be after them. Scanning the surface closely from a boat also may pay dividends; look for the tiny dimples left by backswimmers or water bugs coming to the surface for air, or for leeches swimming close to the surface.

(165)

Since many of the creatures trout feed on are most abundant in the shallows, over weedbeds or shoals of rock or marl, those are the places to look.

And once you have some idea of what's on the menu, the next problem is to offer the proper imitation and fish it in the proper way. And once you have solved that, you'll discover the opportunities in store for a stillwater angler who knows his business.

The scud usually is the most important item on this menu of miscellany, especially in the fertile, alkaline waters of the Far West. If it is present in a lake at all, it usually exists in enormous numbers and provides a year-round staple in the diet of trout. It is a primary reason why the Kamloops trout of British Columbia grow so fast and fight so well. Typically, a scud-fed trout is fat and thick and well conditioned, with firm, red flesh.

Fishermen usually call the scud a shrimp because of its superficial resemblance to the large true shrimp—the kind that ends up in curry, creole, or cocktails. But aside from being a member of the same general class of animals (Crustacea), the scud and the true shrimp have little in common. The misnomer of shrimp comes from the scud's habit of holding itself in a curved, crescent shape while at rest. But the scud's body is elongated in swimming, and free-swimming scuds are those most often taken by trout.

The various species of *Gammarus,* widely distributed in cold-water lakes across the North American continent, are of most importance to anglers. *Gammarus* is most common in shallow water, where a full-grown individual measures 20 to 25 millimeters in length. Its color usually ranges from dark to light olive, although specimens of light or dark brown or turquoise are not uncommon. The young are hatched and carried in a brood pouch by the female, and these "pregnant" scuds are easily recognized by the orange color of the brood pouch. The color comes from the young themselves, which are bright orange when they hatch, and some fly tiers have devised imitations of the "pregnant" scud.

The fecundity of these little animals is amazing. A British Columbia angler found that out for himself when he received permission from a neighboring rancher to remove scuds from the rancher's irrigation pond to transplant into a nearby trout lake. Using fine-mesh nets to capture the scuds where the pond flowed out into an irrigation flume, the angler and a few companions easily harvested sixteen *bushels* of live scuds in a single weekend.

No wonder, then, that trout grow rapidly when stocked in lakes with such a rich supply of food. Where scuds are present, it is almost a certain bet that if trout are feeding at all, there will always be some feeding on scuds. So it stands to reason that a fisherman armed with a good imitation ought to do well.

Invariably, scud imitations are called "shrimp" flies. There are a lot of them, but relatively few are really good imitations of the natural. This is especially true of some commercially tied patterns, which usually are either too large or too brightly colored. A couple of popular commercially tied patterns also are dressed on up-eyed hooks, which breaks up the silhouette of the natural. Many anglers also tie these patterns on curved bait hooks, which provide a very realistic imita-

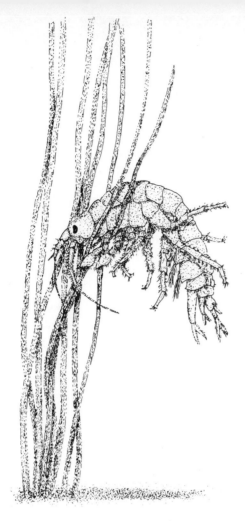

Freshwater shrimp *(Gammarus species)*

tion of a gammarid at rest. The problem with these is that they look unnatural be-ing retrieved through the water because the scud's body is elongated while swimming. The swimming gammarid is best imitated on a straight-shank hook.

Trout can be surprisingly selective when feeding on gammarids, so it is vital to have a good imitation. Based on a lot of trial-and-error experimentation with var-ious patterns, there are three I would suggest: The so-called "Baggy" Shrimp, the Trueblood Otter Nymph, and the Golden Shrimp.

The "Baggy" Shrimp is so named because a transparent polyethylene strip cut from a sandwich bag usually is used to tie it. The hook size is #8 to 14, down-eyed, straight shank. The body is olive or brown seal's fur dubbing or wool. A thin strip cut from a sandwich bag is tied in at the bend of the hook before the body is dressed. When the body is finished, the strip is placed over the top as an overlay and bound with brown or olive silk or fine gold or copper wire ribbing, which imitates the segmentation of the natural. Wool or dubbing fibers then are teased out of the lower body with a dubbing needle to imitate the legs of the nat-ural.

Despite its name, Trueblood's Otter Nymph, originated by Ted Trueblood, makes a better scud imitation than it does a nymph. It is tied on a #8 or 10 hook, down-eyed, straight shank. It has a short tail of partridge hackle fibers and a body of dubbed otter mixed with a pinch of natural seal's fur. The hackle is partridge tied in at the throat. Tan tying silk usually is used to match the color of the dubbed body.

The Golden Shrimp is my own pattern, and I am just as guilty as other tiers of calling it a shrimp instead of a scud. It was developed after years of experimentation on the scud-filled lakes of British Columbia. Various combinations of materials, colors, and hackle styles were tried with varying results. And then came the summer morning on Hihium Lake when I set out with a sample of the latest variation. I found trout over a long gravel bar running out into the lake, apparently rooting for scuds along the bottom, and before noon I had released forty-three trout on the experimental pattern. I haven't changed it since, and it has served me well in any lake where scuds are present.

The fly is dressed on a #8 to 12 hook, down-eyed, straight shank. The smaller sizes seem most effective. Tying begins by stripping the fibers from one side of a ginger hackle feather about twice as long as the hook, leaving the hackle tip intact and a few fibers at the base. Using olive Monocord, this hackle is tied in at the bend of the hook so that the tip extends backward and down to form the tail of the fly. Fine gold wire then is tied in for ribbing and a thick, cigar-shaped body of golden-olive Rayon floss is wrapped on the hook shank. The hackle fiber then is laid along the underside of the body with the stripped side up so that the remaining fibers hang down as legs. The gold wire is then wound on as ribbing and to hold the hackle in place, using a dubbing needle to separate the fibers so they hang down naturally. The butt of the hackle then is tied back behind the eye of the hook so that the fibers extend forward as antenna. Excess hackle is trimmed away, and the fly is finished. Two hackles may be used to give a more realistic double row of legs, but you will find the fly is difficult enough to tie with only a single hackle.

Even the best scud imitation isn't worth much unless it's fished properly. I prefer a fast-sinking line, unless fishing very shallow water or picking pockets in submerged weedbeds; a sinking tip works well then. Avoid using extra-fast-sinking lines; they continue to sink between retrieves, pulling the fly down with them in a motion that is unnatural.

The most dependable technique is to cast and count off the seconds while the fly is sinking. Then, if your retrieve hangs up on the bottom or in weeds, knock a couple of seconds off the count and experiment until you're confident you're fishing the fly right along the bottom or just over the weedtops. A very slow, patient retrieve seems best. Don't get excited when you start to take fish—you might inadvertently speed up the retrieve too much.

It's hard to overestimate the importance of a good scud imitation fished properly. When no hatch is in evidence, a scud often is effective any time from early spring to late fall. I vividly remember a fine spring morning on Lundbom Lake, weeks before the mayfly and caddis hatches were due to start. Using the Golden Shrimp, I landed just five fish—but the smallest weighed five pounds and two were 7½ pounds each. Several others took my fly with them, and when I gave one to another angler he broke it in a fish on his very first cast.

There's another crustacean that sometimes plays an important role in the diet of stillwater trout, and that is *Asellus,* the aquatic sowbug. It looks just like the fa-

Sowbug *(Asellus species)*

miliar land-dwelling sowbug—also called a pill bug or potato bug—that often is found under rocks or boards on damp ground. *Asellus,* however, is wholly aquatic, and thrives in alkaline waters. It probably is more common in slow-moving streams than it is in lakes, but like the gammarids it multiplies rapidly and usually is present in very large numbers.

Asellus ranges up to 20 millimeters in length, but usually is smaller. A dull brown is the most common color, although some gray individuals are found, too. Look for it in thick vegetation in shallow water.

The "Baggy" Shrimp, tied in smaller sizes with brown or gray dubbing, makes a reasonable imitation. The British fly tier C. F. Walker also has devised a good imitation, tied on a #12 or 14 hook weighted with wire. The wire is flattened with pliers to give the body a concave-convex shape. The body itself is dressed from mixed brown and gray hare's ear dubbing and wound with a silver rib. Partridge hackle, tied short, imitates the legs.

Since *Asellus* prefers thick vegetation, the most effective way to fish this pattern is with a floating line. Look for an opening in the weeds, drop the fly in it, and retrieve with very short twitches. You'll hook fish, but how you get them out of the weeds is up to you.

Variety is the spice of life, even for a trout, and they like bugs as well as scuds. Of the various types of water bugs, the water boatmen *(Corxidae)* and backswimmers *(Notonectidae)* are most common. Superficially, these two insects look quite a bit alike, but they differ in habits. Both require surface air for respiration, but the water boatman gets it by sticking his head through the surface and the backswimmer by hanging upside down with its abdomen protruding through the surface film. Both gather air into a shiny silver film that is carried with them under water, and the backswimmer often leaves a tiny dimple or ring on the surface to mark its departure. When you see these, you'll know that the insects are active.

Both insects swim rapidly with a paddle-like motion of their strong hind legs, which gives the water boatman its name. The backswimmer swims on its back, which is how it got its name. There is little difference in the appearance of these two insects at various stages of their life cycle, except in their size and wing development. The water boatman is a stubby insect, preferring shallow, weedy water. Adults range to 15 millimeters in length. They hold their wings flat, beetle-

Water boatmen *John Merwin*

fashion, and typically the wings are a mottled brown or black. Their ventral surface is a creamy yellow, but usually is obscured by the silvery film of air the insects carry with them under water. Backswimmers are longer, thinner insects, ranging up to 20 millimeters long; their coloration is exactly the opposite of the water boatman, and they have cream-colored or yellow wings and brown or black markings on their abdominal segments—an adaptation that comes from swimming on their backs. They are most active in warm weather and it usually takes the trout a couple of days to get onto them.

Although I don't believe it happens very often, I have seen trout feed on these insects with surprising selectivity. Once, on a brown-trout lake that I was fishing for the first time, I went through half a dozen patterns before taking my first fish on a scud imitation. In the process of releasing the trout, I noticed a couple of backswimmers in its mouth. Immediately I changed to a backswimmer imitation and the trout began coming readily until I had released nearly a score of them.

It is fun to fish an imitation of either one of these insects. Again, a sinking line is called for and a rapid retrieve is necessary to imitate the rapid swimming motion of the naturals. And when the fly is moving rapidly in one direction and is taken by a trout swimming strongly in the opposite direction—well, you can imagine.

Not many patterns have been developed to imitate these bugs. *Flies of the Northwest,* a fine pattern book assembled by the Inland Empire Fly Fishing Club of Spokane, lists a water boatman pattern designed by Everett Caryl, Sr. It is tied on a #10 hook with a short tail of brown partridge or turkey, a body of dubbed reddish-tan fox fur over lead wire, and an overlay from a metallic blue mallard drake secondary feather. The "paddles" consist of two flues from the leading edge of a Canada goose wing feather, tied to flare out to either side. Jack Shaw, in his book, *Fly Fish the Trout Lakes,* suggests using a standard Brown Hackle with

Backswimmer adult *(Notonecta species)*

peacock herl body and trimming away the top and bottom of the hackle, leaving only those fibers that extend out to the sides.

I have experimented with several patterns and have arrived at one basic pattern with a body of yellow wool, thick for the water boatman and thin for the backswimmer. This is ribbed with wide embossed silver tinsel to suggest the silvery film of air carried by the insects under water—a feature I think is important to the success of the pattern. The wing consists of eight or ten strips of black Rayon floss, combined and cut to equal length; the strands of floss lay out flat when the fly is being retrieved rapidly through the water. The hackle is one or two turns of large brown pheasant rump hackle. The pattern is tied on a #10 hook to imitate the water boatman. A #8 Hook is used for the backswimmer.

The fishing technique is simple: cast, let the fly sink, and then retrieve with short, violent pulls, pausing occasionally. This is a good match for the quick, jerky motion of the naturals.

The giant water bugs of the family *Belostomatidae* are sometimes locally important to stillwater trout fishermen. These are large, oval-shaped bugs with three pairs of strong legs, a large pair of metallic brown or black wings held flat in beetle fashion, and a cream-colored or yellow abdomen. Adults of 35 to 40 millimeters in length are not uncommon, and they are a real mouthful for a trout. I once caught a 6½-pound rainbow out of a shallow, weedy pond that was literally jammed to the gills with these bugs, many of them still alive. That prompted me to construct an imitation, and it still is the only one I know of.

It is tied on a #2 or 4 hook with a thick yellow wool body, a wing of bronze peacock herl tied in at both ends and legs of the same material—a big, bulky fly that is simple to tie but difficult to cast. It is best fished on a slow-sinking line with a slow, even retrieve. But only occasionally will you find these bugs an important factor in the local trout diet.

The predaceous water beetles of the family *Dytiscidae* also are sometimes locally important. There are more than 400 species and they vary widely in appear-

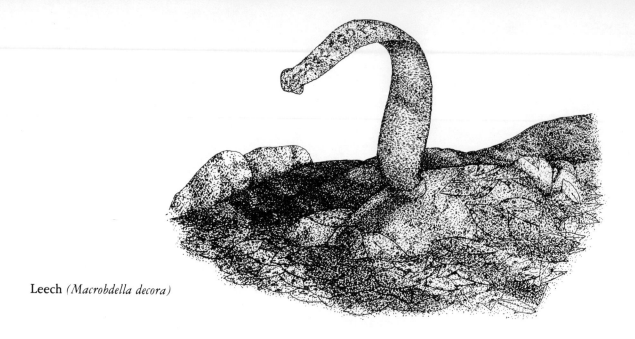

Leech *(Macrobdella decora)*

ance and habits, especially in the larval stages, which is when they are most vulnerable to foraging trout. I know of a number of lakes with large populations of these beetles, and occasionally, when nothing else is going on, the trout will turn to them for food. But because the larvae vary so widely in appearance, the best advice is to try to capture some samples and try to construct an appropriate artificial. If possible, it also pays to try to observe the behavior of the natural in the water because the larvae of different species display a variety of swimming motions and behavior. Again, these insects are only occasionally important.

Leeches *(Hirudinea)* are a staple of the trout diet in many lakes, especially during the summer months after surface hatches have tapered off. Aquatic leeches are flat, ribbonlike creatures that characteristically swim with a motion similar to that of a sidewinder rattlesnake. They are found in a wide variety of lengths, but those measuring between two and four centimeters are taken most frequently by trout.

The most common colors are black, muddy brown, dark gray, and gray with dark green spots. Leeches are mostly nocturnal and during daylight hours they often conceal themselves under rocks or vegetation. However, fortunately for both fishermen and fish, it is not unusual to see solitary individuals swimming leisurely just under the surface during broad daylight. These unwary leeches are the ones that usually end up in trout stomachs.

The best imitation I know of is the Black Matuka Leech. As with most leech patterns, it is tied on a 4X long-shanked hook, either #6 or 8. The body consists of full black chenille with two long, black saddle hackles paired and tied Matuka fashion over the back with the tips extending to the rear. A similar, older pattern is tied the same way except the hackles are not bound to the body Matuka fashion, but are merely laid parallel over the body and secured behind the eye of the hook. The fault with this design is that the hackles easily become tangled around the hook in casting. Both patterns have a few extra turns of black saddle hackle behind the eye. Some anglers also have experimented with dark gray or black marabou leech patterns. These also are tied on long-shank hooks with a body matching the color of the marabou feather, which is tied on top as a wing. The

(172)

lifelike movement of the marabou in the water gives a good imitation of the natural swimming motion of the leech.

These patterns should be fished on sinking or sinking-tip lines with a long, slow stripping motion in the retrieve. When all else fails, a good leech pattern, fished properly, often will bring fish—especially during the warm, late-summer months when trout may be feeding near the thermocline.

The final member of our miscellaneous bestiary is the lowly snail. Every experienced trout fisherman knows that aquatic snails are almost as popular with trout as the terrestrial versions are with French gourmands. And almost every trout angler has had the experience of catching a heavy trout whose belly felt as if it were full of rocks, only to discover it was really full of undigested snail shells.

There are a number of different types of snails found in freshwater lakes, especially lakes with alkaline water. Two of the most common are *Lymnaea* and *Physa,* with their distinctive spiral shells—the former spiraling to the right and the latter to the left. *Goniobasis,* with a heavy, elongated shell, is another common variety, as is *Planorbis* with its flat spiral shell that resembles a miniature chambered nautilus.

Snails attach themselves to plants in shallow water and trout browse for them there. And just how do you imitate a relatively motionless object fastened to a plant? You don't. But fly fishermen have taken trout on snail imitations during that peculiar phenomenon known as a "snail rise." A number of writers have described this phenomenon on British reservoirs, and though I have never witnessed it in this country there is no reason to suppose it does not occur. It usually happens during a prolonged spell of hot summer weather, and the theory is that oxygen depletion caused by the warming water prompts the snails to head for the

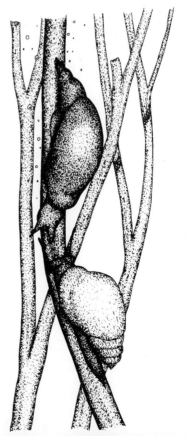

Freshwater snails *(Lymnaea species, upper—Physa species, lower)*

surface where they float upside down with their "foot" clinging to the surface film. Trout rise to take them there, and if an angler can figure out what is happening, he can take them with an imitation.

Such an imitation has been devised by the British fly tyer Cliff Henry and is described in John Goddard's excellent book, *Trout Flies of Still Water.* It is tied on a #10 to 14 wide-gape hook and consists of a cone-shaped cork body that is split and slipped onto the hook shank with the flat base of the cone facing forward. The cork is wrapped with stripped peacock herl except for the final two turns at the front, and these are made with unstripped bronze peacock herl. It's a ratty-looking thing, but the British swear it catches fish. It is fished on a floating line with a dead drift, except for an occasional tiny twitch.

This completes our miscellaneous menagerie, an odd assortment of beasties that have only two things in common: trout like them all, and fly fishermen strive to imitate them. They lack the glamor of the mayfly or the caddis or other more visible organisms, but they are worth studying and their habits are worth knowing; day in and day out, it is almost a certainty that the trout will be feeding on one or more of them. The angler who trains himself to take advantage of that fact is sure to do well.

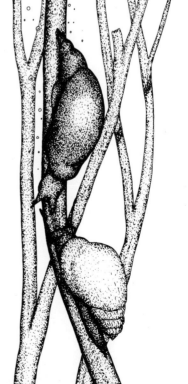

14

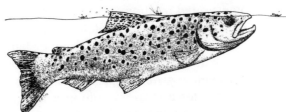

FLY-FISHING
THE
GREAT LAKES

David Richey

PERHAPS NOWHERE IN THE COUNTRY ARE THE STILLWATER FLY FISHER-man's chances for big trout on a fly better than in the Great Lakes. Certainly this area exceeds all others in terms of the range of water available and the numbers of fish it contains. Thousands of shoreline miles surround these inland seas, which are themselves home to chinook salmon, coho salmon, steelhead, brown, lake, and brook trout. Steelhead and browns in particular are available and largely unexplored targets for fly fishermen.

Open-water fly-fishing for these husky trout is still in its infancy; anglers have little in the way of published material on which to base their fishing. Along with several other anglers, I've tried to determine how, when, and where the best of this fishing can be found. The methods we employ and the periods and locations we choose remind me of the tip of an iceberg. I've only touched upon the fantastic possibilities stillwater trout fishing can offer in lakes Superior, Michigan, Huron, Erie, and Ontario.

There are two primary times when trout work within range of shore-based fly fishermen: spring and fall. Inshore migrations of trout will occur sporadically during summer months, but only if the shoal waters are cold. Cold water close to shore is one key to taking these trout with any consistency, but the theory and practice goes far beyond that simple premise. Other factors are at work during spring and fall that contribute as much to trout being within range.

One major reason why trout approach shoal water is that one or more species is preparing to spawn—steelhead in the spring months shortly after ice-out, and browns, brookies, and domesticated rainbows (fall spawners) in the autumn. I've had little success in taking trout on flies in the fall just prior to their spawning run—three or four fish, but not enough to establish a fair pattern. The bulk of my studies have taken place with browns, steelhead, and brook trout in that order. These trout move into shallow waters approximately two to four weeks before an upriver spawning run. This inshore migration is triggered by a last-minute feeding spree, a build-up of eggs and milt in soon-to-spawn fish, and because cold water is close to shore. Establishing a timetable for these trout movements is difficult due to the range of latitudes encompassing the Great Lakes area. It's common in my northern Michigan area for steelhead to move in off shoals and rivermouths about April first, but it can be as much as six weeks later in Lake Superior or two weeks earlier in southern Lake Michigan or Lake Huron. Not all fish run at once so this allows approximately six to eight weeks of top-flight sport providing you can find isolated areas in which to fish without competing with hardware and bait fishermen. A timetable for each species' movement is critical, but anglers must learn to establish these patterns on their own favorite waters.

Smelt, alewives, and small shiners begin massing for their own spawning run in April in most Great Lakes' areas. It's at this time that cold water is also close to shore and off rivermouths; both steelhead and browns may be present. Two factors working to bring trout within casting distance: food supply and trout (steelhead) preparing to spawn. Cold water is the third key, and since it's also present, trout are apt to be nearby. It sounds too simple, and I'd be remiss if I didn't state that certain times exist when all factors are present, but it's impossible to locate the fish. It is a frequent occurrence, and a riddle I haven't solved.

All Great Lakes trout will at times make their presence known by rolling or porpoising in the shallows as they feed on forage fish. A distinct boil or swirl should also attract your attention. I prefer wading and fly-fishing, but the elevation offered by fishing from a boat allows anglers to spot and follow potential action before it passes. It can sometimes be difficult to spot feeding trout, and polarized sunglasses are a tremendous help when scanning the surface.

My first experience with pre-spawning brown trout was in Michigan's Little Bay De Noc near Gladstone and Escanaba. It was two weeks before spawning season, and large numbers of trophy browns had massed in shoal water before ascending the Whitefish and Escanaba rivers. Dawn broke with a red glow that seemed to flow over the calm, unbroken surface. Then the trout moved in, and everywhere I looked broad shoulders bulged the surface. The browns rolled over and down in classic head-and-tail rises as they took the hapless shiners at the surface.

Bob Ryan, a fellow fly fisherman from Minnesota, and I watched in awe as ten-to fifteen-pound browns rolled within thirty feet of us. The water here was shallow, often less than ten-feet deep, and heavy mats of weeds were present. The only hope we had was to make an accurate cast, allow the tiny streamer to sink about two feet, and retrieve it with a minnowlike action. Bob's first cast was on target, and a brown rolled to the fly and surged away on a long run, breaking Bob's 5X tippet. I eased out and lengthened line in the air, trying to keep my backcast high to avoid snapping the fly off on the rocky beach. A brown had been rolling about every six feet in a relatively straight line. I dropped the fly where I assumed he'd be next. It was on target, and the fish took before I started the retrieve. I lifted the rod in a soft salute to the fish, and as the #14 hook bit deep, the fish boiled from the water in a ponderous leap. A brief struggle, and the fish was lost in the weeds. We lost two more fish before Bob was able to turn a nine-pounder to my waiting net.

We ended the day with two fish, not fully what we'd hoped to do, but it had been an exciting two hours in the morning and two hours before dark. The total of hooked and lost browns stood at ten, including one fifteen-pound-plus fish that Bob lost on a long run. We each landed one fish that day, mine a ten-pounder. I made a return trip a week later and found the browns equally receptive, and my luck a little better. Three fish, including one fourteen-pounder, fell to my flies, but the hooked-lost ratio remained about the same. In two days of fishing at sunrise and sunset—the two best times—I hooked fifteen fish and lost them for a variety of reasons. Weeds were the biggest culprit, because hooked fish often bore down through them, and the increased drag on the fly line produced a broken leader.

The initial secret in this type of fishing is to locate areas where trout can be found. I look for secluded beaches off rivermouths where the best action is during the week. Weekend anglers often crowd these areas, and since they can often throw hardware farther than flies can be cast, chances are you won't catch fish. It's possible for newcomers to the sport to check with area department of natural resources (DNR) biologists or tackle shops to determine when runs of trout are expected. Second best is to go on weekends and observe rivermouth anglers. If they catch trout, you'll know that midweek fishing should be good.

After trout are located it still remains a problem to catch them. Schools of browns or steelhead move inshore en masse and all one can hope to do is cast into the middle and hope for a strike. This is hit or miss fishing, usually the latter. I prefer to observe a single fish, try to determine its path of travel and the frequency of its rolling boils, and try to have my fly in the proper place at the right time. Trout will often change directions, so many casts are fruitless, but occasionally you'll guess right and a strike will follow.

Two schools of thought prevail on retrieves. One is to make the cast and allow the streamer to sink naturally, while others (myself included) prefer to cast and begin a slow, twitching hand-twist retrieve. Although I've taken a few fish on a dead sink, more fish have been hooked by bringing the fly back in short jerks to imitate a shiner or other forage fish in trouble.

Lake Michigan brown trout often enter the shallows in the fall, where they can be taken on small streamers—as was this seven-pounder. *Photos by David Richey*

Long, fine leaders are important. I've never fished with less than a ten-footer, and twelve-footers tapered down to 4X or 5X are better. There is little room for error in handling big trout on light tippets, but the number of strikes will soar when you go fine.

Very little feeding by larger trout seems to take place on insects in the Great Lakes. My best success has come while using flies (mostly streamers) tied with an abundance of tinsel or other reflective materials. George Richey, my brother and a professional fly tier, specializes in patterns imitating forage fish. His Rattlelure, a streamer with a built-in sound chamber, is probably going to come into more widespread use, since it appeals to feeding trout by sight and sound. A hand-twist retrieve brings out an appealing noise, and the large amount of tinsel and overall shape imitate an alewife. The combination is effective on pre-spawning trout, especially steelhead off rivermouths.

The Silver Streak is a common Midwestern tie for brown trout. Tied on a #12 to 16 long-shanked hook, it features a red-yarn tail, silver tinsel body, and a thin, streamlined wing of fox or calf tail. It can be either weighted or unweighted.

I've tried on countless occasions to lure jumbo trout to the surface with dry flies, but without success. I've been present when the large *Hexagenia limbata* mayflies have been hatching, but at that time (early July) the inshore waters are usually too warm for anything other than a brief feeding flurry. In time I'm sure anglers will hit this and other hatches at their peak, and the result will be a brand of excitement known only to a select few.

Steelhead represent a slightly different challenge than browns because they like a fast, darting retrieve. Whenever I've hit steelhead off a rivermouth, they have zoomed inshore after minnows like a pack of wolves. They slash out in all directions, and skittering alewives and smelt bolt into the air in an attempt to get away. The only retrieve that has consistently worked for me is to make as long a cast as possible, begin the retrieve slowly, and then speed up with fast, foot-long pulls on the line This once paid off as I fished off the mouth of Michigan's East Branch of the AuGres River. I was the only angler in late October, and schools of salmon and steelhead were breaking water everywhere as I drifted in a small aluminum pram and tried to stay outside of the fish. Whenever I spotted a boil, I'd cover it and begin my long strip. This type of fishing results in hard strikes, and my ten-foot leader was tapered down to 2X. Three fish were covered before my fly stopped with a jolt, and a twenty-four inch silvery steelhead made a long run that ended with a sparkling leap. Ten minutes later I closed the meshes of my net around a chunky seven-pounder. The action continued until I'd landed five trout ranging in size from four to eight pounds. I kept one fish for dinner and released the others.

My blue-and-silver Rattlelure was torn and tattered, but enough flash and noise remained to allow me to finish the day with just the single fly. Blue-and-silver combinations, or red and pink, seem to be most attractive to steelhead off rivermouths.

Fly tackle for the Great Lakes can be basically the same as for big river fish. I normally select one of four graphite rods, which range from eight to nine feet in length. The smallest rod is my favorite, and I use it for working the boulders and rocky ledges of Michigan and Wisconsin for brook trout. A weight-forward seven-weight floating line is used with a nine-foot leader. These fish aren't large; although an occasional fish will top four pounds, the average is closer to a pound-and-a-half. Steelhead and brown trout are usually fished with an eight-and-a-half or nine-foot rod and a nine weight-forward line, also a floater. The reel is the most important item the angler uses. It should have a smooth drag and be large enough to hold at least a hundred yards of twenty-pound-test Dacron backing. A big trout is fully capable of rattling all the fly line and a hundred yards of backing out in one powerful run. I've broken my leader many times by pointing the rod at the fish and holding on when it became apparent the fish would not stop. It's better to lose the fish and a portion of the tippet than to get cleaned entirely.

On a retrieve I'll watch the line-leader connection and whenever it stops, it's time to set the hook. Once in a while the line or leader will jerk sideways as a trout takes the fly. In either case, I'll simply lift the rod until the fish is felt, because the weight of the line rising off the water is sufficient to anchor the hook. A hard set will invariably break the leader point. Keep the set soft and delicate, and many times the fish will fight a dogged battle without panicking away on a line-gobbling run.

It is an art to play a big trout in open water. Many areas are choked with weeds, especially early in the fall when browns are present. A tightly held brown will rampage back and forth, and a tangled and broken leader is often the result. I loosen the drag on my reel, and when a trout is hooked, allow the fish to run toward open water without much restraint. Once the fish clears the weeds, I'll carry the fight to it as much as my tackle will stand. If possible, I'll try to keep the trout as far from shore as I can until it starts rolling on the surface as it tires. Only then will I attempt to bring it within netting distance.

Big steelhead and browns have a last-ditch trick that is as common as the morning sunrise. They will allow themselves to be led almost within netting distance and then speed off on a hard run. The angler who's caught flatfooted will often tighten up in an attempt to hold the fish, and the leader will break. Allow the fish free rein whenever it comes close, and try to make good on your first attempt to land it.

Pinpointing good areas for Great Lakes trout is like predicting the weather; it can be done, but only with a margin of error. Fly fishermen are such a minority that one or even a dozen anglers can't locate all the best areas. I've personally fished perhaps one dozen spots around the three upper Great Lakes, and there are probably fifty times that many waiting to be discovered. These are my favorites:

Steelhead: Michigan has the best waters for fly fishermen. I'd recommend the mouth of the AuGres River (East Branch) near Tawas City. Another good spot is Thompson Creek near Manistique, the mouth of the Two-Hearted River near Newberry, or the mouth of the Little Manistee River in Manistee Lake near Manistee. Wisconsin anglers could find good sport in Lake Michigan near Jackson-port, Algoma, Kewaunee, or the rocky areas in Door County.

Browns: Little Bay De Noc near Gladstone or Escanaba, Michigan, is the key location. I'd also suggest trying upper Green Bay near Menominee, Michigan, and Marinette, Wisconsin. The rocks around Caseville and Grindstone City, Michigan, are an untapped area with plenty of fall browns.

Brook Trout: Try Grand Traverse Bay near Northport, Michigan, or the Cave Point-Bailey's Harbor area in Wisconsin. Brookies are scattered and tough to lo-cate.

15

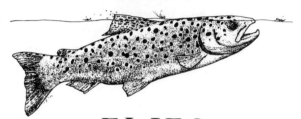

FLIES
FOR
STILLWATERS

John Merwin

MANY OF THE FLIES YOU'VE ACCUMULATED FOR STREAM TROUT WILL ALSO serve well in stillwater. As is true on streams, you could often eliminate many of them and simply fish with a Muddler, Hare's Ear wet fly, and the Adams dry, all in a variety of sizes. I once conducted a fairly extensive survey of fly shops around the country, and those were the best-selling patterns hands down. As a group, they are generally imitative of almost all the trout-food organisms found in stillwaters. That means also that while they work often, they don't always. So as in other sorts of fly-fishing, some special sorts of stillwater flies are in order, designed or adapted to imitate specific creatures and fitting the criteria for stillwater flies that follow.

Animals or birds in a forest are almost invisible until they move. Anyone who's spent even a few minutes in the woods or even a city park has probably not noticed a bird or squirrel until it's hopped. The same is often true for a trout searching for food in quiet waters, especially below the surface. The darting hop of a *Callibaetis* nymph on the weed edges, the wriggling acrobatics of a midge larva, the frantic dash of a caddis pupa to the surface, the silent flashing of an alewife overhead near the mirrored surface; these are all movements that catch a pred-

ator's eye. And so almost all successful stillwater patterns are designed to offer naturally appearing motion in or on the water when properly manipulated.

Whenever its appropriate or possible, the materials used in constructing these flies should themselves be capable of easy movement, complementing the pattern's manipulation in the water. Soft hackles, fur, and marabou are more appropriate—and more alive—than hard quills, flosses, and stiff hair fibers. The question of an artificial's action in the water, a function of its materials, is even more important in stillwaters than in streams. There is no current to add life by moving the hackles; such life depends solely on your own manipulations and your choice of materials.

The flies in this selection have been chosen to support the preceding chapters. Either the patterns have been specifically mentioned or a contributor has mentioned a need for an imitation without stipulating a pattern. Some patterns you'll recognize as being standards, others are relatively new and a few are presented here for the first time. I haven't supplied any step-by-step tying instructions. Anyone who has mastered the fundamentals would find them redundant here, and if you haven't, there are numerous good books on fly-tying basics that will help. One that I like is Eric Leiser's *Complete Book of Fly Tying* (Knopf). Step-by-step instructions for some of these flies, especially the more recent ones, have appeared in other books or magazines, and I've supplied that information when it applies to a particular pattern. If a fly requires a special trick or two, I've mentioned that also in the commentary after each fly.

The attention focused on stillwater fishing in Britain has produced a corresponding proliferation of stillwater fly patterns. The American tier who is fishing for ideas will find plenty in books by John Veniard, Taff Price, John Goddard, Richard Walker, Geoffrey Bucknall, and others. A few British patterns are included in this section.

Finally, a couple of words about barbless hooks. Their use as a conservation measure has been widely urged and rightly so. I want to add something with which you may more readily identify and that's that I pinch down my barbs because I'm lazy. Although I like to eat trout, I don't like the bother of hauling them home and cleaning them. Happily, I can do some good by letting them go for the sake of the fishery and save myself some drudgery at the same time. So I let them go. Removing a barbed hook—and especially the very small ones—from a fish can be time consuming and occasionally difficult; it sometimes means killing the fish. Fish are more easily hooked without the hooking resistance of a barb, the hooks seem to hold just as well—I've never lost a trout for lack of a barb—and when the time comes to remove the hook, it's much more easily done. A happy combination.

The following are prototypical imitations of common stillwater mayflies in this country. Because size and coloration even within a single species will vary from watershed to watershed, there is no substitute for catching a few samples and modifying these patterns to suit local conditions.

Tricorythodes Dun, #20

TRICORYTHODES DUN

HOOK:	Mustad 94859 ringed-eye, #20 to 26
TAILS:	Medium blue-dun hackle fibers
BODY:	Fine blackish-brown or olive-green polypropyl-ene dubbing
WINGS:	Single, upright clump of pale gray polypropyl-ene yarn at thorax
HACKLE:	Medium blue-dun tied parachute
THREAD:	Engerbretson Ultramidge

This is my own pattern, first developed on the Battenkill River when trout were taking these tiny duns before switching to the subsequent spinner fall. It's easier to tie than it sounds. Leaving the yarn wing extending about an inch above the hook and trimming it last will make the parachute hackle easy to wind without any sort of gallows-type holding device. Ultramidge thread is a fine, monofilament nylon, sometimes called "18/0," and although its color is white, the lack of bulk produced in tying makes it almost invisible. The little ringed-eye hooks offer much better hooking properties than either down-eyed or up-eyed versions, and I use them for all my flies in sizes smaller than twenty. This fly has worked on ponds not only as a mayfly imitation, but also when small black midges are on the water.

CAENIS DUN

HOOK:	Mustad 94859 ringed-eye, #20 to 28
THREAD:	Ultramidge
TAILS:	Palest blue-dun (almost white) hackle fibers
BODY:	Fine, pale-cream polypropylene dubbing
WINGS:	Single upright clump, palest gray polypropyl-ene yarn
HACKLE:	Pale blue-dun (almost white) tied parachute

More conventional dressings include pale badger hackle and white hackle-point wings. My seeming obsession with little parachute patterns is because of all the possibilities for minute, hackled mayfly duns, they are the easiest to tie. The poly-yarn wings are durable, and if not tied too thickly, also very effective.

(184)

Caenis Dun, #20

Pale Speckle-wing Quill, #16

PALE SPECKLE-WING QUILL

HOOK:	Mustad 94842, #16 to 20
THREAD:	8/0 white silk
TAILS:	Pale grizzly fibers
BODY:	Bleached peacock quill
WINGS:	Light-barred teal flank, upright and divided
HACKLE:	Pale grizzly

This is Ernie Schwiebert's pattern from his book *Trout,* and it is a specific imitation of a lighter-phased *Callibaetis* mayfly. More general imitations are offered by such standard patterns as the Adams, Mosquito, or Gray Quill. Where these mayflies are prolific, the matching of widely variable local color phases can be important; if you see some duns, take a close look.

(185)

GREAT SUMMER DRAKE

HOOK:	Mustad 94840, #10 to 14
THREAD:	6/0 brown
TAILS:	Medium-gray dun hackle fibers
BODY:	Dark cream-gray fox, ribbed with darker gray dubbing
WINGS:	Dark-gray dun hackle points; upright
HACKLE:	Medium-gray dun

Another Schwiebert pattern, and also from his *Trout,* this is a specific imitation of the larger *Siphlonurus* mayflies that are most important on western waters. A Gray Wulff is often cited as an imitation of these Gray Drakes, and a large Adams is also a rough approximation. For flies such as these with strongly marked bodies, try two layers of dubbing on a single thread. The core color (light gray here) is applied first, and the secondary color is applied in a thin noodle directly over it before winding. The effect can be startlingly realistic, and I tied the illustrated version of this pattern in that manner.

MONTY'S HEXAGENIA

HOOK:	Mustad 94840, #10 to 12
THREAD:	6/0 tan
TAILS:	None
BODY:	Extended; tan poly dubbing over tan polypropylene yarn
WING:	Single wing made with wing-burner from mallard flank dyed lemon woodduck; tied upright
HACKLE:	Dark and pale ginger mixed

This is a new fly developed by Monty Montplaisir of Colebrook, New Hampshire, to imitate the big *Hexagenia* duns that are fairly common on the ponds in his area at the end of June. It has accounted for rainbows better than twenty inches when fished at dark and the fish are hunting the big, flopping duns. Hold a strand of poly-yarn along the shank of a long-shanked streamer hook from which the eye has been removed. Overwrap tightly with tying thread and then cover with dubbing and whip-finish. Slide the body off and tie on the dry-fly hook, covering the wraps with dubbing. Finish the fly in a conventional manner, trimming the hackles underneath to sit the fly low on the water. The polypropelene extended body is light, easy to cast, and durable, unlike more conventional versions that feature extended bodies of bulky deer hair. Only one wing is used, in order to reduce leader-twist when the fly is cast.

Great Summer Drake, #12

Monty's Hexagenia, #10

The following are four spent-wing versions of some dry flies just described, to be used during the spinner falls that sometimes assume more importance than the hatches themselves. I tie all of my spinner patterns with spent wings of polypropylene yarn; more selective fish may demand wings of hen-hackle points (white), pale hackle fibers, or wings cut from such transluscent materials as swiss straw. The poly-winged versions are by far the easiest to make. The most common error, especially in commercially tied versions, is the use of too much material; a bunch of 15 to 20 fibers separated from the yarn itself is plenty.

TRICORYTHODES SPINNER

HOOK:	Mustad 94859 ringed-eye, #20 to 28
THREAD:	Ultramidge
TAILS:	Three pale-blue dun hackle fibers, fairly short
BODY:	Fine black poly dubbing
WINGS:	Palest gray poly-yarn fibers, tied spent at thorax
HACKLE:	None

CAENIS SPINNER

HOOK:	Mustad 94859 ringed-eye, #20 to 28
THREAD:	Ultramidge
TAILS:	Three white hackle fibers
BODY:	Fine off-white poly dubbing, touch of light brown poly dubbing around thorax at wing bases
WINGS:	Palest gray poly, tied spent at thorax

SPECKLE-WING SPINNER

HOOK:	Mustad 94833, #14 to 20
THREAD:	6/0 white
TAILS:	Three white hackle fibers
BODY:	Very pale to medium-gray fine polypropylene dubbing
WINGS:	Palest gray poly-yarn; speckle the forward half of each wing with a fine-pointed permanent marking pen (dark gray)

This is a somewhat simplified version of the *Callibaetis* spinner imitations tied by René Harrop of St. Anthony, Idaho, who uses a leading edge of barred mallard flank ahead of white poly in the wings to imitate the distinctively mottled wings of the naturals. Once again, pay particular attention to local color variations in the naturals.

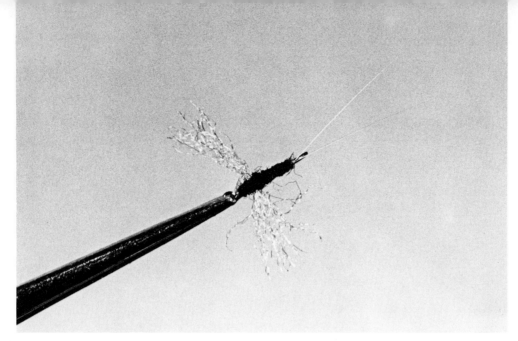

Tricorythodes Spinner, #20

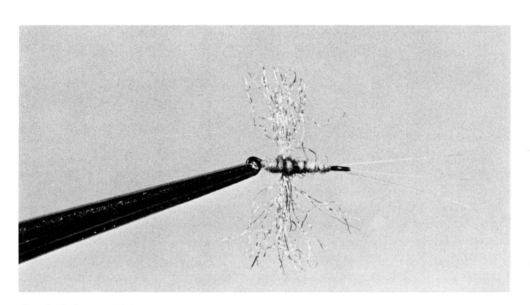

Caenis Spinner, #20

Speckle-wing Spinner, #16

Rusty Spinner, #16

RUSTY SPINNER

HOOK:	Larger sizes: Mustad 94833 #10 to 18
	Smaller sizes: Mustad 94859, #20 to 24
TAILS:	Three white hackle fibers
BODY:	Variable from light rusty-amber to deep rust, fine polypropylene dubbing
WINGS:	Palest gray poly-yarn fibers, tied spent at thorax
HACKLE:	None

This is the most frequently encountered color range of spent mayflies on American waters. No fly box should be without a selection in a full range of sizes. Among many others, it's imitative of the various *Siphlonurus* species, for which a dun imitation was given previously. Included within this color range is the so-called Sherry Spinner, popular on British waters, and often sold here under that name.

Many writers stipulate the heavier Mustad 94840 dry-fly hook for spinner patterns, and if you're more comfortable with the additional strength it offers, by all means use it. The 94833 model offers the advantage of lighter weight and slightly better hooking properties, although a heavy hand will straighten the hook on a large fish. A few eyebrows may also be raised by my use of very pale-gray poly wings instead of the more customary white yarn. The wings of spent mayflies are often transparent with subtle overtones of color refracted from the surroundings. The white versions of poly-yarn are often glaring white, and I've found that a very pale gray is just as transluscent without being harsh.

Caddis adult patterns have proliferated tremendously in recent years. Stillwater versions should most often be twitchable, hackled patterns that can be made to jump around on the surface with subtle rod-tip manipulations. That motion, if not overdone, will attract the trout. The following is my own version of an adult-pattern style that's more of a synthesis of many patterns than really my own. I use it in a variety of colors and styles.

TENT-WINGED CADDIS

HOOK:	Partridge (Capt. Hamilton) fine-wire down-eye, #10 to 20
THREAD:	6/0 nylon to match body color
TAILS:	None
BODY:	Fine poly dubbing, tan, green, black, or other appropriate colors
WINGS:	One hen-hackle tip, coated with vinyl cement, tied folded around body at head and trimmed at rear slightly beyond hook bend; color is as appropriate
HACKLE:	Of appropriate color, wound over tie-in point of wing and trimmed from under hook shank

In general, those caddis patterns with some hackle forward of the wing will hop better when twitched, and so I've stayed with that style. The Partridge hook I mentioned has a slightly wider gap and shorter shank than a Mustad dry-fly hook of the same size, and I like it better for caddis dries for those reasons, plus its exceptionally sharp point. They are now being distributed in this county by Thomas and Thomas in Turner's Falls, Massachusetts.

Tent-winged Caddis, #12

POLY-WINGED MIDGE

HOOK:	Mustad 94833, #14 to 18; 94859 ringed-eye, #20 to 28
THREAD:	Ultramidge
TAILS:	None (ever)
BODY:	Very thinly dubbed polypropylene: gray, olive, black, tan or red
WINGS:	Palest gray strands of poly-yarn; about ten fibers tied in as for a spent-wing spinner, then angled back to 45 degrees from body; wings should be slightly less than body length
HACKLE:	Blue dun or ginger; one turn behind and one turn in front of wings and no more

The illusion must be spare—a gangly suggestion of the adult. Hackle length should be slightly greater than body length; the use of too much material will ruin the imitation. The fly lies in the surface tension more than a natural ready to take wing, but heavily hackled high-riding versions always seemed to me to be worse imitations because of the amount of hackle necessary to get the effect.

WETZEL'S BLACK MIDGE

HOOK:	Mustad 94840, #16 to 18
THREAD:	6/0 black silk
TAILS:	None
BODY:	Peacock quill dyed black, or black moose mane
WINGS:	Starling, tied upright and divided
HACKLE:	Ginger, tied conventionally

Charles Wetzel was one of the first American writers to offer patterns for both midge adults and midge pupae. This pattern most recently appeared in his *Trout Flies,* first published in 1955 and reprinted in 1979 by Stackpole Books.

GRIFFITH'S GNAT

HOOK:	Mustad 94859 ringed-eye, #20 to 28
THREAD:	Ultramidge
TAILS:	None
BODY:	Fine (single strand) peacock herl
WINGS:	None
HACKLE:	Grizzly, palmered for body length; other colors such as badger, furnace, and various shades of dun also work well

Most ultrasmall dry flies will work sometimes, especially if they aren't over-dressed. Once you start hitting midge hatches with some regularity, though, you'll want a more precise imitation, and you can use these patterns as a starting point for your own.

Poly-winged Midge, #16

Wetzel's Black Midge, #18   Griffith's Gnat, #20

MONTY'S DAMSEL

HOOK:	Mustad 94840, #12 to 14
TAILS:	None
BODY:	Extended; bright-blue poly dubbing over strand of same color poly-yarn; other colors also possible are dark green and bright red
WINGS:	Two light-blue dun hackle tips, tied long at an angle above body
HACKLE:	Light blue-dun, fairly heavy

This adult damselfly imitation also comes from Monty Montplaisir. The extended body is tied in the same way is was the case with his previously described Hexagenia dun. His fishing formula is simple: twitch the fly on the surface and then hold on.

SOPER'S CRANEFLY (GANGLE-LEGS)

HOOK:	Mustad 94840, #18 to 20
THREAD:	Yellow or tan, 6/0
BODY:	Beige yarn
WINGS:	Pale blue-dun hackle points, tied spent
HACKLE:	Light to medium-ginger spade hackle, tied parachute; hackle should be considerably over-size, as much as two inches in diameter

A large tan skater or variant-type dry fly will often draw trout when skated on the surface to imitate the spindly adult craneflies that fall sometimes to the water when mating or depositing eggs. This is a more exact imitation developed by Dudley Soper, a good friend and devastatingly effective fisherman who frequents the lower Battenkill. Complete tying directions can be found in *Mastering the Art of Fly Tying* by Richard Talleur (Stackpole).

Adult midges are difficult to imitate because they almost always have their bodies well above the water, briefly supported on the surface tension by spindly legs before they fly away. Many versions, both in this country and Britain, have hackle-point wings, which are a nuisance to tie, and I've included here a poly-winged version of my own that's easier to make. An old Charles Wetzel version has also been included, along with the well-known Griffith's Gnat, named after Michigan angler George Griffith, and to my knowledge first described in *Nymphs* by Ernest Schwiebert.

Monty's Damsel, #12

Soper's Cranefly (Gangle-legs), #18

Next come the wide variety of patterns for subsurface use: wet flies, nymphs, assorted pupae and larvae, and streamers. Many wet flies are representative of a wide variety of stillwater lifeforms, and a possible listing would run many pages. Although I won't describe them here, I really enjoy fishing for small-pond brookies with a Royal Coachman wet, fished with rather rapid twitches. Another favorite is really a series: the Partridge-and. . . . Especially in very small sizes, these little dubbed-fur soft-hackled wet flies are especially effective. Orange, tan, brown, green, and other colors all work at times.

Of the two wet flies described here, the Woolly Worm is an American stillwater standby, although its roots extend well back through the genesis of fly-fishing in Great Britain. The other is sort of a marriage between a Gold-Ribbed Hare's Ear and a March Brown. I have modified and re-modified it for more than fifteen years, and call it a March Hare. It is really my "If-I-Had-Only-One-Fly" pattern.

WOOLLY WORM

HOOK:	Mustad 9671, #2 to 16
THREAD:	6/0 nylon, match body color
TAIL:	Strip of red duck quill (optional)
BODY:	Black chenille (or brown, olive, and others)
HACKLE:	Grizzly, palmered forward

When you palmer the hackle, bury the quill stem between the turns of chenille as the hackle is wound. The sizes range from a monster to a mere morsel. The fly has accounted for untold numbers of trout over ten pounds from lakes when fished with a sinking line and a slow, stripping retreive. A wide number of color combinations are possible; two of the most popular seem to be a black body with grizzly hackle, and an olive body with grizzly hackle dyed olive.

Woolly Worm, #6

March Hare, #14

MARCH HARE

HOOK:	Mustad 3906B, #14 to 18
THREAD:	Brown 6/0 nylon
TAILS:	None
BODY:	Roughly dubbed hare's mask, brownish gray with guard hairs untrimmed; rib closely with tying thread
WINGS:	Medium-gray duck quill, tied conventional wet-fly style
HACKLE:	Partridge breast from reddish-brown-phased bird; tied sparsely and extending no farther than hook point

The differences between this and the popular GR Hare's Ear are the lack of metallic ribbing —I think it's too flashy—and the addition of partridge hackle of a color that complements the fly. The hackle is soft and works easily. I use the fly greased and on top as an emerger, unweighted and with gentle twitches in the middle depths, and fished deeply with a weighted version. The best thing that I can say about it is that it has worked well and often in both lakes and streams.

(197)

Next on the list are nymphs, and once again the list of possibilities is almost endless. I approached this list trying to provide examples of inherent movement in nymph patterns, and most of the nymphs here accomplish that by one or more means.

HEXAGENIA WIGGLE-NYMPH

HOOK:	Abdomen: Mustad 3261 ringed-eye, #8
	Thorax: Mustad 3906, #8
THREAD:	Tan or brown 6/0 nylon
TAILS:	Slim clump of gray marabou, 3/8" long
BODY:	Of chopped marabou; blend four parts brown, two parts yellow, and one part dark purple. Dub tightly and wind in neat tapering cylinder. Rib tightly with fine gold wire and pick out marabou heavily along sides between ribs to represent prominent gills.
THORAX:	(On 3906 hook) weight shank with lead wire. Tie in wire loop with abdomen on other hook attached. Dub marabou over wire tie-in. Tie in wing case, and continue dubbing to hook eye.
WING CASE:	Dark turkey tail
HACKLE:	Medium-brown partridge or grouse, sparse

Wiggle-nymphs are fly-fishing's answer to jointed bass plugs; their action is superb. Carl Richards and Doug Swisher first described the concept, and numerous people have taken off with it since. Detailed directions for a wiggle-style damselfly nymph are given by Dave Whitlock in the first *Fly-Tyer's Almanac* (Crown). The tying procedure for this pattern is the same, except the hook used for the abdomen should be trimmed with wire-cutters immediately aft of the tail. If you're fishing one of the many ponds in the Northeast or upper Midwest in late June and at dark when these big burrowing mayfly nymphs are swimming to the surface, try a big wiggle nymph.

JANSSEN PRE-EMERGER NYMPH

HOOK:	Mustad 9672, #16
TAIL:	Golden pheasant tippets, dyed medium olive
BODY:	Gray rabbit, dyed medium olive, olive thread ribbing, lead fuse wire wound under body
WING CASE:	Dark-brown mottled turkey
HACKLE:	Woodduck fibers tied in at sides

Developed by Hal Janssen, who contributed two chapters to this book, the nymph is generally imitative of the little *Callibaetis* nymphs prevalent in many lakes and ponds. Complete tying directions appear in *The American Fly Tyer's Handbook* (Winchester), edited by Ken Bay.

Hexagenia Wiggle-nymph, #8

Janssen Pre-emerger Nymph, #16

GRAY DRAKE NYMPH

HOOK:	Mustad 3906B, #8 to 14
THREAD:	Gray 6/0 nylon
TAILS:	Light-brown partridge fibers
BODY:	Gray muskrat dubbing
WING CASE:	Dark-gray duck-quill segment
HACKLE:	Brown partridge

This is a simple imitation of the larger *Siphlonurus* nymphs important in western stillwaters; the pattern is generally attributed to Carl Richards and Doug Swisher. Using a fine-wire ribbing to fasten grayish-brown tufts of marabou along the sides of the abdomen as an imitation of gills will greatly enhance the action of this larger nymph pattern. This process is most often suggested in various writings by Ernest Schwiebert; although time-consuming, it has proved worthwhile in the few instances I've taken the trouble to do it.

DAMSEL JIG

HOOK:	Mustad 3906, #8 to 14
THREAD:	Olive 6/0 nylon
BODY:	Olive dubbing over lead wire
TAIL:	Olive marabou fibers, twice body length

This simple damselfly nymph was first shown me several years ago by Dave Engerbretson. The marabou offers a tremendous amount of action in the water, which is multiplied by the jig effect produced by the weighted hook.

JANSSEN'S DAMSEL NYMPH

HOOK:	Mustad 9672, #8 to 12
THREAD:	Olive 6/0 nylon
TAIL:	Brownish-olive marabou, one-third body length
BODY:	Blend and dub 40 percent bleached beaver, 50 percent olive rabbit and 10 percent flourescent orange rabbit. Rib with tying thread.
WING CASE:	Brown-mottled turkey section
HACKLE:	Ginger, palmered over thorax, trimmed top and bottom

This pattern first appeared in *Fly Fisherman* Magazine in June 1976, and was developed to imitate the damselfly nymphs that have helped make Henrys Lake, Idaho, so famous. The fly was produced by Hal Janssen, whose chapter in this book on nymph fishing describes how to use it.

Gray Drake Nymph, #10

Damsel Jig, #12

Janssen's Damsel Nymph, #6

Darrel's Dragon, #6

DARREL'S DRAGON

HOOK:	Mustad 79580, #6 (bend forward one-third of shank slightly upward)
THREAD:	6/0 nylon to match body color
BODY:	Woven from chocolate and olive chenille
HACKLE:	Bronze-green pheasant fibers
EYES:	Bead chain painted glossy black

A simple and effective dragonfly nymph designed by Darrel Martin for the lakes of his native state of Washington. The fly was first described in *Fly Fisherman* in July 1976, in Darrel's excellent feature on dragonfly nymphs in lakes. The fly was unnamed at the time, so I corrected that omission here.

MARABOU DRAGON

HOOK:	Mustad 9575, #2 to 8, shank bent to horizontal S-shape.
UNDERBODY:	Thin cardboard cut to basic body shape and epoxied to hook shank, covered by floss of a color to match dubbing
TAILS:	Five short, broad fibers of stripped goose
BODY:	Brown (or other appropriate color) marabou, chopped and dubbed
RIBBING:	Flat mono, dyed to match body color
WING CASE:	Dark turkey, lacquered and trimmed
LEGS:	Sparse, dark-brown pheasant body-feather fibers at sides
EYES:	Ambroid cement bubbles, painted black.

This is my own pattern in which I set out to provide the distinctive ovoid shape of the natural's abdomen, the gentle action of marabou dubbing, and to over-

Marabou Dragon, #6

come the weight normally added by bead-chain eyes. The eyes on this fly are made by dipping knotted tippet material in wet Ambroid cement. When dried rapidly in a warm oven, the cement droplets become hard, hollow bubbles that allow the effect of large eyes without adding weight. It's the only fly I've ever designed that took a fish the first time it got wet. Full tying directions are in *The American Fly Tyer's Handbook.*

Once again, there are numerous damselfly imitations not included here, as well as a lesser number of dragonfly types. One dragonfly nymph of note is Charles Brooks's Assam Dragon, described in his *Nymph Fishing for Larger Trout* (Crown).

MARABOU MIDGE LARVA

HOOK:	Mustad 9523, #14
THREAD:	Ultramidge
BODY:	None
WING:	Clump of blood-red, olive or gray marabou; about one-half to three-quarters of an inch long

One of the more common midge-larva imitations is a short piece of rubber band, often red, tied to a hook. This marabou version has more wiggle in the water, and the very short-shanked hook offers enough weight to enhance the action. Retrieve in very slow twitches.

Marabou Midge Larva, #14

PHANTOM MIDGE LARVA

HOOK:	Mustad 94840, #10 to 12
THREAD:	Ultramidge
UNDERBODY:	Two small lumps of orange tying thread, one slightly behind hook eye, one just ahead of hook bend
BODY:	Neat, even cylinder wound from clear vinyl strips
HACKLE:	Pale blue-dun hen hackle, a few short fibers sticking backward from under eye

I have never seen or heard of an American imitation for the Chaorborid midge larvae so common in many of our stillwaters. This fly is adapted from a pattern developed by English angler Richard Walker.

The following are six distinctly different styles of midge pupal imitations. I have included so many because the pupal phase is so important and so little explored in this country. The names of the originators are in parentheses under the fly names, and all of them are illustrated along with the other flies in this section. All of them work at one time or another. I like mine best, although you may well develop a preference for something else.

GREEN MIDGE PUPA
(Charles Wetzel)

HOOK:	Mustad 94840, #20
THREAD:	6/0 green silk
BODY:	Pale green floss
THORAX:	Green chenille, tied at rear of shank
HACKLE:	White, very small and fine, wound near hook bend

Wetzel designed this fly to float with the shank hanging down in the water and with the hook-bend at the surface, supported by the little white-hackle collar. It is the only fly in this series so designed.

MIDGE NYMPH
(Ed Koch)

HOOK:	Mustad 94840, #16 to 28
THREAD:	6/0 nylon, match body color
BODY:	Gray muskrat, brown weasel, or cream fox dubbing; thin at abdomen and thicker at head

That's it. About as simple a midge-pupa imitation as can be tied. I suspect that its effectiveness as an imitation increases in proportion to decreasing fly size.

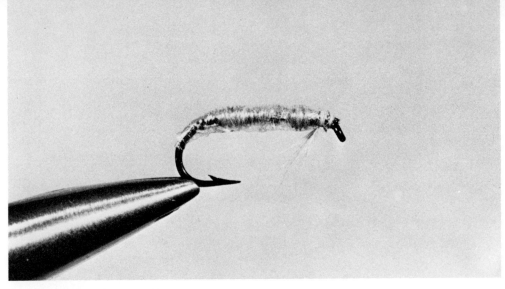

Phantom Midge Larva, #10

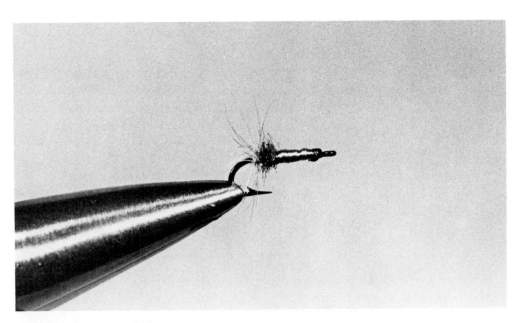

Green Midge Pupa, #20

Midge Nymph, #20

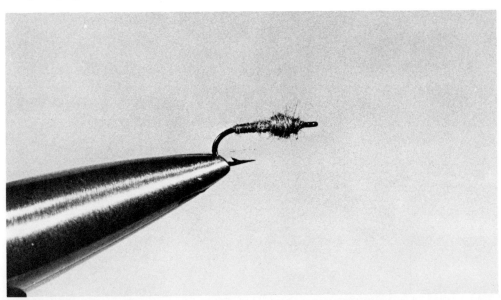

Hatching Midge Pupa, #12

HATCHING MIDGE PUPA
(John Goddard)

HOOK:	Light-wire dry-fly hook with a round bend, #10 to 14
THREAD:	6/0 silk to match body color
BODY:	Black, brown, orange, red, or green floss, tied in on hook bend and wound forward with fine silver ribbing; then cover with clear plastic strip.
TAILS:	White hen-hackle fibers extending one-eighth inch from start of body as tails
THORAX:	Green peacock or buff condor herl
HACKLE:	White hen-hackle fibers extending upward and over the hook eye; tied in bunched, not wound

Goddard is widely known and respected as one of the leading proponents of angling entomology and precise imitation in Britain. Yes, there are midges as large as #10. Condor is not legal in this country; you might substitute buff-colored ostrich herl. The pattern calls for a ringed-eye hook.

FOOTBALLER
(Geoffrey Bucknall)

HOOK:	Mustad 94840, #12 to 14
THREAD:	Gray 6/0 nylon
BODY:	Black and white horsehair wound forward from middle of hook bend to produce slim, alternately banded body. American tiers might substitute light and dark moose mane.
THORAX:	Dubbed mole's fur
HEAD:	Peacock herl

Footballer, #14

According to Bucknall, the fly is designed to be cast directly in front of a cruising fish that's feeding on pupae.

GRAY MIDGE PUPA
(Ernest Schwiebert)

HOOK:	Mustad 94833, #14 to 22
THREAD:	Dark gray 8/0 silk
TAILS:	Soft, dark-gray fibers tied short
BODY:	Bleached peacock quill, ribbed with fine gold wire
THORAX:	Dark hare's mask dubbing
WINGS:	Mallard wing-quill sections
HACKLE:	Soft, dark-gray fibers tied slightly longer than wing sections. Wound, not bunched.
GILLS:	Ostrich herl, dyed black

This delicate imitation comes from *Trout,* where Schwiebert also describes an olive version. Note especially the use of the lightest-wire Mustad hook to reduce the sink rate and make the fly suspend more easily in the surface tension.

Gray Midge Pupa, #16

BLACK MIDGE PUPA
(John Merwin)

HOOK:	Partridge fine-wire dry fly, #16 to 20
	Mustad 94859 ringed eye, #22 to 28
THREAD:	Ultramidge
TAILS:	Ultrasoft white hackle fibers, tied very short at midpoint of hook bend
BODY:	Fine polypropylene dubbing, ribbed with black 6/0 tying thread. Start body at midpoint of hook bend and keep slim to thorax.
THORAX:	Darkest gray dubbing from hare' mask with a few guard hairs included
HACKLE:	Bunched white hackle fibers extending over hook eye for one-third of body length

This pattern came about because I dislike the use of shiny tinsel or wire in imitative flies, and because I feel the translucency of a dubbed fur body is better than that obtainable with floss or quills. This fly, as were the others preceding it, is more of a style than a pattern, and the colors should be varied to suit. The Partridge hooks have more of an open, round bend than do Mustad dry-fly hooks, and are better suited to patterns requiring tying onto the hook bend. After tying, use a fine-bristled toothbrush to tease the thorax fibers down and back under the shank; that's where the thoracic bulk is found on the naturals.

SENS CADDIS PUPA

HOOK:	Mustad 94840, #14
THREAD:	6/0 black silk
TAILS:	None
UNDERBODY:	Gray floss
OVERBODY:	Silver-gray muskrat dubbing, teased out for translucency; two turns of condor quill at forward end of body
WINGS:	Trim end of black duck wing-covert feather leaving a V-shape and leaving lower stem for tying in. Attach on top of shank so wings lie along sides of body, extending back almost full body length.
HACKLE:	One turn only of rusty dun, trimmed away on top. Wind a final turn of condor quill for head. (Once again, dark gray ostrich herl is a substitute for the unavailable condor.)

Black Midge Pupa, #18

Sens Caddis Pupa, #12

As far as I know, this was America's first consciously developed imitation of a caddis pupa, one of the Ed Sens patterns described in Ray Ovington's book, *How to Take Trout on Wet Flies and Nymphs,* which was published in 1951 and centered largely on Sens's work. It is still an effective style of imitation. The number of different pupal imitations are now legion, and many of the important versions are in the fine book, *The Caddis and the Angler,* by Eric Leiser and Larry Solomon. For stillwater fishing, you'll need a series of pupal imitations, in sizes from ten down to twenty, weighted and unweighted, and at least covering the basic colors: dark gray, brownish olive, and tan.

GRAY GHOST

HOOK:	Mustad 9575, #2 to 8
THREAD:	6/0 black nylon or silk
TAILS:	None
BODY:	Orange floss
RIBBING:	Medium-width silver tinsel
THROAT:	White bucktail, one-and-one-half times body length, under which is short golden pheasant crest
WING:	Golden pheasant crest about an inch longer than hook; over this are four olive-bronze blue-dun hackles: center two are one-and-one-half times body length, outside pair are body length
TOPPING:	Five or six strands of peacock herl, full length of wing
CHEEKS:	Silver pheasant with jungle cock or substitute

This American classic was tied as a smelt imitation by the legendary Carrie Stevens in Maine's Rangeley Lakes region. Properly tied, it has a small, well-shaped head of thread that is as inconspicuous as possible. It should offer a long, slim profile in the water. Short, stubby or overdressed versions look silly, are essentially worthless, and, unfortunately, are common.

Gray Ghost, #2

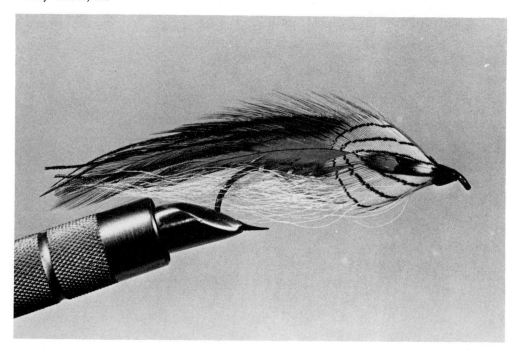

Muddler Minnow, #6

MUDDLER MINNOW

HOOK:	Mustad 79580, #2 to 14
THREAD:	6/0 brown nylon
TAIL:	Peacock primary wing-quill section
BODY:	Gold Mylar tinsel
UNDERWING:	Gray squirrel tail (sparse)
OVERWING:	Matched section of peacock primary, as long as body and tied downwing
HACKLE:	Spun deer hair, about one-third shank length
HEAD:	Deer hair spun and clipped

The fly that does everything, and well. This is probably the single most important stillwater fly pattern in America, and from what I've heard, it also leads the ranks in England.

BADGER MATUKA

HOOK:	Mustad 79580, #6 to 12
THREAD:	Tan 6/0 nylon
BODY:	Medium-width silver Mylar tinsel
RIBBING:	Fine silver wire
WING:	Four light-tan badger hackles with prominent dark center stripe. Tie down Matuka-style with ribbing.
HACKLE:	Two to three turns badger at head (optional)

This pattern is generally imitative of a wide variety of small minnows in ponds and lakes, but especially of dace. It's been most effective for me in smaller sizes and retrieved in a series of quick darts and pauses rather than the slow, deliberate strips sometimes used with other larger patterns. Webby saddle hackle from a hen offers more action in the water than stiffer saddles from a rooster, and take care that the hackle wound near the head isn't too stiff, in which case the fly will

Badger Matuka, #6

ride improperly in the water. Full tying instructions for Matuka-style streamers are given by Dave Whitlock in *The Fly-Tyer's Almanac* (Crown).

SILVER STREAK

HOOK:	Mustad 79580, #12 to 16
THREAD:	Black 6/0 nylon
TAIL:	Short red wool yarn
BODY:	Flat silver tinsel
WING:	Fox or calf tail

This is one fly that Dave Richey described as being effective for large browns in Lake Michigan when they're taking small minnows in the shallows.

Silver Streak, #6

Rattlelure, 3/0

RATTLELURE

HOOK:	Mustad stainless 34007, #1/0
THREAD:	Match wing color
RATTLE:	Put two small lead shot in a piece of plastic tubing slightly shorter than shank. Seal ends with cement, and tie on top of shank, cementing in place. Lead shot should be free to rattle.
BODY:	Large diameter Mylar tubing, slipped over shank and tied in at start of hook bend, frayed ends extending to barb. Tie down other end at head. Press and cement Mylar flat, giving depth to body.
THROAT:	Flourescent red or blue Fishair, slightly longer than body
WING:	Fishair as above, twice body length

The sample flies that Dave Richey sent me were tied on a large hook of the Eagle Claw variety with a turned-up eye. I described the pattern with the Mustad hook because of its more general availability from mail-order suppliers. Those samples also had short (three-eighths inch) prismatic Mylar strips included, one at each side of the head and cemented to the body. It's an intriguing fly, and one with which Richey reports success for open-water steelhead.

MARABOU MATUKA

HOOK:	Mustad stainless 34007, #6 to 5/0
THREAD:	White nylon
BODY:	White Orlon dubbing
RIBBING:	Fine silver wire
WING:	Turkey marabou and thin Mylar strips
OVERWING:	3 to 6 strands peacock or ostrich herl
GILLS:	Red Orlon dubbing
CHEEKS:	Mallard flank
EYES:	Black and yellow enamel over clear cement

This pattern was developed by Dave Whitlock as a specific imitation of a threadfin shad, although it works well as a general attractor pattern in a variety of colors. Its action in the water is superlative. Full tying instructions are in the May 1976 issue of *Fly Fisherman* Magazine.

Marabou Matuka, 3/0

GOLDEN POND SHINER

HOOK:	Mustad 94720, #2 to 10
THREAD:	4/0 white silk
TAILS:	Bright orange hackle fibers
BODY:	Gold Mylar tubing with scarlet nylon throat
UNDERWING:	White marabou
OVERWING:	Pale-ginger, yellow and pale-brown marabou mixed
TOPPING:	Olive ostrich mixed with peacock
HEAD:	White lacquer, painted golden-olive on top
EYES:	Black and yellow lacquer

Golden Pond Shiner, #6

Golden shiners are common brown-trout forage in many ponds. This pattern is Ernest Schwiebert's from *Trout,* and is one of a remarkable series of streamer patterns in that book. They are unusual because they all represent specific baitfish imitations based on multiple color blends in a marabou wing. Most American marabou patterns have been simple attractors, often all black or white. Given marabou's unparalleled action in the water, such flies should prove exceptional. If you happen to fish a lake where trout feed heavily on emerald shiners, as in the Catskills, there's a good imitation offered by Schwiebert in that book.

I'm not going to describe again the various "bestial" imitations Steve Raymond covered in his chapter on miscellaneous stillwater food forms; he gave all the directions you need in his chapter.

I hope these patterns may serve as the basis for your own experiments. When you find something else that works consistently, remember to let the rest of us know.

Valentine Atkinson

ANNOTATED
BIBLIOGRAPHY

I am leaving out some of my favorite fly-fishing books, selecting only those that solve an immediate need created within this book. I am also listing some primary technical references. They are all recent, save one, and their bibliographies will send you on the same, sometimes fruitful search that I and many others have taken from time to time.

General Fishing

LEISER, ERIC. *The Complete Book of Fly Tying.* Alfred A. Knopf, 1977. The best current book for beginners.

MCCLANE, A. J. (ed.) *McClane's New Standard Fishing Encyclopedia.* Holt, Rinehart, and Winston, 1974. Unquestionably the finest single reference on fresh- and saltwater angling in print. Covers numerous topics pertinent to fly-fishing in stillwaters.

SCHWIEBERT, ERNEST. *Nymphs.* Winchester Press, 1973. Deals largely with aquatic forms in streams, but also offers excellent coverage in several chapters of typical stillwater forms. Excellent color illustrations.

————. *Trout.* E. P. Dutton, 1978. Two full and excellent chapters on fly-fishing for stillwater trout plus portions of other chapters on the same topic.

Technical References

EDMUNDS, G. F. JR., JENSEN, S. L. and BERNER, L. *The Mayflies of North and Central America.* University of Minnesota Press, 1976. The most current book on the biology and taxonomy of mayflies.

MERRITT, R. W. and CUMMINS, K. W. (eds.). *An Introduction to the Aquatic Insects of North America.* Kendall/Hunt Publishing Co., 1978. Exceptionally well-illustrated keys for identification of the samples you collect.

NEEDHAM, J. G., TRAVER, J. R., and HSU, Y. C. *The Biology of Mayflies.* Comstock Publishing Co., 1935. A biographer called Needham a brilliant teacher, and this book shines with insight. I have heard of a 1972 reprint (E. W. Classey, Hampton, England), but I haven't seen it as yet.

PENNAK, R. W. *Fresh-Water Invertebrates of the United States.* Ronald Press, 1953. By a professor at the University of Colorado. One of the few current references to treat both aquatic insects and other important stillwater life forms within a single book. Very important.

RUTTNER, F. *Fundamentals of Limnology.* University of Toronto Press, 1966. In a general sense, that branch of ecology that deals with inland waters. One of my favorite books, although some with no scientific background will need Welch's book to understand this one.

USINGER, R. L. (ed.) *Aquatic Insects of California.* University of California Press, 1963. Good general discussions of the life histories of the principal forms. Identification keys are usable for entire U.S.

WELCH, P. S. *Limnology.* McGraw-Hill, 1951. For many years the standard basic text on the topic. Found in many libraries, it has a wealth of technical information on the ecology of lakes and ponds, explained in straight-ahead textbook terms.

WIGGINS, G. B. *The Larvae of North American Caddisfly Genera.* University of Toronto Press, 1977. The most current work on caddis.

And from overseas

CLARKE, BRIAN. *The Pursuit of Stillwater Trout.* A. & C. Black, 1975. One of the most refreshingly original, well-written fishing books of our time.

HARRIS, J. R. *An Angler's Entomology.* A. S. Barnes, 1952 (2nd ed., 1956). A British work with considerable treatment of stillwater forms.

GODDARD, JOHN. *Trout Fly Recognition.* A. & C. Black, 1966. One of the fine books by one of England's finest; deals extensively with stillwater forms.

VENIARD, JOHN. *Reservoir and Lake Flies.* St. Martin's Press, 1970. A collection of patterns—old and new—from the United Kingdom by one of the best-known figures in English fly-tying.

WALKER, C. F. *Lake Flies and Their Imitiations.* Herbert Jenkins, 1970. Now the standard English entomological work.

CONTRIBUTORS

DONALD BALTZ is a graduate research assistant in fisheries at the Davis campus of the University of California.

GEOFFREY BUCKNALL is one of Britain's leading fly-fishing writers; his work frequently appears in *Trout and Salmon* and other British angling publications.

FRED EISERMAN until recently was the state fisheries resource manager for the Wyoming Game and Fish Department; he now works for a Wyoming-based firm that specializes in the transmission of energy in a variety of forms.

BOB ELLIOT was for many years the director of the travel and development department for the State of Maine. He now lives in Florida.

DAVE ENGERBRETSON is the western editor of *Fly Fisherman* Magazine, a contributing editor of *Backpacking Journal,* and an associate professor in the biology department of Washington State University.

JIM GILFORD was formerly a professor of aquatic biology at Hood College in Maryland, and is now the chief of ecological assistance in the branch office of toxic substances in the federal Environmental Protection Agency. He is also the eastern director of the Fenwick fly-fishing schools.

HAL JANSSEN is achieving increasing recognition as one of the most innovative and adept stillwater fly fishers in the Rocky Mountains and West. He is the sales manager for the Sunset Line Company in Petaluma, California.

BERNARD "LEFTY" KREH is the author of *Fly Fishing in Salt Water* and co-author of *Practical Fishing Knots.* His articles have appeared in every major national outdoor publication, and his casting and fishing abilities are legendary.

PETER MOYLE is an associate professor of fisheries at the University of California (Davis). He is the author of *Inland Fishes of California* (University of California Press, 1976).

STEVE RAYMOND is the environmental editor of the Seattle *Times,* and was the editor of *The Flyfisher,* the magazine of the Federation of Fly Fishermen, for six years. He is the author of *Kamloops* and *The Year of the Angler,* and has contributed chapters to several other books. He lives in Seattle, Washington.

DAVID RICHEY has written extensively about Great Lakes fishing for a variety of national publications and has authored several books, among them *The Brown Trout Fisherman's Guide.* He lives in Buckley, Michigan.

EARL WEST is a consulting geologist in Casper, Wyoming, whose work often takes him to the high-country lakes he describes in this book.

INDEX

E

Eagle Lake 84, 85
Emerald shiner 58
Ephemera 59
Ephoron 59
Epilimnion 46, 48–50
Eutrophic lakes 51

F

Fish, feeding habits of 75–82, 84–86
Fisheries 32, 34, 37, 38, 66, 67, 75, 77, 78
Float tubes 105–8
Fly boxes 98, 99
Fly-fishing sundries 97, 98; vests 95–98
Fly lines 92–94, 146–49; reels 91, 92; rods 24, 90, 91
Food chain 42, 43, 49, 58–61
Footballer 36, 206

G

Gammarus 166, 167
Giant waterbugs 169
Goddard, John 35, 174
Golden Pond Shiner (artificial) 214
Grafham Reservoir 34, 38
Grant, William 27
Gray Drake Nymph (artificial) 200
Gray Ghost (artificial) 210
Gray Midge Pupa (artificial) 207
Great Lakes 175–81
Great Summer Drake (artificial) 186
Green Midge Pupa (artificial) 204
Griffith's Gnat (artificial) 192
Gulper fishing 131–33

H

Halford, F. M. 29, 30, 32, 36
Harris, J. R. 152, 156
Harvey leader 136
Hatching Midge Pupa (artificial) 206
Henry, Cliff 174
Henrys Lake 82
Hexagenia 59
Hexagenia Wiggle Nymph (artificial) 198
High-altitude lakes 62–72; fly-fishing in 70–72
Hirudinea 172
Hyalella azteca 76

Hydropsyche 59
Hypolimnion 48–51

I

Isle of Orkney 33

J

Janssen's Damsel Nymph (artificial) 200
Janssen Pre-emerger Nymph (artificial) 198

K

Knots 94, 95

L

Lake Berryessa 85
Lake Pend Oreille 80–82
Lake trout 52, 53
Landlocked salmon 52, 55, 56
Leaders 94, 95, 136, 148
Leeches 172, 173
Leiser, Eric 183
Limnephilus 59
Limnetic zone 42, 43
Little Bay De Noc 176
Littoral zone 42, 43, 49, 51, 71
Lymnaea 173

M

Marabou Dragon (artificial) 202
Marabou Matuka (artificial) 213
Marabou Midge Larva (artificial) 203
March Hare (artificial) 197
Metalimnion 46, 48–51
Midge 139, 150–63; adult 153, 154; larva 154–56; pupa 157–60
Midge Nymph (artificial) 204
Monty's Damsel (artificial) 194
Monty's Hexagenia (artificial) 186
Muddler Minnow (artificial) 211
Mustad hooks 145
Mysis shrimp 78–81

N

Nets 99, 100
Nymphs 116–28